THE PRIVATIZATION DECISION

THE PRIVATIZATION DECISION

Public Ends,
Private Means

JOHN D. DONAHUE

BASIC BOOKS, INC., PUBLISHERS

NEW YORK

For Maggie

Library of Congress Cataloging-in-Publication Data

Donahue, John D.
 The privatization decision: public ends, private means / John
Donahue.
  p. cm.
 Bibliographical notes: p. 225
 Includes index.
 ISBN 0-465-06358-6
 1. Privatization. 2. Privatization—Case studies.
 3. Privatization-United States—Case studies. 4. Privatization-
Great Britain—Case studies.   I. Title.
HD3850.D66   1989   89–42511
353.0071′2–dc20   CIP

CONTENTS

ACKNOWLEDGMENTS

THIS BOOK took shape in the lively intellectual environment of the Kennedy School of Government at Harvard University where I was first a student and later a teacher. While it is impossible to credit every source of support and inspiration I received on this project, a few benefactors must be singled out.

The core of the book evolved from my 1987 doctoral thesis, and I thank the fellow students who provided critiques, suggestions, and moral support, including Steven Johnson, Shelley Metzenbaum, Andrew Nevin, and especially Howard Frant, who, from thesis to book, read virtually every draft. I am immensely grateful to the scholars who for many years were my advisors and whom I am now honored to claim as colleagues. More than anyone else, Richard J. Zeckhauser taught me how to think about public problems. More than anyone else, Robert B. Reich taught me why public problems are worth thinking about. To these two teachers I owe the kind of debt that can be repaid only by transmitting their tradition of committed inquiry to my own students.

Mark Moore balanced the mix on my thesis committee, and as the book developed he provided especially helpful insights on chapter 8. Throughout this whole enterprise, discussions with Dutch Leonard helped refine my ideas, and his advice was invaluable through repeated drafts of chapter 6. Steven Kelman also offered comments and suggestions that improved chapter 6, as did the participants in the Defense Acquisition Project, especially Bruce Gudmundsson. John Meyer's suggestions enhanced chapters 5 and 8, and his warm encouragement through the last year of work is much appreciated. Robert B. Reich and Jeremy Rosner both gave the entire rough draft a thorough, sympathetic, and perceptive reading at a crucial stage. Tony Gomez-Ibanez's comments were illuminating and generously supplied. Raymond Vernon helped keep me honest. Roger Leeds of the World Bank provided a practitioner's perspective. A complete and energetic reading by Maggie Pax as press time neared gave me encouragement, perspective, and a wealth of excellent suggestions, many of which I had sense enough to follow. Others who critiqued, commented upon, or inspired parts of the book include Olivia Golden, Heather Hazard, Michael O'Hare, Mary O'Keefe, Dennis Thompson, Arthur Maass, and Roger Porter.

Assistance from several institutions made this venture possible. The Japanese Corporate Associates Program covered many research expenses. A fellowship from the George S. Dively Foundation allowed me a semester to do the research that informed chapters 2 and 3. A generous grant from the Economic Policy Institute gave me time to read and think when it mattered most. And at several junctures I received crucial logistical and financial support from Harvard's Center for Business and Government. I am grateful to its founding director, Winthrop Knowlton, and to acting director John T. Dunlop.

No author could hope for a more perceptive publisher than Martin Kessler, nor a more responsive project editor than Charles Cavaliere. Finally, Paula Holmes has assisted me with research for nearly two years and—supported at times by Lye-Keong Tho and by Center for Business and Government administrator Rita Gordon—has done everything from compiling arcane statistics to tracking down half-remembered quotes with diligence, intelligence, and good humor beyond the call of duty.

PART ONE

THE STAKES

CHAPTER 1

THE ARCHITECTURE OF

ACCOUNTABILITY

T WO POLITICAL legacies of the 1980s will color and constrain the economic policies of the 1990s. One is a renewed cultural enthusiasm for private enterprise. The other is an enduring, deficit-induced imperative to limit government spending. The confluence of these two trends has led to great hopes and claims for "privatization," the practice of delegating *public* duties to *private* organizations.

The virtually worldwide cooling toward collectivism and a growing readiness to experiment with market approaches are trends that are rooted in forces far more complex and profound than American ideological fashion, as the Soviet Union, Eastern Europe, and even (haltingly) China grant a greater role to private business. But this celebration of the private sector is manifest in the United States in peculiarly American ways. Popular distaste for government, though never wholly absent from American politics, reached a level in the 1970s and 1980s that had not been seen for over a half century. Ronald Reagan gained and retained immense popularity in part by tapping the electorate's hostility to politicians and its contempt for bureaucracy. The antigovernment themes of both Jimmy Carter and George Bush were subtler and less strident than Reagan's, but were in some ways nearly as central to their electoral successes.

Yet, while government plumbed new depths of disfavor, the appetite of the citizenry for roads, schools, basic research, military force, and other public benefits failed to slacken. As federal spending outpaced revenues and the budget deficit soared to stunning levels, virtually any stratagem for reining in government budgets while cutting public services as little as possible—and preferably not at all—

took on great political appeal. The collapse of the Reagan administration's fiscal
policies committed his successor to continue the campaign to shrink the domain
of government and to promote private alternatives. Conservative writer Stuart
Butler observed in 1988 that "even for people who are philosophically opposed,
privatization is the least unpleasant of all the choices they can make."[1].

HISTORY AND CONTEXT

The privatization movement is not solely a response to late-1980s fiscal panic, of
course. Business writer Peter Drucker was using the term as far back as 1968
and a Rand Corporation analyst discussed in detail the private delivery of public
services in a 1972 study.[2] Large fractions of federal, state, and local budgets have
always gone to purchase goods and services from suppliers outside government.
The durable American taste for free enterprise has long imposed a bias for the
private alternative. The former Bureau of the Budget issued a directive in 1955
discouraging federal agencies from producing for themselves any "product or
service [which] can be procured from private enterprise through ordinary business
channels."[3] This policy was restated routinely and amplified periodically; the
successor agency, the Office of Management and Budget, reformulated it as Circular A–76 in the late 1960s. Circular A–76—which would become familiar as
the institutional label for federal-level privatization—was revised and amended but
essentially reaffirmed by both Democrat and Republican administrations.[4]

But privatization, as today's fiscally ambitious, ideologically charged phenomenon, began as a British import. English academics and Conservative party officials
prepared a sweeping privatization agenda as Margaret Thatcher took office in
1979, and the British government shed major assets and responsibilities throughout the 1980s.[5] Conservative intellectuals in the United States set out to emulate
the British example. A senior Reagan appointee, E. S. Savas, was accused of
writing his book *Privatizing the Public Sector* with the assistance of his civil service
staff. Savas's private application of public resources shortened his tenure as assistant secretary of Housing and Urban Development, but it also served to spotlight
privatization as a prominent administration policy.[6] Manuel Johnson, an author
of *Better Government at Half the Price*—a vigorous brief for privatization—became
an influential governor of the Federal Reserve.[7] The Privatization Task Force of
the Private Sector Survey on Cost Control—better known as the Grace Com-

mission—called for cutting the federal payroll by half a million jobs, or roughly one-sixth, through contracting out governmental functions. A torrent of privatization proposals and briefing papers by the conservative and well-connected Heritage Foundation culminated, in 1985, in *Privatizing Federal Spending: A Strategy to Eliminate the Deficit*, by Heritage director Stuart M. Butler.[8] By the second Reagan term, officials took to joking that virtually any proposal could become administration policy if it carried the label of privatization.[9] Others concentrated on promoting privatization at the state and local levels with less hoopla but with at least as much to show for their efforts.[10]

As was perhaps inevitable, given the grandeur of the movement's hopes and claims, privatization fell well short of expectations through most of the Reagan years.[11] Yet federal privatization proponents did achieve significant victories in the 1980s. The most visible was the 1987 sale of Conrail, the government's once-sickly freight railroad, after steady infusions of federal money restored it to profitability. Less symbolically resonant but more important in financial terms was the selling off of five billion dollars in government loans. There was also a notable increase in the use of private firms to perform tasks previously left to civil servants. A new office within the Office of Management and Budget was formed specifically to promote privatization, and a blue-ribbon presidential commission celebrated the theme and issued a volume of specific proposals.[12] Outside contractors were hired to check the backgrounds of applicants for government jobs, to collect on bad debts owed the federal government, and to audit the books of the General Services Administration.[13] The Superfund environmental cleanup program, launched in 1981, has devoted 80 to 90 percent of its annual budget to private contractors. Two important instances of this trend were an explicit bias toward privately run transit operations in the allocation of federal subsidies for state and local mass transit, and a sharply increased use of private contractors for performing support services for the military.[14] The White House hired freelancers to write some major Reagan speeches. And the Iran-Contra debacle might be considered privatization run amok.

DEFINITIONS AND DISTINCTIONS

Privatization is not only an inelegant term; it is also lamentably imprecise. The word can signify something as broad as shrinking the welfare state while promoting self-help and voluntarism, or something as narrow as substituting a team of private workers for an all-but-identical team of civil servants to carry out a particular task. One major source of confusion is the difference between privatization in the United States and privatization in most of the rest of the world.

In other countries, privatization has been mostly a matter of selling off parts of an abundant stock of public assets. Through the mid-1980s the Thatcher government sold British Gas, British Telecom, Jaguar, British Airways, the Sealink ferry service, all or part of its stakes in British Sugar, British Aerospace, British Petroleum, and British Steel, as well as nearly one million public housing units and various public utilities.[15] France meanwhile divested Saint-Gobain, a materials producer, and Paribas, a leading bank, before the market crash of 1987 and a change in governments curbed its privatization campaign.[16] Spain, under a Socialist government, sold off SEAT, an auto manufacturer, as well as the state oil company. Italy sold off Alfa Romeo, its stake in the national airline Alitalia, and other assets. In Japan, the Nakasone government privatized Japan Air Lines, Nippon Telegraph and Telephone, and other public operations.[17] Turkey sold its Bosphorus bridge as a prelude to a broader privatization campaign; Malaysia took steps to get out of the airline, telephone, and railroad businesses; and Argentina, Singapore, Mexico, and Brazil all set out to radically cut back the number of state-owned enterprises.[18]

As American enthusiasts mourned the meager accomplishments of domestic privatization in the late 1980s—meager relative to the steps taken by other countries, as well as to the battle cries of the early Reagan years—calls arose to redouble efforts.[19] But America never could equal other countries in selling off government enterprises and assets for one simple reason: America has never *had* all that many government enterprises and assets. In the late 1970s (perhaps the high-water mark of postwar socialization in the noncommunist world), state-owned enterprises claimed an average of 6.7 percent of the labor force in the other developed market economies, but only 1.5 percent in the United States.[20] America was the only major country with an entirely private telecommunications industry. No other industrialized nation except Japan and Canada had *any* privately owned railroads, and even Japan and Canada had only modest private sector involvement in rail; the United States had an overwhelmingly *private* rail industry, with only modest public sector involvement. Only Japan, Spain, and Belgium matched America's scant governmental involvement in electricity generation and transmission, and only in Canada, Japan, and South Korea did the private sector so thoroughly dominate gas distribution. In only a handful of other major countries was there no public oil or coal production, no public steel plants, and no government-owned civilian shipyards.[21]

In short, most of the activities that tend to work badly in the public sector, as both industrialized and third-world countries learned to their sorrow in the post-war decades, America had kept private in the first place. Accordingly, as other countries were pondering or pursuing their version of privatization—severing the government connection with segments of the commercial economy—in the United States, privatization had a quite different meaning. Aside from a strictly limited number of asset sales, it meant (and continues to mean) enlisting private energies to improve the performance of tasks that would remain in some sense public.

The choice between public and private has two basic dimensions. The first dimension concerns *financing*: Should we pay for some good or service individually, out of our own resources, or should we pay for it collectively with funds raised through one form or another of taxation? The second dimension concerns *performance*: Should the good be produced or the service delivered by a governmental organization or by a nongovernmental organization? Figure 1.1 illustrates the choices.

FIGURE 1.1

Dimensions of the Public/Private Choice

	Collective Payment	Individual Payment
Public Sector Delivery		
Private Sector Delivery		

The northwest quadrant of figure 1.1—public financing *and* public sector delivery—covers much of what the typical American has in mind when he speaks of "the government"—the FBI, public schools, state police departments, American embassies abroad, and so on. The southeast quadrant—individual payment and private sector delivery—covers the large share of the economy in which the government role is limited to enforcing contracts and otherwise regulating, monitoring, and certifying private exchange.

The northeast quadrant—private financing but public delivery—may at first seem to be an odd and unimportant category, but a little thought will reveal many instances in which the output of governmental organizations is paid for in individual transactions. Perhaps the most important is the U.S. Postal Service, an essentially public organization that raises its resources not through taxation but through the sale of services. Admissions fees cover about one-fifth of the costs of the National Park Service system. While the Apollo moon landing and robot probes to explore the solar system have been paid for with tax dollars, the National Aeronautics and Space Administration has long charged fees for launching commercial satellites and other private payloads, and the space shuttle was originally expected to pay its own way in this manner.[22]

The Bureau of the Census and dozens of other public agencies package and sell information. The National Security Agency markets some of its encryption technology to banks and other private organizations concerned with the security of electronically stored and transmitted data.[23] National laboratories sell licenses and technical information to private firms. (For example, technology developed for the military to detect submarines turned out to be adaptable for commercial brainscan devices, and was transferred, for a price, to a firm able to exploit it.)[24] There is often no *technical* reason why a far broader range of functions that are performed by government cannot be paid for individually. Boat owners could be billed for the search-and-rescue services of the Coast Guard, either through license charges or on a fee-for-service basis. Travelers might be expected to defray more of the costs of overseas embassies, and so on.

The southeast quadrant of figure 1.1 includes goods and services financed with public money but privately produced. This category covers all of the intercontinental ballistic missiles, patrol cars, and pencils the government procures, the services of consultants to the Environmental Protection Agency or municipal development offices, and airline tickets bought for official travel. Indeed, it includes nearly half of all government spending on goods and services. The American public sector—federal, state, and local levels combined—spent $965 billion in 1988 (excluding interest and transfer payments). Of this sum, $462 billion went to buy goods and services from outside organizations.[25]

Several points merit emphasis at the outset. First, the distinction between public and private—on both dimensions—is a good deal messier than figure 1.1's tidy matrix suggests.

Every government agency is made up of private individuals driven by their own hopes and fears; every private firm is deeply political both internally and in its dealings with the broader society. While it would be going too far to say that there is *no* mileage left in the distinction, comparisons of public and private forms of organization must be either hedged about with qualifications, or taken as slightly artificial statements of tendency.

There is an almost infinite variety of possible organizational forms, with varying mixes of "publicness" and "privateness." Public servants may be elected, appointed, drafted, hired (under civil service rules or not), bound by contracts (long-term, short-term, cost-plus, performance-based) or not. Public institutions range from traditional federal, state, or municipal departments to exotic commissions and authorities with complex and sometimes murky official status. For example, when the Postal Reorganization Act of 1970 transformed the federal Department of the Post Office into an "independent governmental corporation" called the U.S. Postal Service, the change was hard to map along any single-dimensional public-to-private scale. *Private* organizations include profit-seeking firms, nonprofit corporations, voluntary service organizations, religious and neighborhood organizations, and so on.

Consider, too, collective versus individual funding, which at base concerns the distinction between *taxes* and *prices*. If a payment is attached to something essential, or nearly so—a driver's license, say, or the services of customs agents when citizens return from abroad—then the payment may be called a fee or price though it remains, in essence, a tax. Similarly, a tax that can easily be avoided by a change in behavior—like building a home or factory on one side or the other of a jurisdictional boundary—looks very much like a price. Trading on the ambiguous distinctions between prices and taxes can be politically expeditious—the Bush administration, for example, seems to follow the premise that a tax by some other name loses much of its sting—but it should not obscure the central issue: Should the item in question be paid for individually or collectively?

In principle, *financing* and *delivery* decisions are separable. One can conceive of a peculiar sort of collectivist economy where state-owned enterprises monopolize every industry, but where there are no taxes and citizens make all spending decisions on their own. (In this economy, transactions would be clustered in the northeast quadrant of figure 1.1.) Or one can imagine an economy in which a very small number of public officials—no doubt equipped with a very powerful computer—tax citizens at lofty rates and run nearly all of the economy through contracts with private firms. (Here the action would be in the southwest quadrant.) We are accustomed to thinking of the public-private tradeoff in terms of choices along a northwest-to-southeast continuum—that is, a large public sector and high public spending versus a small public sector and low public spending. But there is nothing inevitable about these connections. Indeed, the scenario of increased privatization leading to *higher* government spending is by no means implausible, for reasons that will become clear in later chapters.

At the same time, financing and delivery decisions *are* connected, sometimes in complex and indirect ways. Choices about what to pay for collectively are usually made through political processes. People involved in carrying out public programs—whether organized in corporations or in agencies—are likely to care about both the level and the disposition of public spending. They will also be political actors in their own right, entitled and inclined to make their voices heard. Choices about *how* to carry out collective undertakings may reconfigure the political forces that fix the pace and the pattern of public expenditure.

This book aims to develop and illustrate a set of principles to guide the allocation of publicly financed tasks between governmental and nongovernmental organizations. Most discussions of privatization have treated *public* and *private* as more or less coherent packages of functional, philosophical, and symbolic attributes. Here, I set out to unbundle the packages. By examining particular strengths and defects of public and private institutions—in specific contexts and for specific tasks—I try to get beyond the tidy labels and to engage the more complex but more interesting networks of *relationships among individuals* that are, at base, the substance of any institution.

The logic of the inquiry is fairly simple, though the application often is not. Different kinds of tasks call for different kinds of relationships—expectations, obligations, rights, and duties—among the people who carry out those tasks, and between the people who perform them and the people on whose behalf (and at whose expense) they are performed. Private companies and public agencies tend to differ in the kinds of relationships they encourage and allow. For each collective task, choosing the right kind of organization often requires comparing public and private alternatives by the criterion of efficiency. In chapters 2 and 3, I tap a rich lode of past theoretical work on the comparative efficiency, in varying contexts, of alternative organizational forms.

But efficiency, at base, is merely one aspect of a more fundamental quality—*accountability*. People depend on one another. One person's behavior affects another's well-being. The term suggests the idea of taking "into account" the consequences of one's actions for the welfare of others. Accountability is a central attribute of almost every definition of the "good society," and a central desideratum of almost every moral code. The proper weight to accord to the interests of others depends, of course, on the culture, the context, and the nature of the relationship. One's obligations to a child, a parent, or a lifelong friend differ from one's obligations to a stranger encountered on the street. The definition of accountable behavior differs accordingly. There are intermediate levels of obligation in between the simple civility due a stranger and the expansive accountability due an intimate. An employer owes an employee fair pay and respect, and the employee in turn owes honest work and loyalty. Their mutual obligation is important, extensive, but bounded. The accountability of merchant to customer, teacher to student, physician to patient, attorney to client is similarly set and delimited by convention and expectation.

A special burden of accountability accompanies grants of public authority. This is so for three potent reasons. First, some of the most crucial functions of any society must be carried out collectively. Because weighty choices are at stake, we worry about accountability in public tasks. Second, the public at large—precisely because it is so large and diverse a category—is particularly exposed to failures by authorities to take into account its interests. Third, the individual is inherently vulnerable before the powers of government in ways that history richly illustrates, which the Constitution (and America's other defining documents) seek ingeniously to remedy. While accountability is a fundamental aspect of social existence, it is most often seen as a *problem* in the area of government.

This book is concerned with the challenges that arise as a group of individuals defines itself as a community, discovers collective interests, measures the value of mutual undertakings, and authorizes some of its members to act—on the group's behalf and with the group's resources—to accomplish common ends. Sometimes this arrangement is strictly and simply governmental. Sometimes it is mediated and indirect, and we speak of private involvement in the public realm. The underlying problem, however, remains the same: structuring efficient arrangements that enforce accountability on those who act on behalf of their fellows. It is a question of organizational architecture, and the measure of that architecture is how well it deters opportunism and irresponsibility and promotes faithful stewardship.

Is that all there is? Efficiency and accountability are all very well, one might object, but is this not a rather abstract and bloodless basis for assessing privatization proposals? Are not other issues at least as important? Can the symbolic implications of admitting profit-seeking into the public realm, or of letting government expand at the expense of private business, be ignored? Are there not some values inherent in publicness or privateness *per se*, beyond the purely instrumental?

The symbolic dimension *does* matter, and it is taken up at several points throughout this book. But reasonable people might differ on which way the symbolism cuts: When the options are equivalent (or nearly so) on pragmatic grounds, should the bias be toward public or private arrangements? What appear to be ethical or symbolic concerns, moreover, are frequently prudential concerns in disguise. Employing government workers, or private contractors, for some particular task is sometimes condemned as wrong *not* in an absolute ethical sense, but because of an often tacit judgment that such an arrangement will probably not work very well. Ethical imperatives are too important to be abused, and so whenever possible I try to get behind moralistic language to the pragmatic anxieties that inspire them.

The *efficient* alternative need not be the *cheapest*, and "accountability" covers a lot of ground. It means evaluating alternative arrangements for carrying out public business by the yardstick of *fidelity to the public's values*, whatever they may be. If the citizenry cares about *how* goods and services are produced, about how equitably they are distributed, about the pay, benefits, and working conditions of those who produce them, then any legitimate measure of efficiency must incorporate these concerns.

This and the following chapter provide a framework for thinking about privatization, mapping the terrain on the entire western half of figure 1.1—the domain of social spending. Chapter 2 defines the public realm, examines various rationales for paying for goods and services collectively, and discusses the special difficulties surrounding common spending decisions. The next three chapters take up issues of organizational architecture and assess alternative institutional structures for enforcing accountability in public tasks. Chapter 3 introduces the idea of "agency" arrangements and depicts public and private organizations as, essentially, variants of the basic agency relationship. Chapter 4 reviews the evidence on the economic advantages that profit-seeking organization promises. Chapter 5 then establishes a set of propositions about when privatization is likely to make sense, and when not.

The next four chapters look to specific public tasks where private delivery is being tried, or considered, or has become the norm. Chapter 6 turns to our experience with weapons procurement, one of the most important (and most thoroughly analyzed) areas of government activity where private supply predominates. Chapter 7 looks at service contracting at the city and county levels. Chapter 8 engages (in both theoretical and empirical terms) the controversy over prison privatization. Chapter 9 assesses a recent initiative in American manpower policy that relies upon the private sector to define criteria for subsidized training programs, and to do much of the actual training.

This book offers both good and bad news. The good news is that—while privatization is by no means the universal corrective that some more fervent proponents assert—there *are* real opportunities to make public undertakings more efficient and accountable by enlisting the private sector. It is possible, moreover, to map out with some confidence the features that make certain public tasks promising candidates for privatization.

The bad news is that the imperatives of organizational design and the imperatives of political feasibility are at odds. Sadly, there is no reason to expect the political process to lead to the right pattern of privatization. Unless we are luckier or more careful than we are likely to be, political pressures will tend to retain for the public sector functions where privatization would make sense, and to privatize tasks that would be better left to government.

Yet, a broader appreciation of which public tasks can be effectively delegated, and which cannot, will improve our odds for getting more of the right kind of privatization, and less of the wrong kind.

CHAPTER 2

PRIVATIZATION AND
PUBLIC SPENDING

CHOOSING HOW to accomplish the public's business would be a far simpler matter if it were clear just what the public's business ought to be. But the border between the private and public realms is at once ill-defined, shifting, and disputed. And choices over the public or private performance of collective tasks, as later chapters aim to demonstrate, often affect choices about which tasks come to be designated as collective responsibilities.

This chapter surveys the factors that come into play in collective spending decisions. It is, necessarily, a brief treatment that cannot do full justice to the compelling problem of social choice, but it does set a context, and suggests the stakes, for our central inquiry into the risks and rewards of putting public tasks into private hands.

Every culture, guided by the values it cherishes, builds its own institutional structures for creating and distributing wealth. This organizational architecture is greatly influenced by tradition, ideology, and inertia. But it happens, at times, that analysis and deliberate design enter into the process as well. The range of eligible economic arrangements—surveyed either theoretically or historically—is very broad, and no simple set of categories can cover the whole array. But by limiting the field to more or less modern, more or less capitalist cultures, one can distinguish three organizing principles for production and exchange.

The first is *voluntarism*. People act in the interest of others uncompensated and uncompelled, animated by tradition, or by a sense of religious, social, or familial duty, or out of empathy, joy in the work itself, or the thrill of power implicit in magnanimity. While participants in a culture of voluntarism may anticipate benefiting in their turn, they do not keep accounts, expect reciprocity for each transaction, or have any recourse should they end up, over the course of their lives, as net benefactor rather than net beneficiary. The volunteer fireman, for example, is doubtless motivated in part by the prospect of assistance should his own house catch fire, but he does not insist upon a pledge of reciprocal aid from each fire victim before he connects the hose.

The most obvious instances of voluntarism may seem economically marginal. The gardener next door shares his tomato harvest with the neighborhood; you give a panhandler a quarter, or pledge some small fraction of your income to the United Way. But in fact transactions based partially or predominantly on voluntarism are pervasive. Except in the most peculiar of families, they include the bulk of the production and exchange that occurs within the household. They include philanthropy in cash and in kind.

There are also mixed transactions in which voluntarism figures prominently but not exclusively. When a soldier steps forward for a dangerous assignment, the extra degree of commitment is voluntary, even if he is compelled to military service by the draft and is paid a salary for his time in uniform. There is an element of voluntarism when people choose work—as ministers, schoolteachers, or general practitioners, for example—because they feel that it is meaningful or noble, and in spite of the greater ease or compensation other occupations offer. The American system of public finance, while formally based on mutual compulsion, in fact relies to a great extent on voluntarism. Most people pay their taxes without making elaborate calculations of the risk and reward of various stratagems of evasion, and enforcement costs are comparatively low. Similarly, many business people take greater care to avoid environmental damage than regulations require.

The second broad principle for organizing production and distribution is the price system, the manifestation, in Adam Smith's words, of our species' "propensity to truck, barter, and exchange one thing for another." Modern man "stands at all times in need of the co-operation and assistance of great multitudes, while his whole life is scarce sufficient to gain the friendship of a few persons." Thus price-mediated interdependence—the market—operates (to a greater or lesser extent) in every culture. The organizing principle is reciprocal, self-interested exchange. The result is often a marvel of coordination. "Give me this which I want, and you shall have this which you want," Smith wrote. "It is in this manner that we obtain from one another the far greater part of those good offices which we stand in need of." When the circumstances are right, market forces orchestrate a community's material interactions with astonishing speed and precision.[1]

The market's virtues as an organizing device are not due solely, or even perhaps primarily, to the scarcity of benevolence that Smith posits. Even a society of altruists would require some reliable means for members to learn what would make their neighbors happy. (Anyone doubting this should recall the last time he or she put together a Christmas shopping list.) Prices convey information. Unless my neighbor the gardener is particularly adept at drawing inferences from my diminishing enthusiasm as August wears on, he will be imperfectly informed as to the value I place on his gifts of zucchini, and will not know to adjust his production accordingly. If my neighbor makes his living by selling vegetables, however, the price of zucchini will deliver a good deal of information by which to guide his endeavors. Similarly, if he is thinking about removing a mildly troublesome tree stump from his yard and asks my assistance, I may volunteer to help him, out of neighborliness, even if I loathe stump pulling with a depth of feeling that far outweighs his annoyance at having to dodge the stump each time he mows his lawn. The world would, on balance, be a better place if the stump were left alone, and were I a professional landscaper the fee I would charge for removing the stump would make this clear. (People also find neighborliness itself valuable, of course, and if there are limited occasions to exercise that virtue, it may be worthwhile to put up with too many zucchini or too much stump pulling.)

In a market, prices signal scarcity and desirability as an indirect, decentralized process allocates human efforts to accord with human wants. Many good minds have thought hard and written at great length about where and when this primal bargain of "give me this which I want and you shall have this which you want" is society's most promising coordinating device. But it is important to emphasize at the outset that *the market* is not an institution, but rather an organizing principle. The exchange relationships that prevail in any given culture are social artifacts. The laws of property, enforced by rules against theft and fraud, set the basic terms of exchange, without which no coherent decisions could be made about production or distribution. Rules concerning patents, pollution, wages, child labor, and so on limit options for production. Rules against selling whiskey to children or weaponry to felons limit options for distribution.

The third broad organizing principle is *government*. Political decisions backed by authority, rather than benevolence or price signals, determine what is produced and how it is distributed. The general concept of government-organized endeavor is hopelessly broad, including—if we count clan and church authority as more "public" than "private"—the bulk of economic activity throughout human history. I limit my attention to systems in which those who formulate, issue, and carry out economic directives are in some sense answerable to the citizenry at large, thus excluding feudal, theocratic, Stalinist, and fascist systems. In a more or less democratic culture, government, like the market, is a mechanism of coordination, a device for ascertaining desires and allocating resources.

"The legitimate object of government," in Abraham Lincoln's words, "is to do for a community of people whatever they need to have done, but cannot do in their separate and individual capacities."[2] The archetypal bargain of government spending, complementing the individual promise of "give me this which I want, and you shall have this which you want," is the collective "we mutually pledge to pay for this which we all want."

How are we to know when this is the right arrangement? How shall we strike such bargains? Once they are struck, how are they to be appraised, amended, or annulled? Scholars have engaged such questions for centuries, generating a vast literature, a number of glittering insights and powerful generalizations, and, not too surprisingly, no durable consensus. Politicians and citizens, meanwhile, have to make do. Each culture, in each generation, for each proposal, must make decisions about the realm of common responsibility. These decisions are inescapably troublesome. The dream of purifying public choices into a kind of arithmetic purged of politics will forever elude us. We can, at best, improve the quality of the politics—make it less fractious, more efficient in its use of available truth, less vulnerable to manipulation and obfuscation.

Proposals for government spending are made on three different grounds. The first, which economists term "market failure," refers to prudential judgments that some desirable result is only achievable, or more expeditiously achieved, through collective rather than individual means. The second ground is moral, and manifests a consensus of collective responsibility for nonmarket goals. The third ground is opportunist: The proponent anticipates personal gain from some collective endeavor, irrespective of the broader balance of gain or loss to his fellows.

MARKET FAILURE MOTIVES

Even a culture devoted to the price system will find that there are some tasks that cannot be organized through the market. The market system fails on its own terms when prices lie—that is, when the prices of goods and services give false signals about their real value, confounding the communication between producers and consumers. Market failure is the subject of a voluminous economic literature ranging from towering mathematical constructs to homey parables.[3] Edith Stokey and Richard Zeckhauser distinguished six causes of market failure.[4] First, information relevant to exchange may be incomplete, inaccurate, or suspect, frustrating a central requisite of market efficiency. Second, transaction costs may deter exchange. Third, some markets simply may not exist—because of the inadequacy or asymmetrical distribution of information, or because no authority can enforce certain contracts (such as transactions across generations). Fourth, the market power of some buyers or sellers can undermine the conditions for proper pricing. Fifth, some transactions feature externalities—positive or negative consequences that are not incorporated into prices. Sixth, some goods and services are inherently public, in the sense that each person benefits from their provision whether he helps pay for them or not.[5]

For present purposes, the most interesting category of market failure concerns *public goods*. While this terminology is relatively recent, the essential logic was laid out more or less completely in *The Wealth of Nations*, in which Smith spoke of the state's duty of "erecting and maintaining certain public works and certain public institutions . . . because the profit could never repay the expense to any individual . . . though it may frequently do much more than repay it to a great society."[6] Smith's intellectual heirs have made several attempts to define public goods with more operational precision, ranging from the purely conceptual (Robert Dorfman's Zen-like definition of goods or services that are "enjoyed but not consumed") to the purely descriptive (Edward Birdsall's "any good or service . . . provided for or subsidized through government budget finance").[7] Most definitions turn on *nonexclusivity* (once a public good is provided, nobody can easily be prevented from benefiting from it) or on *nonrivalry* (one person can enjoy a public good without diminishing the benefit to anyone else).[8]

There are three complications to this general line of thinking. First, publicness is a matter of degree. Fireworks displays, for example, are nonexclusive (within broad bounds) and nonrival; nobody in the vicinity can be barred from enjoying the explosions aloft, nor does one more watcher diminish the pleasure everyone else takes in the display. Thus fireworks are generally paid for by some public organization or by a philanthropic group. But in Boston, and doubtless in other cities, a for-profit company puts on splendid fireworks displays. Revenues collected by selling access to music coordinated with the aerial bursts covers the cost of the fireworks with a good profit to spare; tens of thousands of freeloaders benefit serendipitously. It is often hard to predict what private initiative will accomplish (or fail to accomplish) on its own, particularly since the potential and limits both of the price system and of voluntarism are so intimately shaped by policy. Citizens might muster a volunteer militia to repel an invasion if there is no public provision for defense. Or they might not. If the government *does* organize an army, there will almost certainly be no volunteer militia, nor any sure way of telling if there would have been one but for government initiative. The cautionary point here is that identifying substantial public aspects to a good or service does not, in itself, establish the case for collective financing.

The second complication is, in a sense, the converse of the first. There are very few transactions wholly free of external effects. For most of human history, clan and village organization left little to strictly individual choice. In the past few centuries, in the minority of cultures strongly influenced by liberal thought, this realm has expanded. But many Americans sincerely feel themselves to be wronged when their neighbors read *Fanny Hill* or *The Communist Manifesto*, and they assert a right to intervene. Some people care much more deeply about their neighbors' observance of the Sabbath than about these same neighbors' contributions to the national defense. Homeowners in designated districts in the United States and England are required to conform to historic-preservation codes; in some European cities, residents are required to adorn balconies with flowers. In modern America we require each other to teach our children to read, but, with few exceptions, we leave *what* to read up to individuals. We deny each other the right to fill the air around us with hydrogen cyanide; we selectively constrain the right to fill the air with tobacco smoke; and with very limited exceptions we grant an unlimited right to fill the air with conversation, even when it is offensive or inane. There are powerful reasons why we set the borders between individual and society as we do, but they are not *economic* reasons. The limits of the collective realm are established by collective decision, and they tend to be matters of dispute. When we complain that an issue has become "political," we mean that other people are insinuating their preferences into some issue that we feel entitled to settle alone. When we complain of "unaccountability," we mean that other people are failing to grant due weight to our preferences.

The third complication is more empirical. Theoretical definitions of public goods bear only the faintest resemblance to descriptions of what the public sector actually does. Several scholars have pointed out that providing truly nonrival, nonexclusive goods and services accounts for only a small fraction of total government spending.[9] A great many things are paid for collectively that citizens could pay for individually with little or no loss in efficiency. Moreover, public and private aspects are normally bundled together in the same good or service. A child's learning to read affects her future income and her parents' economic security, the efficiency with which she will complement the efforts of her future colleagues, her future accomplishment as a conversationalist, and the quality of her future voting decisions. The logic of external benefits, that is, imparts a measure of publicness to primary education, but the case for financing schools *entirely* through tax revenues cannot be made on market failure grounds alone. Similarly, public financing for national defense *per se* can be justified on pure public goods grounds—citizens driven by individual self-interest tax themselves to pay for items where market mechanisms happen to fail—but government action to intimidate the politically objectionable elements in strategically irrelevant foreign locales cannot. It cannot, that is, unless the concept of a public good is broadened considerably beyond the egoistic, utilitarian premises of standard economics to include *any* action that can be considered conducive to a better world. And in fact, this kind of language, far more than the logic of market failure, characterizes debates about public spending.

MORAL OR PHILOSOPHICAL MOTIVES

Analytically elegant definitions of *public goods* represent economists' attempt to domesticate the messy concept of *the public good*. It is a quixotic endeavor, at once noble and doomed to frustration. Noble, because it seeks a rationale for collective action more plausible than invocations of some organic common will, and more palatable than the stipulation of the public good by king, church, or party. Doomed, because motives other than the individualistic and the utilitarian demonstrably affect what kinds of public action citizens support.

Members of democracies see government not only as a mechanism, complementary to the market, for serving individual appetites but also as the expression and the instrument of moral and philosophical aspirations. People have preferences about the world around them—for more fellowship, less hunger, more democracy, less torture, and so on. They can and do pursue these goals privately. But a citizen may also press for public action to advance his values. First, some moral or philosophical goals may be pursued most efficiently by the state. Private initiatives work fairly well to feed earthquake victims, less well to support ideologically congenial guerrillas, and quite badly to explore the moons of Mars. Second, an individual's willingness to pay to promote certain goals may be conditional on others' joining in the campaign—either to ensure a large enough effort to make a difference or simply to confirm his conviction that the endeavor is worthwhile. It is not irrational for a citizen to support a $100-per-capita tax to fund a program to eradicate malaria, even if he might hesitate to donate $100 to the same cause on his own. (Of course, he might also be willing to donate but unwilling to be taxed; compulsion could undermine voluntarism.)[10] Third, an individual might press for public financing for some enterprise—saving the whooping crane, say, or broadcasting libertarian propaganda in Lithuania—if he cares intensely about the issue, knows that most people do not, and seizes on the government as a device to compel others to help advance his values.

Economists often relegate public action animated by moral motives to a murky category labeled "merit goods"—anything judged, for whatever reason, by whatever authority in a position to make such pronouncements, as more deserving of resources than market signals suggest. On the criteria for legitimatizing such spending, economics is largely silent. The decision rule for public spending based on market failure motives is (at least in principle) straightforward: Identify the flaw in the market, specify the public action proposed to fix it, tally up the estimated costs and benefits, and adopt the proposals that promise net benefits. Moral and philosophical motives are immensely more complicated. What is their source of legitimacy? The Platonic tradition commissions intellectual elites to discover the good through philosophical inquiry. Theocracies rely on revelation, usually routed through religious leaders. Some early economists—especially in Germany—entertained a Hegelian conception of an organic collective will embodied in the state.[11] Classical welfare economics posits a social welfare function mapped and maximized by disinterested government officials. Americans (and many others) reject such devices. But democracy can be admitted only at the sacrifice of conceptual tidiness. Ultimately, politics is the mechanism, and political appeal is the measure.

In 1916, the United States joined a foreign war in order to "make the world safe for democracy." In 1919, it declared drinking illegal and devoted considerable resources to enforcing the ban. In 1946, it thanked the soldiers who had defeated Hitler and Tojo with the generous GI Bill. In 1949, it launched the Marshall Plan to rebuild Europe. Each endeavor can, with some ingenuity, be cast as a response to market failure. But this does not explain how these initiatives gained legitimacy, it merely translates the question into the language of economics. Each was debated and endorsed in moral terms, and found its legitimacy as the expression of values held strongly by a sufficient proportion of the electorate. Within the limits on state action set by the Constitution—the value-based code embodying our culture's choices as to the general boundaries of the public realm—the political process must be accepted as the mechanism for designating public endeavors.[12] It is an imperfect mechanism indeed, but if we believe at once in democracy and in collective moral action in the world, it is the best we can ever hope for.

Yet, even granting the broadest potential grounds for legitimacy, it is clear that governments do some things that are not very wise, not very fair, not very efficient. Every spending decision affronts *some* citizens; this is to be expected in our diverse society. The point is that some spending decisions affront *most* citizens who examine them closely, including people who are predisposed to believe governments can and do accomplish useful things. Even—indeed, especially—for those who see in government a force for good, a keen awareness of the threat of ill-advised collective spending should inform thinking not just about where the government should act, but how. In particular, the organizational arrangements for carrying out public business should reinforce, or at least not pervert, our processes for designating collective tasks.

THE PROBLEMS OF PUBLIC SPENDING CHOICES

By keeping terms sufficiently vague, it is possible to set criteria. Good public spending advances the material or moral goals of the citizenry. Bad public spending is wasteful or exploitative, setting in motion resource flows that are inefficient (helping beneficiaries less than they hurt those who pay), or unfair (allocating burdens and benefits in a manner at odds with the society's values), or both. A community is better off—more prosperous, more able to attain its members' ideals—to the extent that it can discriminate between good and bad spending proposals.

This is hard to do. No democracy will succeed in adopting all the right proposals and in rejecting all the wrong ones. There are three overlapping types of impediments to sound collective decisions. Each set of problems is sufficient to undercut the expectation that we will ever achieve a perfect pattern of public spending. Taken together, they should make us less surprised about widespread unhappiness with existing public policies, more humble about sweeping proposals to improve the process, and more vigilant against introducing new sources of error into the system. The first set concerns problems of principle: What criteria should govern public spending decisions? The second involves problems of procedure: How should collective choices be made? The third set includes problems of information: How can we choose when none of us knows the full range of choices and ramifications, when some know more than others, and when so many are so easily misled?

Problems of Principle

We have failed conspicuously to arrive at any workable, consistent set of principles for judging public action. This is no news to any philosopher, but in light of the frequency with which political rhetoric refers to "justice" or "fairness" as if these terms were matters of simple common sense, it is worth underscoring that controversies over budgetary levels and priorities spring not just from a failure to live up to principles of social action, but also from a failure to formulate them.

Human beings no doubt have been debating about the public good for almost as long as they have had words with which to debate. Yet, as has often been noted, the past two millennia of staggering technological advances have witnessed virtually no progress in defining the good society. In small groups bound by familiarity and affection, the problem of social choice is eased considerably by empathy. But in larger societies, principles for collective decision must be to some degree guided by communicable general rules. Efforts to extend and modify the logic of *individual* choice to encompass *social* choice, though, have met with little success.

The problems of principle troubling contemporary economics can be traced to philosophical disputes that raged in the nineteenth century; these were never really resolved, but only submerged beneath an accretion of analytical technique. These disputes go well beyond the scope of this book, but to illuminate the philosophical ambiguity that complicates public spending decisions it may be useful to identify three closely related issues: individual sovereignty, distribution, and compulsion.

INDIVIDUAL SOVEREIGNTY. Societies are collections of individuals who depend on each other (in varying ways and degrees) but who differ (in varying ways and degrees) in their interests and beliefs. Hence the basic dilemma. There are some issues the resolution of which matters for society as a whole, and hence must be resolved collectively. But *collective* decisions must be governed by *individual* values, which means that public criteria must somehow be derived from private criteria. Accountability means that government action accords with the will of the people the government represents—not the will of individuals who happen to work in the government, and not what those individuals *think* the citizens should want, but what the people, by their own criteria, count desirable.

In a culture that rejects the notion of social welfare as something different from or greater than individual welfare, the guiding principle of social choice must be respect for the principle of individual choice. Yet, even assuming the best intentions on the part of public decision-makers, making that principle effective in collective choice is an elusive ideal.[13]

DISTRIBUTION. "The greatest good for the greatest number" remains the philosophical polestar of economic reasoning. And while utilitarianism cannot be made operational through one grand calculus of social welfare, we still have to judge alternatives. We must somehow do it, moreover, without recourse to unanswerable questions about just how much an individual values one option over another, or about the relative intensity of desires as *between* individuals. A principle that fits within these constraints is the Pareto criterion, which in its classic form is about as morally cautious a precept as can be imagined: If at least one person prefers A to B, and nobody else cares one way or the other, then from society's perspective A is better than B. If a millionaire gives a starving beggar a dollar because it makes him feel magnanimous, they are both happier— the one morally gratified, the other fed—and the world is a better place. If the millionaire ponders the choice between giving the beggar a dollar and kicking him off the sidewalk, finds himself indifferent, and makes the donation after flipping a coin to decide, at least the beggar is happier and the world is a better place. But if the government taxes the unwilling millionaire a dollar to feed the beggar at a public soup kitchen, one person is better off, the other is worse off, and the Pareto criterion has nothing at all to say about the utilitarian balance.

This kind of reasoning strikes most noneconomists as bizarre, since social choices almost always involve net benefits to some people and net costs to others. Economists know this, of course. It is not obtuseness, but rather philosophical scruples and methodological fastidiousness, that deter economists from judging tradeoffs across individuals. Economists defend the Pareto criterion and its variants by pointing out that they really only work as measures of efficiency *improvements* within a social state that is *already* considered just. The Pareto criterion concerns only the incremental efficiency promised by a new flood control dam; it does not consider the prevailing level of distributive justice in the society as relevant in deciding whether to build the dam. The position is logically quite defensible: If a community is unhappy with the distribution of wealth and income, let it redistribute resources and leave the economist to her specialty, the search for efficiency gains. If society cannot or will not redistribute to meet its standards of fairness, why demand that the economist rig her calculus to account for distribution? From the economist's perspective, everybody always talks about distribution but nobody ever does anything about it.

Unfortunately, most societies have proven unwilling to undertake significant lump sum redistributions; most societies seem to care about the distributional consequences of economic decisions; and economists remain not much better equipped than barbers to make judgments about distribution. Economists who, out of taste or necessity, seek to offer practical policy advice typically abandon the pure form of the Pareto rule in favor of the *potential* Pareto criterion, which gains a good deal more applicability at the cost of a certain moral recklessness: If one person prefers A to B so much that he would be willing to pay off everyone that prefers B to A if they will let him have his way, then from society's perspective A is better than B *even if* no compensation actually happens.

COMPULSION. Max Weber defined government as "the human community that successfully claims the monopoly of the legitimate use of physical force."[14] The state relies on a (usually latent) capacity to use force to defend the realm, to ensure that citizens adhere to their private contracts, and to exact common support for common purposes. It is this last function that concerns us here. To deter "free riders" from starving public undertakings, the government must require every citizen to pay his share. For example, I might rationally refuse to help pay for the Central Intelligence Agency or for the Legal Services Corporation, even if I approve of and benefit from their activities, if I predict that withholding my contribution will have no effect on my share of the benefits, and only a tiny effect on the program budgets. But if everybody reasons this way, we have too few spies and poverty lawyers. Citizens thus agree to let government compel the recalcitrant to pay taxes to support public activities.

Some people object to compulsion itself as antithetical to a free society. Most do not, at least in a reasonably responsive democracy. But even if we accept the principle of mutual compulsion for mutual benefit, there remains a major problem with obligatory taxes: We lose information. If a citizen voluntarily donates $100 to buy a trenchcoat for a CIA agent, we can infer that suitably clothing a spy is worth at least $100 to at least one citizen. But when the citizen's resources are tapped via taxes, all we can say is that he would rather pay for the trenchcoat than go to jail for tax evasion. The real value of the expenditure becomes much harder to gauge.[15]

Problems of Procedure

In the United States and other democracies, taxing and spending policies are proposed or approved, or both, by elected officials. This broadly admirable system, representative democracy, has some notable shortcomings as a device for determining what should be paid for collectively. Consider, first, some basic limitations of elections as a means for signaling citizens' desires.

BALLOTS AS BLUNT INSTRUMENTS. Perhaps the most obvious limitation is that if there are more issues than candidates, the voter cannot mark her ballot in a way that signals her full range of desires. In selecting a candidate, she chooses a bundle of policy options, some but not necessarily all of which she endorses. She cannot affirm one candidate's position on highway spending, the views of another on housing subsidies, and the platform of a third on leukemia research. Nor, on any single issue, can the voter signal the *intensity* of her views or her preferred *level* of spending on a program. She simply selects the candidate whose position most closely approximates her own, and in so doing she must filter out a good deal of information.

The problem is further complicated by the fact that spending issues share platforms with other issues. If a voter happens by some improbable coincidence to agree dollar for dollar with a candidate's budget priorities, but votes against him out of revulsion for his position on abortion or capital punishment, her ballot conveys no valid information about her preferences for public spending.

So public spending decisions, at best, will be *imprecise* reflections of popular desires. Imprecision may not be so bad, if it simply means that the actual pattern of spending will approximate the ideal but with a degree of random error—a bit too many tanks, a bit too few air-traffic controllers. Matters are more serious if our procedures are prone to systematically misinterpret the views of the citizenry on spending issues. Sadly, there are reasons to fear that they are.

DEFECTS OF MAJORITY RULE. One obvious, oft-cited peril is the tyranny of the majority, which de Tocqueville characterized thus: "If it be admitted that a man possessing absolute power may misuse that power by wronging his adversaries, why should not a majority be liable to the same reproach?"[16] Were majority rule to apply strictly and without constraint, deplorable results would become possible. Brown-eyed people could vote to enslave blue-eyed people; those whose names begin with A through N could vote to confiscate all the property of those whose names begin with O through Z. But in most democracies, the rule of the majority is constrained either by explicitly putting some issues out of bounds—through devices such as the Bill of Rights—or by requiring certain kinds of issues to be approved by more than a majority. In practice, minority interests are also safeguarded in some measure by the fact that it is often difficult for majorities to recognize their favored status and to organize to exploit it.[17]

Communities must reach some consensus about what language to speak, and the linguistic troubles of Quebec, Belgium, and parts of the southwestern United

States are the inescapable costs of reaching and enforcing a collective decision. We have judged individual discretion as too costly or divisive in many areas, and mandate instead a measure of conformity: what language to speak, which side of the road to drive on, whether or not to follow daylight savings time, where to get on and off a limited-access highway. In each case, somebody may be unhappy with the collective decision, and that unhappiness is a true social loss—counterbalanced, presumably, by the overall social gain. But in most areas we judge that the balance cuts in favor of individual discretion. It would be less costly to print a smaller number of book titles, and less divisive to practice a common religion, but we judge that in these and other cases the value of choice outweighs the value of commonality.[18]

Problems of Representation

Most spending decisions are made by elected representatives, not directly by citizens, although representation is neither logically necessary for budget decisions nor universally practiced. Cities, for example, frequently require referendum approval for major investments. There are no rigid *technical* limits on the extent to which societies can settle spending issues through plebiscites.[19] In 1967, the citizens of Basel voted by referendum to buy Picasso's *L'Arlequin Assis* and *Les Deux Frères* for the city's art collection.[20] But the voice of the people seldom pronounces on spending priorities with this kind of specificity.

The chief arguments for representation, as laid out by James Madison in *The Federalist Papers*, are to keep the deliberative body of manageable size, and to permit what an economist would call specialization in policy-making, or in Madison's words, to "refine and enlarge the public views by passing them through the medium of a chosen body of citizens whose wisdom may best discern the true interest of their country and whose patriotism and love of justice will be least likely to sacrifice it to temporary or partial considerations."[21]

But at the same time representation creates two more sets of problems for public spending choices. The first set concerns the form of representation. Does each piece of real estate inhabited by some specified number of souls send a delegate to the assembly? This preserves the one man, one vote rule, but at the cost both of submerging conflicts among the represented, thus jettisoning information about the ultimate value of public spending options. Or should the unit of representation be preexisting associations, such as unions or trade groups (as in corporatist and guild socialist systems), states or provinces (as in legislative assemblies like the U.S. Senate), countries (as in the United Nations), clans, ethnic groups, special-interest organizations, and so on? This makes it more likely that representatives will speak for groups united by common desires, but at the cost of breaking the one man, one vote rule and disenfranchising the unorganized.

The second set of complications concerns the long-debated role of the representative. Is he a *delegate* who simply conveys the desires of his electors to the deliberative body, or a *trustee* with the right and duty to interpret, amend, or even ignore those desires as his own judgment directs? There is, of course, a continuum between the extremes of slavishly serving the whims of constituents, on the one hand, and of consulting no authority but personal conscience, on the other. But the distinction raises complex issues about the functioning of representative democracy as a device for setting public spending priorities. The delegate model seems, on its face, to offer the more direct link between the interest of constituents and budget decisions. But the electorate may hold deeply opposing views, or it may be misinformed about its interests. And achieving long-term benefits for constituents may require strategic short-term sacrifices. The trustee model offers greater scope for balance and bargaining, but at the risk of hampering the transmission of citizen priorities. Most of us would concur with Madison and prefer for legislatures to be populated by men and women of vision, public spirit, and courage. But any departure from the straightforward delegate role, however essential for political stability, legislative harmony, and considered deliberation of noneconomic issues, compromises the reliability of representative democracy as a device for discerning citizens' desires.[22]

POWER BEYOND THE BALLOT BOX. Even if citizens could affect collective decisions only through the formal apparatus of democracy, there would be little reason for confidence that public spending choices would closely reflect the priorities of the community. The links between individual interests and public decisions about what to pay for collectively become correspondingly more complex when political influence flows from sources other than the ballot box and, in particular, from *organization*.

One can argue that the basic unit of political life is not the individual but the group—the church, union, professional association, corporation, and so on. Collective decisions are not exclusively or even primarily a matter of aggregating the desires citizens express in the isolation of a voting booth, but are rather the results of intricate negotiation and accommodation among groups within the community. One way in which groups concentrate political power is by coordinating their members' voting decisions. They do this by shaping the values that govern votes— either subtly and systematically (the Appalachian Mountain Club encourages in its members certain attitudes about nature and public land)—or directly and specifically (the Catholic church decrees abortion to be morally wrong). Or they attempt to interpret candidates' positions in light of their professed values, as when Americans for Democratic Action and other issue groups rate legislative voting records. Or they explicitly endorse candidates or policy proposals, and run "get out the vote" drives to increase the political weight of their point of view.

Groups may also affect elections by influencing the ballot decisions of non-members. The National Rifle Association runs advertisements soliciting broader public sympathy for its positions. The AFL-CIO organizes union members to canvass door-to-door in support of selected candidates. And, perhaps most importantly today, groups make campaign contributions, both to promote the election of candidates they favor and to gain access to incumbent legislators.

Organized groups also influence public choices in ways that have little direct connection with elections. They can pool members' resources and hire polished spokesmen to present their views to government officials. They can stage protest demonstrations. They can attempt to influence the government through boycotts or strikes. Finally, they can bribe, threaten, or blackmail officials—tactics that are, in principle, open to ambitious individuals, but may be more promising when undertaken by groups.

Interest groups may enable citizens to communicate both the nuances and the intensity of their preferences, compensating to some degree for the informational paucity of the ballot box. Ballots are binary, but other political tactics involving group organization—appeals to public sentiment, campaign support, protest demonstrations—can be calibrated to match the importance people place on a spending decision. By broadening citizens' repertoire of political expression, interest-group activity may make collective spending decisions more responsive to the true interests and values of the populace.

Or it may not. Interest-group activism will only improve the quality of public spending decisions if each group's ability and willingness to bring political resources to bear on a decision closely parallels its members' real stake in the outcome. Suppose a group prints and broadcasts its message, organizes members to ring doorbells, donates money to the campaigns of sympathetic candidates, and stages rallies in the streets. This could mean that group members care especially deeply about the issue, suggesting that society should grant more weight to their desires than a simple vote count would indicate. Or it could mean that the group is especially well positioned to apply political pressure, however flimsy its claims. Similarly, a group's quiescence may mean either that it has little at stake in some decision, or that its members are deficient in resources or organizational capacity. Group politics, in short, can help to overcome the imprecision and unfairness of majority rule spending decisions. It can also introduce a whole new set of distortions into the expression of citizens' desires.[23]

SPECIAL INTERESTS AND COMMON ACTION.   Where does this leave us on the narrow question of how to make decisions about public spending? Critics of interest groups charge that their actions tend to warp spending choices in ways that are economically destructive and distributionally perverse. The Madisonian scenario of the common interest emerging out of the struggle between factions, this critique goes, overlooks the reality that for most issues it won't be a fair fight. Some interests never organize. Those that *do* gain political clout are distinguished by ease of organization, and not by any special claim to legitimacy.

Yet disparaging collective action as irredeemedly warped by special interests is the wrong response to the pathologies of pluralism. To the extent that important classes of citizen aspirations—both material and moral—can only be pursued collectively, then to surrender our ambitions for *common* action is to limit our *individual* lives. In *Civilization and Its Discontents*, Sigmund Freud argued that humans confront a choice between two sharply divergent strategies for coming to terms with an uncertain world: One path seeks pleasure, the other flees from pain. The first involves openness and risk; the second insulation and wariness. Freud speculated that "under the pressure of the possibilities of suffering, men are accustomed to moderate their claims to happiness [so that] . . . in general the task of avoiding suffering pushes that of obtaining pleasure into the background."[24]

Perhaps communities face a comparable choice. Market-mediated activity retains secure links between individual desires and economic outcome, but it is constricted in what it can accomplish. Politically organized activity expands our material and moral horizons, but it renders us vulnerable. Insofar as we renounce the common realm and restrict ourselves to endeavors that do not burden our weak and vulnerable procedures for collective choice, we opt for a safer but bleaker path.

This reasoning suggests that it is not simply the emergence and entrenchment of special interests that has bedeviled postwar American politics, but also the erosion of traditional public values and the failure to restore them or to replace them with a new consensus on the claims citizens can make on their fellows. It also underscores that the assessment of spending proposals requires attention not only to the material goals citizens seek, but also to the moral purposes they endorse. Thus the accurate flow of information about public policy becomes at once more vital and more problematic.

Problems of Information

Recent years have seen an explosion of work on the economics of information.[25] This is a significant departure for a profession that had long proceeded from the assumption that information is cheaply acquired, readily verified, and widely shared. Information on citizen priorities and the pattern and consequences of collective spending, in fact, is generally costly to collect, confirm, and transmit. The American system of representative democracy, coupled with a free and energetic press, is markedly superior to any other arrangement for generating and disseminating the information essential to accountability. Yet it falls well short of the ideal of well-informed citizens served by fully candid officials who oversee transparently comprehensible spending programs. There are at least three reasons why citizens are imperfectly informed as to the options for collective action and their likely consequences.

IGNORANCE BY DEFAULT. First, key questions may be simply unanswerable. The data may not exist, or may be too complex to process. Commentators lamented the seeming public indifference to the debate over the landmark tax code revisions of 1986. But nobody could be certain about the consequences for long-term economic growth and stability, and only a few people were equipped to have well-informed opinions, so public inattention to all but the narrowest issues—"Will my tax bill go up or down next year?"—is understandable.

Second, and perhaps more importantly, the costs to the citizen of obtaining information may exceed the benefits he anticipates from such expertise. Informed democracy is *itself* a public good. The costs of gaining wisdom about collective spending choices, and of acting upon it, fall on the individual; but the benefits tend to be spread throughout the polity. Indeed, if citizens acted solely as calculating individualists, they might invest less effort in learning about competing fiscal plans than about competing floor polishes, opting to get a free ride on their fellows' informed choices. Many people, fortunately, feel a civic duty to stay informed, or simply enjoy keeping up with the issues.

Third, individuals may not *know* that they are ignorant. Since the opinion of any one citizen is seldom decisive, and since the consequences of any one decision are likely to be ambiguous, citizens may be able to maintain false, incomplete, or inconsistent beliefs for a long time before clear evidence of error inspires revision. Whatever the mix of reasons, the result is that, for a large fraction of issues, a large fraction of the citizenry is uninformed. That Americans so enthusiastically celebrated tax revolts in the late 1970s, and then with such puzzled dismay lamented decaying roads, bridges, and school systems in the late 1980s, illustrates the extent of this more or less rational ignorance about the details of cause and consequence in the public realm.

One result of the imperfect public understanding of government programs is that perceptions are quite responsive to myth, anecdote, and metaphor. Alston

Chase argues in *Playing God in Yellowstone* that the National Park Service is held in high regard, despite egregious management practices, simply because no level of ineptness can destroy the majesty of the real estate it holds in trust.[26] Conversely, as there will always be some percentage of the population poorer than the rest, antipoverty programs will always be vulnerable to charges of ineffectiveness. A few stories about help for malnourished children shifts public sentiment to favor such programs, a few stories about fraud and abuse discredits them; but there is no sturdy connection to objective needs or results.

ENGINEERED IGNORANCE.   Quite apart from such *natural* ignorance—the technical and organizational barriers that deny the public a complete picture of what is being done in its name—there is also *engineered* ignorance, the result of deliberate deception by political subgroups, public officials, or by organizations assigned responsibility for public business. Most voters would like the realm of collective responsibility to be wide and the cost of government to be low. They reward claims that the common realm can be expanded at little cost, or that costs can be cut with little diminution of that realm. They frequently punish concessions to the contrary. (Research shows that citizens who favor large tax cuts seldom want to shrink the size of the government or cut the pay of public workers.)[27] There are, accordingly, powerful incentives and considerable opportunities for politicians and public servants to mislead citizens.

Around the turn of the century, the Italian economist Amilcare Puviani applied the term "fiscal illusion" to the tendency for governments to endeavor, often with a fair degree of success, to obscure the costs and to highlight the benefits of public expenditures.[28] Costs can be hidden by means such as making taxes complex and indirect; by inflating the currency; by shifting costs to the future through borrowing or by neglecting upkeep; and by imposing "temporary" levies that endure and expand as the public becomes accustomed to them. Benefits can be magnified by tactics such as attractive labeling; painting alternatives in the blackest possible tones; and by claiming credit for results that really spring from other causes. Anyone who pays attention to budgetary politics can think of dozens of examples and even suggest new categories. In *Checks Unbalanced: The Quiet Side of Public Spending*, Herman B. Leonard argues that "avoidance and obfuscation of the public's financial business are a national pastime approaching an art form."[29] Leonard enumerates several major types of "quiet spending," including unfunded promises to pay social security and public pension benefits, tax expenditures, concessionary loans and loan guarantees, off-budget financing, and deferred maintenance.

Max Weber wrote that government organizations seek to "increase the superiority of the professionally informed by keeping their knowledge and intentions secret." He related how the "treasury officials of the Persian shah have made a secret doctrine of their budgetary art and even use secret script."[30] Those who have occasion to consult federal budget documents are familiar with a modern American analogue.

Defensiveness and deception are not the only reasons why the language of public budgeting is complex, paralyzingly dull, and booby-trapped with acronyms and forbidding jargon. But they are often important reasons. It is a reliable rule of thumb that the less comprehensible is a spending program, the more questionable is its overall worth.[31] In part, this could result from a sort of perverse fiscal natural selection: The more obscure and confusing a program is, the more likely it is to escape the attention of reformers, while comprehensibly wasteful programs will be weeded out. But there are also any number of cases of confusion consciously engineered for defensive purposes.

For example, during the 1971 hearings on the ill-fated supersonic transport aircraft, one congressman lamented that the obviousness of the subsidy mechanism had invited unwelcome attention to the SST. "Should we be putting such things as incentives for technological development into a process that risks their being vetoed someplace along the line, such as a subsidy was in the case of the SST, or should we put them into tax-incentive areas fundamental in the law so that this kind of thing can continue to develop without closer scrutiny?"[32] Similarly, when the Pentagon was embarrassed by reports of overpriced weapons in the mid-1980s, it proposed breaking down its budget requests and accounting reports on the basis of subcontracts rather than weapons systems, ostensibly to enable Congress to monitor individual contracts more easily. But as a single weapons system can involve some hundreds of subcontracts, one observer concluded that "the real objective was to render the procurement budget an incomprehensible maze of line items."[33] A vigilant press is a significant corrective to these tendencies, of course. But the press is itself somewhat biased against coverage of the mundane, the ambiguous, and the complex. When officials seek to conceal something shocking or criminal, it is very likely that the American press will bring it to public attention. But undramatic deceptions may remain long submerged.

Of course, citizens are broadly aware that partisans, lobbyists, and public officials are tempted to mislead. The general result, however, is a generalized skepticism about "political" claims. Unable or unwilling to discriminate among different degrees of hyperbole, speculation, and rhetorical license, citizens simply take everything they hear from public officials with a grain of salt. Political leaders attempt to compensate for this discount factor by further inflating their claims, which only motivates citizens to discount political statements more sharply. Small wonder, then, that information about public undertakings is typically of low quality and difficult to verify.[34]

All this would be less of a problem if the consequence for collective choice was simply a degree of imprecision. But the tendencies for some people to be better informed than others, and for most people to be well informed about certain issues only, has important implications for the division of public business between the public and private sectors. These two basic means of carrying out collective undertakings will often differ in transparency. If private contracting is more readily comprehensible—because competitive bids and unit prices better summarize information about true costs—or if public arrangements are more transparent—because of sunshine laws and a more complete accounting for external effects—then the implications for citizens' understanding of what is being done in their names and at their expense may matter greatly—indeed, may matter more than do conventional efficiency comparisons.

The question this book seeks to illuminate is this: When is private performance of public tasks a good idea? The total public sector in the United States—federal, state, and local—accounts for roughly 35 percent of the nation's economy. About one-third of this spending is transfer payments such as social security checks, aid to the disabled, and general relief. Another one-third goes to compensate government employees, ranging from the president of the United States to the basketball coach at Indiana University to the man who mops the floors at Cambridge City Hall. The final one-third goes to purchase goods and services—from pencils and pothole repair to supersonic bombers and environmental impact statements—from nongovernmental entities.

Private organizations have been involved in public undertakings throughout history. Weber discusses "tax farming," in which entrepreneurs collected taxes on a commission basis in ancient Greece and Rome as well as prerevolutionary France. Mercenary armies, organized by profit-seeking entrepreneurs, have figured prominently in medieval as well as modern conflicts.[35] One academic, after surveying a number of empirical studies, concludes that "private suppliers are always more efficient than public suppliers."[36] Maybe so. It is conceivable that this is the case, and that we would do well to delegate virtually all public tasks to private organizations. It seems much more likely, though, that any private advantage is selective, and the right organizational form depends on the task.

PART TWO

EVIDENCE AND

ARGUMENTS

CHAPTER 3

ORGANIZATIONAL FORM
AND FUNCTION

HOW SHOULD public tasks be accomplished? Which should be performed by government itself, and which by hired outsiders? The essential starting point for this inquiry is the recognition that to speak of "government" producing something is to employ a convenient but potentially misleading figure of speech. "The government" is a shorthand term for a collection of people acting within some particular network of rules and expectations. To examine any instance of "government production" is invariably to discover *people*, variously organized and variously motivated, doing the producing. The document that codifies federal policy on privatization declares that "the government should not compete with its citizens."[1] But unless government is staffed exclusively by aliens, this ringing declaration has no real meaning. Government produces by arranging relationships whereby individuals and organizations, motivated at least in part by the promise of compensation from common funds, devote resources to designated public purposes. Some of these relationships we call "government jobs," while others we call "government contracts."

Consider *Air Force One* taking off from Andrews Air Force Base to carry the president to a summit meeting—a relatively pure case of government in action. The airplane was made by hourly wage workers at Boeing who were supervised by salaried managers, who in turn reported to Boeing investors who had put up their capital in exchange for profits. Other people, comparably organized and compensated, pumped, refined, and shipped the jet fuel. A salaried Air Force pilot handles the controls, while hundreds of military and civilian workers are involved in maintaining the aircraft and in staffing the navigation and traffic control systems that will keep it safely on course. Each of these people is carrying out his part in a diplomatic mission; each of them, including the presidential passenger, is being paid with money collected from the public at large.

The previous chapter dealt with the overarching problem of selecting and evaluating public tasks. Now the focus narrows to the organizational means of accomplishing them. Assume that this trip is really necessary, and consider the options. The president can book a ticket with a travel agent, hop a cab from the White House to Dulles, and fly TWA to Geneva. Or he can hire a jet and crew from a private charter company. Or—as he does in practice—he can use government-owned (but privately manufactured) equipment operated primarily by workers on the public payroll, while continuing to rely upon an intricate background network of goods and services organized chiefly through the market. A comparable range of options exists in principle for virtually any publicly funded activity, from retraining dislocated workers to performing surgery on elderly veterans to designing intercontinental ballistic missiles. Once we have decided to pay collectively to accomplish some task, we have to decide on the form of the contract with the people who will carry it out.

THE IDEA OF AGENCY

Selecting the right structure of accountability for public tasks raises the basic problem of agency. (The word *agency*, confusingly, holds several meanings. Here it refers to a type of relationship, not a governmental office.) The central idea is simple: A *principal* commissions an *agent* to act on the principal's behalf. In general, the agent's interests do not entirely coincide with those of the principal; the principal does not have complete control over the agent; the agent has only partial information about the principal's interests; and the principal has only partial information about the agent's behavior. The agency *relationship* consists in the reliance of a principal upon an agent with an agenda of his own. The agency *problem* is the difficulty, in all but the simplest such relationships, of ensuring that the principal is faithfully served and that the agent is fairly compensated.[2]

The agency approach is one formulation of the fundamental problem of mutual responsibility in human society: Individual interests are overlapping but not identical; we must constantly rely on others whom we can influence to a degree but cannot fully control. It engages the root social challenge of accountability to which cultural devices like law, ethics, and the market are meant to respond. A culture's capacity to get things done depends greatly on the quality of the institutions it develops to allow people to delegate tasks to others, or to undertake tasks for others, without fear of exploitation.

The basic agency dilemma has a long pedigree. The parable of the steward related in the gospel of Matthew concerns the problems a voyaging landholder must face when he delegates the management of his estate to an agent who cannot be monitored in the course of his duties, and whose performance can only be evaluated imprecisely after the fact. John Stuart Mill summarized the central problem when he wrote that "experience shows, and proverbs attest, how inferior is the quality of hired servants, compared with the ministration of those personally interested in the work, and how indispensable, when hired service must be employed, is 'the master's eye' to watch over it."[3] For Adam Smith, the chief sources of the agency problem are specialization and the consequent division of labor, and the chief solution the set of institutions making market exchange possible.[4] Smith's primal bargain of "give me this which I want, and you shall have that which you want" is a soundly structured agency relationship whenever you know what I want, I know what you want, I can be sure when you have delivered, and you are assured that I will deliver in turn. Under less ideal circumstances, agency relationships are more complex and more problematical.

The range of institutions involved in carrying out public work includes bureaus wholly controlled by government; semiautonomous governmental corporations; lower levels of government or private nonprofit groups to which tasks and resources are delegated; and direct or indirect contracts with private businesses. The central presumption of this book is that different kinds of public tasks call for different kinds of relationships with the agents who carry them out.

Pure types are rare. In practice, *publicness* and *privateness* are contingent, even slightly artificial categories. But to get a sense of the repertoire of organizational alternatives, it is worth examining in some detail two basic types of agents—profit-seekers and civil servants. The next two sections elaborate on one basic distinction: The profit-seeker, in exchange for a *price*, agrees to *deliver a product*. The civil servant, in exchange for a *wage*, agrees to *accept instructions*.

THE PROFIT-SEEKER

In the classic profit-seeking agency relationship, the customer is the principal and the entrepreneur is the agent. The agent delivers to the principal some specified product in return for a price. The art of the entrepreneur is to carry out his commission as efficiently as possible, so that the resources he uses up in the process are worth less than the price he receives. The remainder—the profit—is his motive and his reward. The agent's sole obligation to the principal is to deliver the goods as promised; how he does it is up to him.

Accountability is enforced transaction-by-transaction through the principal's abilities to judge the quality of the product, and to opt out of the relationship with agents who fail to deliver. Accountability is enforced economywide through competition. Principals can select among numerous agents on the bases of price and quality. Those agents best able to transform resources into valuable goods and services will prosper and expand; the less talented will drop out of the market. The dictates of efficiency are met as agents gravitate toward areas of endeavor where their talents matter most, and are squeezed out of areas for which they are unsuited.

Complications—Measurement, Risk, and Incentives

This idealized model obviously bears small resemblance to the kinds of economic relationships we encounter in the real world. Pure output-based transactions, in which the agent's payment depends solely on the value he delivers to the principal, are uncommon. Consider, for example, a taxicab ride. In Washington, D.C., cab fares are fixed fees based upon the distance between the points of origin and of destination. But in Boston and most other cities, fares are based upon time or distance traveled. The agent is paid not according to *output*—getting the principal from here to there—but according to *input*—miles on the road or time spent traveling. Similarly, the physician as an agent is not paid according to the length of the patient's life or how good he feels in the course of it, but according to the time spent in consultation and treatment. Stockbrokers are not paid by how rich they make their clients, but by how many trades they undertake on their clients' behalf.

The simplest apparent explanation for the rarity of pure output-based agency arrangements is that most people are not entrepreneurs but hired employees. But this begs the question of *why* this particular form of organization is so much more common than freelancing.[5] Moreover, employees as well as independent entrepeneurs can, in principle, be paid precisely the net value of their contribution to production; indeed, in the economist's ideal of competitive equilibrium, they must be. Yet, in practice, workers receive an hourly wage or an annual salary that is, at best, an indirect measure of the value of production. Nor does this explanation account for the frequency with which independent entrepreneurs—doctors, stockbrokers, plumbers, taxi drivers—although answerable directly to the principal, are paid on the basis of input rather than output. Two sets of reasons—one concerning *measurement*, the other concerning *risk*—underlie this pattern.

Measurement of output is often difficult even when only one principal and one agent are involved. Unless the principal has some expertise in the application of asphalt shingles, he will not know if his agent the roofer has delivered a new roof that will last for ten years or one that will leak within months. And even if the principal and his agent the barber share the same information on the physical characteristics of the product, they might disagree as to whether it constitutes a good haircut. Measuring output is still more problematic when the efforts of more than one person are involved. If one agent wields the pick and another the shovel, how is the foreman to gauge each worker's contribution to the excavation job?[6]

This difficulty of measuring contributions to joint production is further complicated by risk. If the final product is the result of an agent's effort and *something else* as well, output-based contracts get messy. In many cases, the product delivered to the principal depends not only on the agent's exertions, but also on external factors over which the agent has no control. When the agent's compensation depends solely upon output, he is paid in part according to the productive effects of his efforts, and in part according to accidents of good or bad luck. If the taxi driver is paid a flat fee for a ten-mile trip, he bears the risk of heavy traffic, forced detours, or bad weather. If the stockbroker's pay is based on how well his client's stocks perform, he bears the risk of a slump in the overall economy. If the surgeon's fee depends on his patient's health after the operation, he bears the risk that the patient will take an unforeseeable turn for the worse, or will disregard doctor's orders. Under such circumstances, the prudent agent may decline to enter into a purely output-based contract, or may demand a steep premium for accepting the risk. The principal, then, may do better to bear the risk himself, and to offer a contract paying the agent according to input rather than outputs.[7]

Thus measurement and risk problems often force a departure from simple output-based contracts. But once the bond between payment and ultimate results is severed, the agency relationship is vulnerable to breakdown. There are good reasons why taxi drivers are paid by the mile instead of by the trip; why stockbrokers are paid by the trade rather than in proportion to the client's net worth;

and why surgeons are paid by the operation and not according to the patient's health. The consequences, though, may include meandering routes that drive up the meter, blindly churned stock accounts, and too many operations performed with too little care.

When it is impossible (because of measurement problems) or inappropriate (because of risk) to pay an agent according to the output he delivers, the principal will seek to devise contracts that come as close as possible to the pay-for-performance ideal. One approach is to look for *proxies* for output value. Sometimes proxies are reliable. When a pest eradication program aims to induce hunters to kill coyotes, county officials can pay a bounty for each pair of coyote ears delivered with reasonable confidence that the hunters are not simply tackling the animals, snipping off their ears, and letting them go. John Stuart Mill favored government support for a few outstanding "scientific discoverers, and perhaps some other classes of savants." But he worried over how the government could identify the right savants to subsidize. Mill proposed a proxy: Assume that the *desired* output of superior research is closely associated with the more *visible* output of superior teaching. He called for attaching teaching responsibilities to the posts of scientists-laureate since "the public at large has the means of judging, if not the quality of the teaching, at least the talents and industry of the teacher."[8] (Interestingly, the faculty evaluation procedures of most modern universities are based on precisely the opposite assumption that the quality of teaching cannot easily be measured, but that the quality of research can be. Faculty are selected and paid largely on the basis of their publications, as a proxy for the value of their teaching.)

The danger is obvious: When the proxy is not perfectly linked to what is really desired, the agent may be motivated to deliver the one at the expense of the other. If the passenger *wants* progress toward his destination but *pays for* miles traveled, he risks a roundabout route. If the government wants pioneering research but pays for good teaching, scientists-laureate might neglect the lab to polish their lectures. And if the dean wants top-flight teaching but pays on the basis of publications, faculty members might deliver perfunctory lectures and retreat to their offices to pound out papers. Moreover, the proxy may not only be loosely linked to the product desired, but also hard to measure in itself. Taxi meters can be rigged. A long list of publications may not be a sound measure of original thinking, and the yearly profits on which executive bonuses are based may reflect accounting gimmicks rather than enduring increases in shareholders' wealth.

Overcoming Agency Problems

Many of the institutions that make the real economy so much more interesting and untidy than the world described in an elementary economics text—franchises, civil courts, standards and regulations, licensing and certification, and so on—can be seen as social devices to forge an adequate measure of accountability and efficiency in the face of measurement problems, risk, and temptations to opportunism.

One particularly significant device for overcoming agency problems is a *layered* structure of accountability—the profit-seeking, wage-paying private firm. Ownership is wholly or partially distinct from operations. Production workers are accountable to managers, and are paid a wage in exchange for time on the job. Managers, in turn, are accountable to owners, and are paid a salary for directing and supervising production. Finally, the owners are accountable to customers, and collect a profit—the excess of revenues over costs—in exchange for organizing and monitoring the whole process. From the customer's point of view a classic profit-seeking agency relationship prevails, but with layers of more complex contracts nested within it.

Somewhat paradoxically, one reason why enduring business organizations predominate in the economy, instead of shifting, task-specific teams of producers, is the pervasiveness of change and uncertainty. In all but the simplest undertakings, participants will not know at the outset just what will be needed at each stage along the way. New information—about the task at hand or the goals to be pursued—may make original contracts obsolete. A clothing wholesaler who contracts with independent knitters to make argyle socks may find that fashions have switched from argyle to stripes. I negotiate with a taxi driver to take me to the airport by what I calculate to be the shortest route, then discover that an unexpected traffic jam makes another route look better. When circumstances change, following through on old contracts is often wasteful, or worse.

Several options confront the principal entering into a contract when uncertainties loom.[9] First, he can simply write a contract that fits the most likely course of events, and resign himself to living with the consequences if the world subsequently refuses to cooperate. (A skier rents a slopeside cabin for the last weekend in January and hopes it snows.) Second, he can write a *contingent* contract spelling out in detail the agent's obligations in each conceivable event. This strategy tends to require a great deal of time, imagination, and paper. If details are left open to lighten the chore of writing the contract, moreover, there may be disputes over interpretation as events unfold. And some contingencies may not be foreseen, thereby unhinging the agency relationship should they occur. Consider the medieval French farce that portrays a domineering wife who demands her husband hew to a detailed list of his household duties. When the wife tumbles into a deep washtub, the husband consults the list and reports, over her muffled pleas for help, that extricating spouses from washtubs isn't one of his chores.[10]

A third option is to write a *series* of contracts step-by-step, building in new information as it emerges along the way. This works if the principal and the agent retain the same kind of arm's-length, independent relationship at each stage in the process that they had at the start. In particular, the same regulating force of *competition* must operate with equal strength throughout. But once a transaction begins, an agent may develop advantages that insulate him against the threat of replacement. Familiarity with the task at hand or with the principal's desires, gained in the course of the contract, may make it costly for the principal to replace him in midstream. Knowing this, an agent may opportunistically drive a hard bargain with a principal who reopens the contract after events have limited his options.

A fourth option is a response to the deficiencies of the first three: employment contracts. Rather than agreeing to deliver to the principal a predetermined product, the agent agrees to *follow the instructions* of the principal, within specified limits and for a specified time. The principal can amend the agent's mandate in line with shifting priorities and opportunities.[11] Flexibility in the face of uncertain circumstances is only the most obvious advantage of the employment relationship. The employee has less need than an independent agent to demonstrate the value of his output, and thus less incentive to misrepresent that value. He has only limited opportunity to exploit the principal in renegotiations if circumstances change once a task is under way, so long as his new duties remain within the agreed-upon range. While a freelancer may often find it advantageous to conceal or distort information, employees will usually be more willing to share information with the principal and with other agents. A more structured relationship may permit better monitoring, and ease communication between the principal and the agent. It will allow more complete social contacts and richer human ties, which may be valuable both intrinsically, and as a means of forging trust, and instrumentally, as a management approach to overcome opportunism. Finally, a principal might care about *how* a product is delivered, and hiring employees (instead of contracting with outside suppliers) gives him the discretion over means that would otherwise go to the agent.

Employment relationships have some basic defects as well. As the principal becomes committed to a particular agent, the discipline of competition erodes. Insulation from the check of the market invites inefficiency, and may constrict the flow of information about outside opportunities and alternatives. (This is one reason why employment contracts are usually at least in part output-based, and performance ratings matter for retention and promotion decisions.) The principal also bears full responsibility for choosing how to carry out the project, and loses whatever value the agent's independent judgment has for the task at hand. (This is why independent contracts are especially common in areas where the expertise of the suppliers exceeds that of their clients, such as law, medicine, architecture, and other technical professions.) Finally, by moving from output-based relationships to employment relationships, the principal is left with the chore of ensuring that his orders are carried out. Sometimes it is easier to monitor fidelity than to evaluate production; sometimes it is not.[12]

The relative appeal of *employing* people, as opposed to *contracting with* them, increases (1) the more the task at hand is uncertain at the outset and prone to revision, (2) the harder it is to measure the value of production, (3) the more disruptive it is to switch agents in midstream, and (4) the more the principal knows about the best means to accomplish his task. Conversely, arm's-length contracts with outside suppliers are more attractive (1) the more precisely requirements can be specified in advance, (2) the more the principal cares about *ends* over *means*, (3) the more difficult it is to monitor fidelity to instructions (or the easier it is to measure results), and (4) the more readily incompetent or unfaithful agents can be replaced.

A central theme of this book is that very similar considerations should govern the public-policy choice between (input-based) civil service and (output-based) private contracting. The concepts of agency illuminate some of the basic issues involved in carrying out the public's business. How concretely can the principal— the public—specify what is to be accomplished in its name and at its expense? Does competition discipline suppliers and thereby ensure the public a fair price? Is the product sufficiently measurable to allow for output-based contracts? Or do factors beyond the control of the agent affect outcomes too strongly to permit payment by results alone? If measurement or risk problems require input-based contracts, are agents tempted to inefficiency or deception and, if so, how well can the public discern and control these tendencies? Such factors determine how confidently and efficiently public officials can use contracts with profit-seeking agents to fulfill common needs. But before exploring these factors further, let us examine more closely the governmental alternative to private contracting— bureaucracy.

THE CIVIL SERVANT

Bureaucracy is one particularly important way of arranging to accomplish the public's business. In novels such as Joseph Heller's *Catch-22* and Franz Kafka's *The Trial*, as well as in the typical American street-corner commentary, bureaucracy is depicted less as an institutional form than as a social malignancy—at best mindlessly inflexible, at worst chillingly unaccountable. Many scholars, especially economists, share this perspective. In the words of conservative economist Ludwig von Mises: "The terms *bureaucrat, bureaucratical,* and *bureaucracy* are clearly invectives. . . . Nobody doubts that bureaucracy is thoroughly bad and that it should not exist in a perfect world."[13] Von Mises's declaration is quite meaningless if taken literally, of course; antibiotics, dentists, and diapers would also have no place in a perfect world. If taken less than literally, the declaration is unduly sweeping. In our own highly imperfect world, there are purposes that no other arrangement fulfills quite so well. The ubiquity of bureaucracy in divergent economies and cultures suggests that humankind has found no better way to organize itself for accomplishing certain kinds of tasks.

Max Weber, probably the preeminent scholar of bureacracy, wrote that the "fully developed bureaucratic mechanism compares with other organizations exactly as does the machine with the non-mechanical modes of production."[14] Bureaucracies, like machines, are costly to build and keep in operation, prone to break down if neglected or misused, but capable, if carefully designed and maintained, of prodigious efficiency when performing functions for which they are suited.

Weber specified three fundamental characteristics of bureaucratic organization: First, duties are clearly defined; second, authority is delimited and hierarchical; third, procedures, rights, and roles are formalized. The organization operates according to "general rules which are more or less stable, more or less exhaustive, and can be learned."[15] The bureaucratic agent agrees to follow the directions of his superiors "as if the order agreed with his own conviction."[16] The bureaucrat's accountability is ongoing, subject to continual redefinition, bounded by the terms of the authority relationship rather than by the achievements of a specific task.

There are obvious problems, however, with defining bureaucracy strictly in terms of hierarchy, authority, and routine. In many governmental bureaucracies—including the Air Force, the Federal Bureau of Investigation, and the National Aeronautics and Space Administration—at least some agents exercise a great deal of discretion. Even more glaringly, many nongovernmental organizations—the

Catholic church, the accounting department at Macy's, the United Parcel Service—display an extreme degree of structured authority and procedural routine. Indeed, many of the classic studies of bureaucracy have concerned themselves as much with private as with public organizations. Max Weber went so far as to claim that "it does not matter for the character of bureaucracy whether its authority is called 'private' or 'public.'"[17]

Bureaucracy and the Market

Later scholars, seeking definitions that would discriminate among General Motors, Massachusetts General Hospital, and the Department of Defense, have stressed *insulation from the market* as a key characteristic of bureaucracies. Anthony Downs, for example, posited four features that distinguish bureaucracy from other forms of organization: a relatively large size, a full-time paid staff, formalized hiring and promotion rules, *and* evaluation by some set of criteria other than market prices.[18] Such definitions are still not particularly restrictive. They include as "bureaucracies" not only government agencies and state-owned enterprises but also most schools and hospitals, charitable and religious foundations, and other large formal organizations whose performance is measured by any metric other than profitability. They include as well those parts of profit-seeking corporations that provide unpriced goods or services to other parts within the corporation. They do, however, distinguish between United Airlines and the United States Air Force. One entity depends for its revenue on the spending decisions of individual customers while the other does not. The compensation of some of the participants in United Airlines—the stockholders, primarily, and also some managers—depends on the organization's profitability, while no Air Force officer gets a bonus pegged to the service's budget surplus. The continued existence of United Airlines is ultimately determined by individual judgments of value; the continued existence of the Air Force depends in a far more complex and mediated way on citizens' perceptions of its worth.

Employment contracts insulate *individuals* from market pressures—partially or entirely, for reasons sound or unsound. In a public bureaucracy, the *organization* is walled off from the price system. The Chrysler Corporation keeps engineers on the payroll (instead of contracting out for each design job) because familiarity with Chrysler's specific products, processes, and administrative style matters too much to reduce the design process to a series of separate contracts with rival design firms. By paying engineers a fixed salary to accept assignments as they come, Chrysler retains the option of ordering last-minute changes without haggling. But the arrangement is still evaluated with reference to profitability. An employment relationship, somewhat separating engineers from the outside market, is simply the best way of pursuing the goal of good returns. Even if Chrysler cannot perfectly calculate the relative advantages of hiring engineering services versus contracting out for them, and even if considerations other than economic ones (such as loyalty to current employees) affect the decision, the profitability criterion, at least in principle, provides a metric to govern the choice between internal and external suppliers.

The same is not true of civil service bureaucracies. For most publicly financed endeavors, market prices are presumed to be misleading measures of value. The mandate of a public bureaucracy is defined, and its performance evaluated, in terms other than the balance between the market cost of the resources it requires and the market price of the product it delivers. "Efficiency" becomes a complicated quality in these circumstances.[19] Employees of Disneyland can be evaluated largely in terms of the effect their performance has on the organization's net income; employees of the National Park Service cannot. A civil servant who sets admission prices to Yellowstone at levels that maximize revenues, or who sells off choice parcels of land at handsome prices, may be increasing income while subverting the organization's mandate.

The absence of relevant market criteria shapes and limits options for managing public workers. A civil service organization must develop direct institutional means for collecting, transmitting, and interpreting the kinds of information brought to bear indirectly, for profit-seeking organizations, through market prices. An organization closely tied to the market can structure mandates to employees around the basic goal: "Increase net revenues." While few firms care *only* about profitability, and while private management is by no means a simple matter, the barometer of profit and loss does greatly facilitate managerial evaluation and control. In governmental organizations, communicating to participants the precise goals of the organization and ensuring compliance tend to be at once more important and more difficult. For an organization devoted to nonmarket goals, mandates are apt to be a good deal more complicated, success or failure less self-evident, and directives and evaluation more detailed and explicit. Unlike the case in profit-seeking organizations—where renegade or incompetent employees are often betrayed by high costs or low returns—deviation from the goals of a public organization only occasionally entails financial consequences that clearly signal problems or spur correction.

THE PUBLIC REALM'S SPECIAL ACCOUNTABILITY PROBLEMS

To set these features of public bureaucracy into perspective, consider the particular vulnerabilities to breakdown of any public endeavor, whether civil servants or profit-seekers are entrusted with its accomplishment. Chapter 2 surveyed some barriers to aligning governmental action with the real interests of citizens. Overcoming these barriers (to invoke the current chapter's terminology) can be cast as an agency problem. What kinds of contracts should govern the relationships between citizens and the agents—whether civil servants or profit-seekers—who carry out the public's business? How should these contracts vary according to the type of task? And how are such relationships prone to go wrong?

There are several degrees of potential breakdown. Attenuated responsibility for results invites simple inefficiency. Or contracts may be too loosely drafted, or too weakly enforced, to keep agents' claims on the public reasonable. And the circular agency relationship peculiar to collective undertakings—where suppliers are also political actors—may give agents potent incentives and opportunities to shape public spending decisions.

Inefficiency

Even when no specific peril looms, management is a struggle against entropy. Productive institutions, like productive machines, break down without maintenance. Harvey Leibenstein, in a much-cited and much-debated article, argued that all organizations, no matter how sensibly designed at the start, are prone to a gradual loss of discipline and rationality, which he termed "X-inefficiency."[20] By this Leibenstein meant the natural tendency of human organizations to depart from the *un*natural state of purposeful industriousness. Albert O. Hirschman employs a similar notion to which he gives the simpler label of "slack." "Firms and organizations," he wrote in *Exit, Voice, and Loyalty*, "are permanently and randomly subject to decline and decay."[21] In the more prosaic language of this chapter, the contractual ties binding principals and agents tend to weaken, loosening the links between agents' behavior and principals' interests. This sad tendency for productive relationships to go slack is controlled only to the extent that someone is both inclined and able to resist drift, deter waste, and focus resources on the organizational mission.

In the private sector, theory assigns this role to *owners*. An owner is entitled to determine the membership and to direct the activities of the productive team, as well as to claim the net return from the team's endeavors. With profits tied intimately to the owner's wealth, his mind is concentrated upon finding ways to turn resources into results as efficiently as possible. Nobody would argue that so simple an arrangement is the norm in the private economy. In most firms of any size, ownership is dispersed, and several layers of agents (an executive team, a board of directors, often an investment fund manager) separate stockholders from shop-floor managerial functions. At each level, the same sorts of monitoring, risk, and incentive problems discussed here threaten to sap accountability. Yet one need have no illusions about the level of slack in the private sector to recognize that the attenuation of ownership poses special problems in the public realm.[22]

In a democracy, governmental organizations are "owned" by the citizenry. The quality of public management *does* affect citizens' welfare: Efficiency improves public services or lightens the tax burden, or both. But public management is a matter of millions of specific policies and procedures. Except for a handful of vital public duties, the difference between superb efficiency and egregious slack translates into only an infinitesimal effect on *each citizen*'s well-being. Even if a citizen knows precisely how a change in some specific policy or procedure would enhance efficiency, he is unlikely to find it *economically* worthwhile to lobby for the change. (Citizens frequently do try to affect public management, of course, because of public spirit, or the pleasure of venting indignation, or because they stand to gain disproportionately from the reforms proposed.) In large part this motivational issue is simply a matter of size, and of the shrinking stake each member has as an organization grows. The "diluted interest" argument would enshrine the mom-and-pop grocery store as the model of efficiency. It would predict slightly more waste and slack in a small partnership, yet more in a midsized business or a small town's public-works department, distinctly more in a big stockholder-owned company or a midsized city government, more inefficiency still in the federal government, and, finally, colossal mismanagement in global organizations.[23]

But while absentee ownership of a private firm involves a dilution of interest similar to that which afflicts governments, there is one crucial difference. In the private sector, ownership rights can be bought and sold, and thus can become concentrated in the hands of a sufficiently small number of people, each of whom has a great deal to gain from efficiency improvements.[24] If a private company becomes grossly inefficient, alert investors are motivated to buy up ownership from dispersed shareholders; to alter the corporate structure, mission, or management to wring the slack out; and to reap the gains of greater efficiency.

In the public sector, *ownership* comes with citizenship, and its inalienability (unless one emigrates) makes a concentration of ownership rights impossible. For obvious reasons, no democrat would have it any other way. Dispersed accountability is not a remediable flaw of public management, but an essential (albeit complicating) feature of the common realm. The potential for chronic inefficiency, then, is a special peril for collective endeavors.

The attenuation of ownership inherent in public undertakings may slacken the entire chain of agency relationships binding citizens with those who ultimately do the work. Politicians are pressed in a general way to make government more efficient. But only rarely can a powerful constituency be found that intensely favors specific improvements. It is unlikely that the electoral prospects of any politician will be measurably enhanced by his role in negotiating a better deal on the paint used for National Park Service buildings, or by his streamlining the procedure for getting a passport. He will put correspondingly little pressure on the appointed officials reporting to him to monitor the economic and managerial details of the public's business. These officials will, in turn, tend to adopt a less vigilant management style with contractors and lower-level workers than they would if the consequences of inefficiency were more concentrated.

At best, activities will drift out of alignment with the public interest in a more or less random way. A city government is probably more likely to repave Park Street, even when Maple Street gets more traffic and has more potholes, than is a private company to make blue sweatshirts when customers are clamoring for red ones. The federal government will probably be slower than IBM to correct expensively flawed financial procedures. A state government is less likely than is General Motors to keep up on the preventive maintenance of its buildings. This type of managerial slack invites not only random drift, however, but also the displacement of the weakly enforced public purpose by narrower agendas.

Excessive Compensation for Agents

The executives of both private and public organizations prefer, by and large, to have comfortable salaries, livable offices, and humane work loads. Production workers generally like high pay, good working conditions, and interesting duties. Suppliers prefer remunerative prices, loose deadlines, and broad-minded quality standards. And, by and large, the members of productive organizations like to make life pleasant for others as well—supervisors enjoy granting raises and days off, purchasing agents like to gratify sales representatives with lucrative orders, and so on. While most people are also strongly driven by pride in accomplishment, there are powerful pressures within virtually any organization for costs to escalate and for productive activity to ebb or to lose focus. To the extent that outsiders have valid claims on organization—by way of having contributed its resources, or through reliance on its promises—the assertion of agents' interests at the expense of the organizational mission is both inefficient and unfair. In a private company, competition and the concern of owners for their invested wealth tends to constrain the self-interest of agents. The public sector must make do with different, and frequently weaker, formal devices for keeping agents' claims reasonable.

Reasonable has a rather specific meaning in economic theory. An agent's compensation should equal the value the agent creates. It should also approximate what the agent could collect in the *next best* use of his powers. In other words, the economic return to a productive asset (including the time of a civil servant or a profit-seeking contractor) rightly depends on its *opportunity cost*—the value it would create if devoted to its best alternative use. An agent's compensation is *unreasonable* if it exceeds the remuneration others would ask to do the work. The principle is neither very subtle nor very radical: Public agents—whether profit-seekers or civil servants—should receive only what is required to induce them, or their equally able rivals, to perform as required, and no more.

THE NOTION OF "RENTS." There is one important refinement to the theoretical ideal that fair compensation should be equivalent to the agent's next best alternative. Sometimes an agent is so well-suited to a particular task that his productive value would be much lower in any other job. If pay levels in his chosen occupation are set by the competitive bids of less specialized agents, his compensation will exceed his opportunity cost. The excess of actual payment over the minimum needed to keep him on the job is what economists refer to as a *rent*. The terminology is regrettable, since most people have another perfectly good meaning in mind for that word.[25] But references to this meaning of rent are, unfortunately, as ubiquitous in most works on the economics of institutions as they are alien practically anywhere else.

Rent, in this specialized sense, originates in *differences*. By temperament or training, people are differentially suited to various tasks. Suppose Bruce Springsteen's range of talents pose for him a career choice between entertaining and tax accounting. If his capacity to create value, as well as his earnings, are greater in entertainment than in accounting, he enjoys a rent, legitimately. Society signals that it wants him to write and to perform songs rather than to prepare Schedule B forms. If some new artist appeared who could perform just like Springsteen for half the price, Springsteen's rent would shrink. If every tax accountant had his talent as an entertainer, Springsteen's rent would disappear.

Cambridge, Massachusetts, has a tight labor market (as this is written) and unskilled jobs go begging. A clerk in a fast-food store knows he can easily find another job just as good as his present one. So even if he is earning twice as much as someone similarly skilled and similarly employed in, say, Shreveport, Louisiana, he is collecting no rents. But clerks at the Harvard Square post office—substantially better paid, and only a little more skilled—might have a hard time finding equally good jobs if they lost their positions, so some fraction of their compensation can be counted as rent.

Since most people tend to gravitate toward the job they like and do best, or grow into the job over time, rents are very common; only those workers right on the verge of quitting are collecting no rents at all. Rents are a problem—unfair or inefficient or both—when an agent is given, for no good reason, a more lucrative deal than would be required to obtain an equally competent replacement. The public realm is especially subject to this problem. Elected officials and public managers may, for diverse reasons, fail to bridle the self-interest of agents, allowing public undertakings to become rich with rents. Some agents are paid more—in money, security, leisure, or other currencies—than they could earn in alternative occupations.

Part of this excess is a simple transfer: Agents do somewhat better than they otherwise would, at the citizens' expense. If the public *intends* to transfer income to its suppliers, of course, such an arrangement is perfectly legitimate (albeit roundabout). Interestingly, economic theory has no comment to make on this transfer in itself. Economists are agnostic about the relative value of different people's welfare, and balk at comparing alternative distributions of income. If the government pays an engineer or a cement company twice what is required to secure their participation in some valuable dam project, an economist can only note that the distribution of income is slightly different than it would have been with competitive pricing.

What *does* worry economists is that *changes in resource use* occur as suppliers respond to the prospect of rich returns. Much has been written about the perverse incentives, set in motion by public budgeting, to engage in wasteful "rent-seeking" behavior.[26] Consider the hypothetical dam project again. If civil service engineers are paid more than the going rate, there will be more applicants than jobs. Applicants might try to get an edge in the competition by taking impressive-sounding but unhelpful courses, or by hanging around the hiring office, or by taking project managers out to lunch. Rent-seeking behavior uses up resources without producing value in return, and thus warps the workings of the economy.

While the terminology of rents and rent-seeking behavior is foreign in any context but economic theory, the idea is commonplace. Government workers invoke the notion when they observe that transferring public functions to private contractors usually means lower wages. Civil servants would still be willing to teach, guard, nurse, survey, analyze, or design under private rather than public management, but they would be worse off. In short, a rent is at stake. The real issue, of course, is what this means in moral and political terms. Public employee organizations frequently argue that rents to *people*—relatively good pay and benefits, job security, congenial working conditions, and so on—are good news, while rents to *corporations*—bonus profits, low risk, and safety from competition—are bad news. Civil servants resent the implication that the desirable features of government work are somehow unmerited, and they underscore that veterans, the handicapped, and victims of past discrimination are major beneficiaries of public employment. The question, of course, is to what extent citizens consciously endorse transferring wealth through government employment policies.

DISTORTED SPENDING DECISIONS

To gather up the threads of this chapter's argument, the weakened accountability that tends to plague the public realm often allows "slack." This slack can take the form of random inefficiency. It can also result in economically needless and morally unwarranted rents to agents. Worse, agents seeking such benefits may be inclined to press for spending on rent-rich public undertakings, whether or not they are good for the community as a whole. When agents are also principals— with the right to vote and otherwise affect policy—they will have the opportunity, as well as the incentive, to influence public spending decisions.

This scenario, with bureaucrats monopolizing the villain's role, has long preoccupied conservative scholars. James Buchanan has warned of "breakdowns in the transmission of individuals' demands through the political-fiscal process, including the possibility that the transmission institutions may be deliberately perverted by self-seeking politicians and bureaucrats."[27] "What are the effects of allowing bureaucrats to vote?" he speculated. "Is this not a direct conflict of interest?" Richard Craswell, writing in the journal *Public Choice*, diagnosed a dynamic of ever-increasing public spending fueled by the self-interest of producers. With each increment in the common realm, he contended, "more people are brought into the class of those receiving private benefits. . . . These people will now take their private benefits into account, and their preferred level of spending will increase."[28] Such indictments, though, are at once too narrow—damning civil servants and, by and large, sparing profit-seeking suppliers—and insufficiently discriminating in their analyses of both types of suppliers' motives and their abilities to distort public spending.

Distort, to be sure, is a loaded word. One might acknowledge the urge of suppliers to lobby for spending programs from which they benefit without conceding that there is much wrong with this. One citizen supports an antiballistic missile defense system because he fears the Soviets, another because he is a laser technician whose job prospects depend upon the program. One citizen favors more public housing because she is deeply troubled by the plight of the homeless, another because she owns a construction company poised for government building contracts. One citizen wants spending on Medicaid increased because he believes in a right to quality medical care regardless of income, another because she owns a large block of stock in a hospital management corporation. Is not the political system supposed to simply register and act on citizens' preferences? Does it matter *why* people want what they do?

The problem is that self-seeking agents may be able to dominate the spending agenda to the detriment of the public at large. *Concentrated* interest in an issue motivates political activism. Other citizens, each only a little affected, may not find it worthwhile to become informed enough, or active enough, to counter agents' pressures. Producers often forge themselves into organized and sophisticated constituencies. Compact coalitions of rent-seeking agents, even if their total benefit from a spending decision is relatively small, can often prevail over much larger groups with a greater, but more dispersed, stake in the issue. The agency relationship breaks down entirely because the agents have, in effect, silenced the principals.[29]

Producer groups seeking to control spending decisions often make common cause with other special interests. Coalitions can include suppliers as well as organized citizen groups that benefit disproportionately from certain publicly financed endeavors: weapons firms and stalwart anticommunists, Veterans' Administration hospital staffers and veterans' groups, teachers' organizations and the parents of young children, building contractors and housing advocates, and so on. Suppliers may also forge alliances with politicians who find it politically expedient to serve the interests of concentrated producers instead of the dispersed interests of other constituents.[30] The "iron triangle" of producer groups, key constituencies, and well-placed legislators is a staple phrase in the policy analysis literature. As such coalitions gain control over the public spending agenda at the expense of unorganized citizens, the system of democratic accountability erodes.

Four points summarize this survey of the special risk for breakdown in agency relationships where the public at large is the principal. First, a degree of *slack* is almost inevitable. Collective endeavors lack the regulating factors of competition and of individual vigilance over spending decisions, as the dispersal of *ownership* weakens pressures for productive efficiency. Second, slack creates opportunities for agents to strike unduly rich deals for themselves. Third, it is the opportunity to collect rents that tempts agents to distort public spending decisions. If public work were not exceptionally lucrative, suppliers would be indifferent to public spending—no slack, no rents; no rents, no reason to lobby. Fourth, and most importantly, these problems are inherent in *collective endeavors*, and *not* in bureaucracy *per se*. While this summary seems to echo familiar analyses of the defects and dangers of government bureaucracy, the problems of slack, rent-seeking, and political opportunism apply (albeit in different forms) however public agents are organized. Thus an important set of issues arises as to how civil servants and profit-seeking agents tend to *differ*, both in efficiency and in fidelity to the public interest. The next two chapters take up these issues in turn.

CHAPTER 4

THE EVIDENCE ON
EFFICIENCY

E XCEPT FOR a handful of ideologues, few people would be very interested
in privatization unless private suppliers promised superior efficiency. Theory suggests that they should. Now theory is all very well, of course, but what about
the real world? *Are* profit-seeking organizations more productive? This chapter
surveys some evidence on the relative efficiency of public and private organizations
performing similar tasks.

Before reviewing some empirical studies, a few caveats are in order. The first,
which ideologically fervent commentators of every political stripe too often neglect,
is that no set of studies can prove any *universal* assertion about either public or
private institutions. There are exceptions to even the strongest, simplest pattern—
and the conclusions suggested by the review in this chapter are subtle and complex.
The best that any empirical survey can hope for is to find some suggestive
tendency in the way the evidence falls. There will always be counterexamples;
there may be a meaningless muddle of clashing results. The only ways to avoid
ambiguity are to restrict attention to a narrow range of phenomena, or to ignore
all inconveniently conflicting data or studies.

Second, theoretical distinctions are satisfyingly crisp; empirical comparisons are
messy, tentative, and hedged about with conditions. Comparing public and private
efficiency in the real world has obliged the analysts whose work is surveyed here
to come up with operational definitions of "public," "private," and "efficiency"
and to apply analytical techniques that allow for a fair comparison by accounting
for factors *aside from* publicness and privateness. I try here to give a sense of how
each investigator tackled these problems.

Finally, this review of the evidence is inevitably incomplete. Only a tiny fraction of the "experiments" that reality incessantly presents has ever been formally analyzed. And while this compendium covers a respectable portion of the studies published in English, by no means does it include all of the available research. Readers are invited to continue examining the evidence.

GARBAGE COLLECTION

I begin with a relatively detailed survey of garbage collection, both because the topic is exceptionally—even curiously—blessed with formal analyses, and because it offers to readers unfamiliar with statistical cost studies a chance to develop a feel for their style and their perils.

Americans dispose of over 150 million tons of trash each year. The average person, on the average day, generates 3.4 pounds of refuse—composed of roughly 37 percent paper, 17 percent leaves and lawn trimmings, and 10 percent each of glass, metal, and food detritus.[1] (Technically, *garbage* is a term of art meaning leftovers, bones, vegetable peels, and other things that rot, as distinct from paper rubbish, yard trimmings, and bulky refuse; here I use the terms interchangeably.) In 1952, most of the overall cost of getting rid of garbage was found to be due to collection, with disposal accounting for only 15 percent.[2] But as American society has become more discriminating about where and in what form the trash gets dumped, disposal costs have risen sharply. Per ton disposal costs in Philadelphia tripled between 1983 and 1988, for example, and other cities have seen similar increases, while Wall Street now values the stock of solid-waste management companies primarily on the basis of how much landfill space they own.[3]

Garbage collection is in many ways an ideal task for which to compare public and private efficiency. Two-thirds of all American cities have some type of private trash collection, whether through free competition among firms, exclusive franchises, or contracts with city governments. In 45 percent of the cities, *only* private firms pick up the garbage, while in 33 percent, municipal sanitation departments have a monopoly. Adjusting these figures by the sizes of the cities suggests that between one-third and one-half of American households have their trash collected by private firms.[4] The private sector role in waste management, moreover, has grown steadily in the past few decades. In 1964, 18 percent of surveyed cities contracted with private firms to pick up residential garbage; in 1982, the proportion had risen to 27 percent.[5]

Intuitively, private garbage collection seems like a good idea. A well-established tradition affirms that a competitive market is a good device for discovering the best and cheapest means of carrying out clearly defined tasks. The enterprise at issue here is readily described: Pick up the garbage and take it away. If the quality of service can be monitored, price competition should lead to the best deal for consumers. Since entering the industry requires no massive capital investments or esoteric knowledge, it seems reasonable to expect a good deal of competition. Meanwhile, theory suggests a number of drawbacks to governmental delivery. Lack of competition is only the most obvious. The more layers of organization that stand between the principal (the citizen) and the producer (the trash collectors), the more diffused are the incentives for efficiency. Crews and supervisors—presumably voting citizens—may be paid much more than they could make in other jobs, and there may be more of them than the work requires. The sanitation department might pass up the chance to upgrade the truck fleet, even when the change promises net savings, if the new technology implies laying off a quarter of the crews.

On the other hand, public and private collection may not be precisely the same product. If municipal collectors collect rents in forms such as high pay, ironclad job security, leisurely schedules, and so on, these represent real benefits, whether or not their incidence is strictly warranted. Collecting trash requires a work force of only modest qualifications. Private contractors, if they know their business, will offer a wage just high enough to attract such personnel. If municipal trash haulers are better compensated, they may also be more qualified. The attractive jobs will draw excess applicants, and there will surely be *some* criteria for selecting crews. Often, no doubt, the key criterion will be political; choice sanitation jobs will go to the well connected. But it could be otherwise. Public sector garbage haulers might be hired for congeniality and attitude. Or they might be chosen for their powers of observation, to double as an early morning security squad. At a minimum, the implicit job description could demand sufficient delicacy of feeling to forswear the playing of boom boxes or recreational lid-rattling. Alternatively, the sanitation department could serve as an informal local welfare system. An untalented fifty-five-year-old with limited options might be given a job that a teenager could do as well and more cheaply. In short, if public sanitation departments provide valuable services of any sort—aside from moving the garbage from here to there—and if private alternatives do not, then the cheaper private service is also in a real sense an inferior service. This refinement—while open to abuse—is well kept in mind for any comparison of public and private.

Of course, quality of service can be contractually specified. If it is thought important to bundle other services into trash collection, the agreement between the city and its private contractors can embody these concerns, including, if necessary, hiring the mayor's brother-in-law. But as such requirements mount, so will the fee required to attract bidders. As the gap between public and private costs narrows, and as the complexities of writing and enforcing contracts increase, any original private sector advantage would shrink. A socially balanced, politically sensitive specification of inputs would essentially eliminate the public-private distinction. More to the point, however, it seems questionable whether assigning supplemental functions to the sanitation department—multiplying mandates and complicating accountability—is really the most sensible way to achieve public goals apart from getting rid of the garbage.

The Evidence on Costs

Laissez-faire theory invites the presumption that efficiency in garbage collection means letting citizens make their own arrangements. James T. Bennett and Manuel H. Johnson attempted to prove precisely this point. The two economists compared the costs of public and private garbage services in Fairfax County, Virginia. Collection is handled publicly in parts of the county, while in other parts private firms compete for each customer's business. Bennett and Johnson found that "when the public sector cost of refuse collection is compared with that of the private sector within a given jurisdiction so that the analysis is not confounded by the anomalies of the public budgeting process, [the] contention that the private sector should be more efficient than the public sector is confirmed."[6] Of the twenty-nine private competitive firms operating in Fairfax County, all but one charged less per household to get rid of the garbage than did the Solid Waste Division of Public Works. (The county charged an average of $127 a year versus an average of $87 for the private firms.) Bringing a battery of statistical tests to bear on their data, Bennett and Johnson demonstrated that the cost edge of private competitive firms is significant at impressive confidence levels.

This study is a fitting one for beginning this review since it displays so well the perils of incautious calculations. While the analysis by Bennett and Johnson is conceptually plausible and suffers from no computational errors, it is a good deal less conclusive than they assert. The key problem is that they simply average all the private costs, average all the public costs, and compare the two numbers. This analysis does not control for distance from the dump, dispersal of households served, quality and frequency of service, and other factors aside from organizational form. (Bennett and Johnson noted in passing that the part of the county with public collection was farther from the landfill, but private firms collected more frequently, so it remains unclear what difference a more comprehensive study would make.) Finally, even if we were to grant that their analysis is persuasive as far as it goes, it goes no further than Fairfax County. (Bennett and Johnson themselves emphasize the complexity of cost comparison by raising one interesting point: Since the cost of public waste collection is included in property tax bills, it is deductible from state and federal taxes. Nearly one-third of the cost of public collection in Fairfax County, then, falls on outside taxpayers.)[7]

Werner Z. Hirsch has examined the same issue, but with a larger and less casually selected sample, as well as methods that control for several factors other than public or private organization.[8] His study, based on data from twenty-four communities in the St. Louis area, attempts to explain the average annual cost of residential trash collection in terms of public versus private organization *and* five other variables: size of the community served, frequency of collection, backyard versus curbside pickup, population density, and financing arrangements (payment by individual households or out of general revenues).

The Hirsch model succeeds in explaining roughly 75 percent of the city-by-city variation in trash service costs. While Hirsch found no reliable evidence of economies of scale, pickup frequency was relevant: An increase from two to three weekly pickups boosted the cost per household by about one-quarter. Another significant factor was pickup location: It cost over one-third more to have crews go to the back of the house than it did if citizens took cans out to the curb themselves. Population density was not a significant variable, a result Hirsch found "somewhat astonishing," since it seemed obvious that the shorter the distance between pickup sites, the lower transportation costs should be.

Contrary to the results Bennett and Johnson found for Fairfax County, Hirsch concluded that the efficiency distinction between public and private organization was statistically insignificant. Whether a city used private contractors or city workers to pick up the trash had no detectable effect on average costs—at least in greater St. Louis. Interestingly, while the form of *organization* did not seem to matter, the form of *financing* did. In principle, the more citizens are made aware of costs, the more inclined they will be to insist on efficiency. Hirsch found, though, that paying for trash collection out of general revenues *cut* costs significantly. This could indicate that city governments are able to strike a better deal on behalf of citizens than the citizens can if they negotiate on their own. Or it might signal something else altogether: some problem in the data or (as Hirsch himself suggested) the model. Some of the peculiar results Hirsch found for other variables—scale and density as well as organizational form—led him to worry about the validity of his own results, and he called for further study.

One difficulty in defining the differences between public and private trash collection is that *public* and *private* are not neatly distinguishable in practice. Dennis Young, in a book with an admirably straightforward title—*How Shall We Collect the Garbage?*—pointed out that the possibilities include unrestricted laissez faire; private collection with free entry but licensing or certification requirements; private firms competing for customers within an area, but with restrictions on the number of competitors; franchise systems, in which governments grant a firm exclusive rights to serve an area (with or without price regulations); government contracts with private firms; and strictly public collection systems.[9]

E. S. Savas studied the costs of four of these alternatives: public sanitation departments, private contractors, private franchises, and open competition.[10] His main data came from a 1975 survey of 1,378 communities selected as representative of the country as a whole. In a relatively simple model (table 4.1) that aimed to explain average household cost in terms of variables representing scale, organizational form, and backyard-versus-curbside pickup, Savas found that the relative efficiency of public and private trash collection depended on the type of private collection at issue.

TABLE 4.1
Garbage Collection:
Options and Costs

Organizational form	Cost per ton
Public	$28.28
Private—contract	$25.78
Private—franchise	$28.23
Private—competitive	$38.54

SOURCE: E. S. Savas, "Policy Analysis for Local Government: Public vs. Private Refuse Collection," *Policy Analysis* 3 (Winter 1977): 66, table 6.

Savas found that municipal *contracting* with private firms was about 9 percent cheaper than direct municipal collection. But franchising—in which households, not the government, pay a single authorized collection company—offered no savings, and private competitive arrangements cost a third *more* than municipal collection.[11] Savas argued that the extra cost of municipal service could not be attributed to superior quality, reliability, or other factors (although he did not attempt to demonstrate this quantitatively).

A study by Peter Kemper and John Quigley, this one limited to cities in Connecticut, found cost differences in the same direction as Savas's results but of greater size: The cheapest form of garbage collection was municipal contracting with private firms. Public sanitation agencies cost roughly 25 percent more than private contractors, while freely competing private firms cost about 30 percent more than public agencies and over 60 percent more than contractors.[12]

The most ambitious appraisal of alternative organizational arrangements for garbage collection—at least in the United States—was done by Barbara J. Stevens. Stevens attempted to measure the determinants of average household collection costs. Mindful of the inconsistent and often misleading accounting systems used by local governments, she got her data from on-site compilations (rather than from agency budgets or financial reports) and included costs such as depreciation and overhead, which may be missed in studies using budget numbers.[13]

Stevens's model includes eight explanatory variables: organizational form (public, contractor, or competitive), monthly wages of garbage crews, total quantity of trash collected, quantity per household, number of collections per week, proportion of backyard to curbside collections, population density, and weather conditions. Her sample consists of 1974–75 data on 340 trash collecting operations, with no single type of organization dominating the sample.

She found (unlike Hirsch) that scale matters. An operation serving fewer than twenty thousand people, or using fewer than four trucks, is apt to operate somewhat inefficiently. Economies of scale get smaller above that point, and the cost curve flattens out at a scale of around fifty thousand people or five trucks.[14] This suggests that, aside from any other differences between civil service and profit-seeking organizations, smaller cities start with a technological disadvantage if they try to run their own sanitation departments. Costs increase, as expected, with the quality of service. Backyard pickup costs about one-third more than curbside pickup; twice-weekly pickups cost about one-quarter more than weekly pickup. Stevens concluded (as did Hirsch) that the density of settlement does not matter much, nor do weather conditions.

Private municipal contractors, she found, are more efficient than public sanitation departments, and both are less costly than house-by-house competitive arrangements. For cities of more than fifty thousand people, Stevens's calculations suggest that contracting out costs about one-quarter less than public trash service.[15] In all but the smallest and the biggest cities, *competitive* garbage collection scored worse than public collection, and for all cities it was more costly than contractual arrangements worked out between city officials and private haulers. Competitive firms cost 10 to 25 percent more than municipal sanitation departments, and 25 to 50 percent more than contractors.

James C. McDavid performed a comparable analysis on data from 126 Canadian cities. About one-fifth of these cities had strictly public garbage collection;

another two-fifths relied entirely on private contractors; and the rest used some mixture of government and profit-seeking organizations. McDavid found the same pattern as did American researchers, albeit somewhat more pronounced: Controlling for scale, service level, and other factors, public garbage collection cost over two-fifths more than private contracting. Interestingly, in cities where public agencies faced private rivals, their costs were substantially lower than those of unchallenged bureaucracies—indeed, they were virtually the same as those of profit-seekers. Meanwhile, the *highest* recorded cost was for a private monopolist. Part of the private sector cost edge came from paying wages about 10 percent below civil service levels. But technical improvements mattered more, especially the contractors' larger trucks, smaller crews, and more flexible scheduling.[16]

Finally, three British scholars studied trash collection data from 317 jurisdictions in England and Wales. Like most of the analyses reviewed here, this one accounted for the number, location, and frequency of pickups, population density, and other factors. Also fitting the pattern was its finding that cities contracting out for waste disposal saved roughly 22 percent over what they would have spent for public collection. The jurisdictions where public workers challenged and prevailed over private rivals in bid competitions, significantly, saved almost as much—around 17 percent. The researchers found that a small fraction of the public-private cost difference was due to wage gaps, while more important factors were differences in scheduling and crew sizes, specialized vehicles, and other technical and managerial innovations.[17]

Table 4.2 summarizes the studies on public and private garbage collection. Except for Hirsch (who worried about the validity of his own findings) and Bennett and Johnson (whose study involved a small, unsystematic sample and no efforts to control for factors other than organizational form), the researchers have found not only the same *pattern*—contractors are cheapest, followed by public agencies, then open competition—but also roughly the same size cost differences as among the organizational forms. Since they used widely varying data and somewhat different methodologies, this broad consensus argues for a fair degree of confidence in the proposition that private contracting is usually the best way to get the garbage picked up.

Why Is Open Competition More Expensive?

In principle, private garbage haulers who must struggle for every customer in competition with other companies have stronger incentives to control costs than do municipal contractors, who enjoy at least temporary monopolies, and whose link to consumers is mediated by local government. Why, then, did all the

TABLE 4.2
Garbage Collection Cost Studies: Summary

Study	Conclusions
24 St. Louis-area cities (Hirsch, 1965)	No significant cost difference between public and private.
Major Connecticut cities (Kemper and Quigley, 1976)	Contractors most efficient; public 25 percent more costly; open competition 63 percent more costly.
1,378 cities nationwide (Savas, 1977)	Contractors most efficient; private franchise and public collection both cost 12 percent more; open competition cost 50 percent more.
340 organizations nationwide (Stevens, 1977)	Contractors most efficient; public cost 25 percent more; open competition cost 26 to 48 percent more.
Fairfax County, Va. (Bennett and Johnson, 1979)	Open competition cost less than public collection.
126 Canadian cities (McDavid, 1985)	Public cost 41 percent more than contractors; public agencies in "mixed" systems cost only 8 percent more than contractors.
317 U.K. cities (Cubbin, Domberger, and Meadowcroft, 1987)	Public monopoly 20 percent less efficient than contracting; public bid winners nearly as efficient as average private contractor.

researchers except Bennett and Johnson find that open competition involved even higher costs than government collection? There are a number of possible explanations (aside from simple measurement errors) why private competitors may have higher costs. First, private competitive firms may be just too small to be efficient. Stevens considered and rejected this possibility. She found that all private garbage firms, competitors or contractors, had similar capital equipment, crew sizes, and management practices.[18]

A second possible explanation turns on the economics of information. Garbage service may be so small a part of household budgets, and so boring a purchase, that consumers seldom bother to inform themselves about the options or to switch suppliers in response to price. At least one Wall Street analyst has attributed the profitability of garbage hauling to limited cost consciousness on the consumer's part, which gives the haulers wide latitude for boosting rates.[19] The sophistication of city officials as to true costs and alternatives in the garbage industry could so exceed that of consumers that, despite the indirect and attenuated stake of officials in price or quality, they can strike better deals than can citizens on their own.

Third, competitive firms must bill each customer, while both municipal sanitation departments and contractors obtain their resources from general revenues, thus saving several steps of paperwork. One might not expect these transaction costs to be particularly high, but Hirsch found user charges to have a large and significant effect on total costs, and Stevens estimated that competitive firms' costs of billing and collection approached 15 percent of revenue.

Several researchers have cited a fourth factor: If a number of rivals operate in the same area, each will lose the "economies of contiguity" that a single firm enjoys when it picks up the garbage at each house in turn. The superior incentives of market competition could be swamped by the waste of having a number of garbage trucks going through every neighborhood, with each stopping at only a fraction of the houses.

A final possible explanation is that what looks like a competitive market in garbage collection is often a hidden cartel, or a network of local monopolies held together by convention, collusion, or what one expert termed "strong-arm tactics and gangster influence."[20] There is reason to believe that such arrangements are quite common in the commercial trash collection industry. Federal racketeering trials in the mid-1980s featured testimony about garbage cartels involving secret market-sharing schemes enforced by sabotage and violence, and about industry leaders with names like "Matty the Horse."[21] In short, the extra cost attributed to competition may in many cases reflect the excess profits of a cartel. Indeed, New York City, in an attempt to break the Mafia's grip on commercial trash collection, engineered a partial shift from open competition to neighborhood-by-neighborhood contracting, with a city agency bidding against private firms to deter collusion.[22]

Why Is Contracting Cheaper?

An example: National Serv-All is a small family firm that was launched in 1957 when an Anderson, Indiana, car-wash owner, irked by sloppy trash service, called the city's bluff and bid to take over garbage collection for Anderson. Today National Serv-All displays precisely the type of aggressive, innovative behavior that theory advertises as a cardinal virtue of competitive enterprise. Its revenues, profits, and the personal wealth of its managers are intimately related to the technical efficiency with which it collects and disposes of garbage. Concentration of ownership motivates cost control in each individual contract. Moreover, since National Serv-All, unlike municipal governments, can replicate valuable innovations in each of the cities it serves, it can multiply the gains from any technical improvements it devises in a way that local operations cannot. For instance, it undertakes joint ventures with equipment companies to improve the design of garbage trucks, an investment that would not be rational for any but the largest municipal sanitation departments, no matter how devoted they were to cost control.[23]

Two other factors, explaining contractor's cost edge in several of the studies, are the relatively high pay and restrictive work rules in public sanitation departments. Labor groups tend to have a good deal of power over public trash collection agencies, largely because the prospect of a garbage strike is so thoroughly distasteful to politicians. There were disruptive garbage strikes in New York City and Memphis in 1968 and in Washington, D.C., in 1970; in 1986, bitter strikes in Detroit and Philadelphia, accompanied by piles of rotting garbage in city streets, sparked violent protests and an uncomfortable degree of pressure on elected officials.[24] This threat leads to somewhat better pay and benefits, on average, for public workers. Wage premiums are not nearly big enough to account for all of the government cost disadvantage, however. More important are differences in work rules and management practices reflecting workers' preferences rather than the imperatives of cost control. The result is a tendency for public sanitation departments and private garbage operations to display quite distinctive styles of work. Contractors use bigger trucks and smaller crews; require employees to accept more flexible, less desirable work schedules; and invoke a fuller set of incentives and penalties.[25]

What prevents contracting for garbage collection from degenerating into cozy, expensive arrangements in which incumbent firms are practically, if not formally, immune from competition? One key is the absence of barriers to entry. The service involves low economies of scale, technological simplicity, and moderate investment costs. If a contractor's fee gets too high or its quality too low, municipal officials seem to be able to recognize the problem and hire a new contractor the next time out. In some cities, more than twenty bidders compete for the average trash collection contract.[26] If the technical feasibility of replacing contractors *allows* officials to enforce accountability, the visibility of the service motivates them to do so. The manager of a family-run collection company with contracts in several states explains his position in these terms: "Garbage is perhaps the most visible public service. The city fathers hire us, but we work for the taxpayers. They're the ones who complain if service is bad."[27] Unlike with some other public services, citizens almost automatically do much of the work of monitoring contractors.

There is considerable evidence that competition, rather than organizational form, is the crucial factor in efficient trash collection. Recall that the Canadian and British studies show that city sanitation departments competing against private rivals more closely resemble private contractors in cost structure and organizational style than they resemble other public agencies. When a new law banned on-site trash burning in Minneapolis in 1970, garbage collection was divided between municipal crews and private refuse haulers. At first, the city sanitation department had higher costs, while the private haulers started out causing more complaints about service quality. But during the system's first five years, the costs of the city operation dropped toward the standard set by the private firms, while the quality of the private service converged toward that offered by the city.[28] In Phoenix, Arizona, the city is divided into four sectors. Two are reserved for the city's sanitation division—to ensure some local capacity for garbage collection—but the other two are put out to bid. The city auditor prepares sanitation division bids, costing out everything down to a prorated fraction of the city manager's salary in order to avoid giving the public organization an edge due to underestimated true costs. And the author of *How Shall We Collect the Garbage?* concludes that the ideal arrangement is competition for contracts (each covering a part of the city) among a public agency and two or more private firms.[29]

The evidence on garbage collection, in sum, is fairly clear. Open competition and monopolistic private franchises are often plagued by inefficiency or illicit collusion. Contractors chosen by fair and honest bid contests typically outperform public monopolies. But competition improves the performance of both public *and* private garbage operations. Public sanitation departments (especially those immune from challenge) are frequently plagued by inefficient size and by work rules that drive up costs. Happily, it appears that local officials are adept at devising means to hold contractors accountable and to ensure that taxpayers benefit from private efficiency advantages.

PENTAGON SUPPORT SERVICES

Defense Department policy has long included some preference for using private suppliers, but the Reagan era witnessed a sharp increase in delegating support functions to outside organizations. Under the provisions of Office of Management and Budget Circular A-76, the Defense Department structured a series of competitions, including both private contractors and Pentagon workers who had traditionally provided the service under review. The Army, Navy, and Air Force awarded a total of 235 support-service contracts in the period October 1980–October 1982. Follow-up cost studies found that, on average, competitive contracting saved the services 22 percent.[30] (The Pentagon housekeeping budget is so massive that this adds up to about $250 million dollars in annual savings.) One of the more striking results of the Pentagon initiative in contracting out was the efficiency gains the *public* suppliers displayed when faced with private rivals. In-house bidders won a sizable fraction of the competitions, improving on their own precompetitive costs by an average of 18 percent.[31]

Some legislators worried that support-service contractors would boost prices once they took over from government workers. Asked to test this suspicion, the General Accounting Office did in-depth studies of twenty functions newly performed by private suppliers, including laundry service at Fort Dix, New Jersey; standardized testing at Fort Riley, Kansas; motor vehicle maintenance at a Florida naval base; and management of the flight-simulation program at Vance Air Force Base in Oklahoma.[32] The General Accounting Office found that, indeed, costs did rise above initial estimates—because of contractual omissions and ambiguities, or because initial low-bidders proved unable to do the work—in all but one of the twenty services studied. Yet even taking midcourse cost increases into account, competitive contracting *still* offered substantial savings in all but a few cases. The exceptions were the more complex and hard-to-specify services. Problems with the initial statement of work for handling photography and audiovisual equipment duties at Florida's Eglin Air Force Base required costly revisions; instead of saving $70,000, contracting out cost the Air Force an extra $300,000. Managing the precision-measurement equipment lab at a Georgia installation presented a yet more complex contract, causing still messier problems. The Air Force was disappointed with the low bidder's work, and the replacement contractor turned out to offer no savings over in-house staff. Worse, the *first* contractor complained that the problem lay not with its performance, but with ambiguities in the contract, and demanded compensation for its time and trouble. Settling legal claims and other transition costs added up to an extra $800,000.[33]

Legislators also feared that unemployment compensation and other government payments to displaced public workers would wipe out the savings from privatization. But the GAO found that only a small fraction of the civil servants involved were forced into joblessness. Most were reassigned to other government jobs; many retired voluntarily; some were hired by contractors to do their old jobs under new management. The majority of the former civil servants who went to work for outside contractors, however, *did* report lower wages, leaner benefits, and less satisfying working conditions. So, while most of the government costs savings represented real efficiency gains, part of those savings came at the workers' expense.[34]

OFFICE CLEANING

The General Services Administration—which handles housekeeping functions for much of the federal government—managed nearly 200 million square feet of building space in 1980. Civil servants did the cleaning in about one-third of these buildings. For roughly another one-third, the General Services Administration contracted with private cleaning firms. The final one-third were buildings that the government rented rather than owned, and in these, the private landlords were responsible for cleaning chores.

The General Accounting Office studied custodial services in GSA-managed buildings in Boston, Atlanta, Chicago, and Washington, D.C.[35] Its analysis revealed that, on average, it cost the General Services Administration $1.18 per square foot to keep a building clean for a year through the use of in-house staff. Contracting out the cleaning chores cost $.73 per square foot. Private landlords, meanwhile, could arrange for cleaning at a cost of only $.63 per square foot. The analysts took care to verify that the lower private sector costs did not simply reflect lower quality, and that standards were similar for all three categories. Much of the difference was due to labor costs; the GSA paid wages 60 percent above that which private firms paid for comparable work. But there were also major productivity differences. Public workers—less well equipped, and following less efficient procedures—accomplished less, on average, per hour of effort.

FIRE-FIGHTING SERVICES

While private firms have long provided fire-fighting services at airports, only in the past few decades have cities experimented with contracting for fire protection. Scottsdale, Arizona, was the first sizable city to privatize fire services when, in the late 1960s, it hired a company called Rural-Metro to respond to alarms. Several jurisdictions now contract out for all or part of their fire protection services, and by the mid-1980s, there were around a half-dozen firms in the industry.[36]

Almost as soon as a private fire-fighting industry existed, analysts set out to compare it to the public sector standard. Roger Ahlbrandt began by identifying the factors affecting the costs of running government fire departments. Assembling data from the Seattle area, Ahlbrandt built a model that explained a community's fire service costs by reference to its region and its population density; the numbers of fire stations, engines, and volunteer and professional fire-fighters; and the nature and value of the buildings in the area. He tested out this model on several Arizona cities to see how well it traveled, and he found that the cost factors identified in Seattle still held true. Finally, Ahlbrandt used the model to estimate what it *would have* cost to serve Scottsdale, Arizona, with a public fire department, coming up with a figure of about $7 per capita. Rural-Metro, the Scottsdale fire-fighting contractor, in reality charged under $4, suggesting a major efficiency difference.[37]

One source of lower costs was Rural-Metro's ability to spread its overhead burden, since it also provided subscription fire services in rural areas outside Scottsdale. Another important factor was technological and managerial innovation. Rural-Metro used a number of part-time workers to handle emergencies requiring extra personnel, so that it was able to keep its full-time work force small. It also designed and built its own equipment, including specialized vehicles improving on traditional fire truck designs.

TRANSPORTATION

Airlines in Australia

David G. Davies examined Australia's peculiar airline industry, which for many years was shared, by statute, between two firms.[38] Trans Australian Airlines was owned by the federal government; Ansett Australian National Airways was privately owned. Australia's Civil Aviation Agreement Act of 1957 made it a matter of national policy that "there are two and not more than two operators of trunk-route airline services."[39]

The government went to extraordinary lengths to achieve this result. Both airlines were required to use the same kinds of airplanes. Each introduced its first DC-9 aircraft not just on the same day, but at the same hour. The central government—which owned the airports—carefully allocated identical takeoff and landing slots to each airline. Only after safety concerns were raised about the prudence of simultaneous arrivals and departures did officials relent from this policy of Solomonic fairness and stagger the schedules by a few minutes. Mail contracts were evenly split between the two airlines. Government officials were required to divide their travel business. Ticket prices were regulated at exactly the same levels, as were wages. The public airline was even required by special legislation to pay profit and sales taxes to avoid gaining any edge over its private competitor. The number of seats and seating arrangements in the aircraft and terminals were almost identical, crews were similarly trained, and in-flight meals were essentially the same. Although the two airlines advertised heavily, neither attempted to claim any real superiority over its rival, with the possible exception of friendlier or more decorative attendants.[40]

After detailing the completeness of this natural experiment, Davies tabulated efficiency measures for both airlines. He compared tons of freight carried per employee; passengers carried per employee; and revenue earned per employee.[41] The results: For every year from 1958 to 1974, for all three measures, the private airline got more output from each worker. The difference was largest for freight (where the private line carried twice as much per employee) but was still significant for passengers and revenue (22 percent and 13 percent more, respectively).[42] Davies concluded that "the private firm, operating under the rules and customs associated with exchangeable private property rights, is more productive than the public enterprise."[43]

Railroads in Canada

Douglas W. Caves and Laurits R. Christensen studied a similar situation: two firms, one public and one private, sharing the regulated Canadian rail industry. Their analysis compares the productivity of the public Canadian National and the private Canadian Pacific from the mid-1950s to the mid-1970s. Both railroads were subject to essentially the same regulations until 1967, when most rate regulations were lifted from both of them. Both operated coast-to-coast, both served all major industrial areas, and both faced similar degrees of competitive pressure from other forms of transportation. The public railroad was also comparable to the private railroad in its mandate. Canadian National had been formed in the early 1900s out of the remains of several tottering private lines. The resulting public railroad was "instructed to operate on a commercial basis under a management insulated from politics." Thus the Canadian National was left free to pursue efficient operations without the complicating requirements of other public goals or, more precisely, without much more burdensome social responsibilities than those borne by its private rival.[44]

After establishing that the Canadian railroads faced similar situations, Caves and Christensen set out to test whether the form of ownership mattered for efficiency. The core of their test was a comparison of "total factor productivity," or real output achieved per unit of real resources applied. The results: The productivity of the public Canadian National was a good deal lower than that of the private Canadian Pacific from 1956 to 1965 (ranging between 81 percent and 91 percent of the Canadian Pacific's productivity) but roughly the same or even a little higher in the period from 1966 to 1975. Caves and Christensen attributed the public railroad's relatively good performance—especially in the later period—to the fact that Canadian National, while publicly owned, has been compelled to compete not just with Canadian Pacific but with cars, buses, trucks, airplanes, ships, and pipelines.[45]

Buses in the United States

One of the most careful studies of public and private transit systems is by James L. Perry and Timlynn T. Babitsky. They examined federal Urban Mass Transit Agency data on nearly 250 urban transit systems in the early 1980s. The majority of the systems were publicly owned and operated, either by a city government or by a special transit authority. About one-third were publicly owned but were managed by private companies under contract to local governments. Roughly 10 percent were both owned and operated by private firms.[46]

Perry and Babitsky used multiple regression analysis to control for the effects of transit system size, service area population density, and other characteristics in order to isolate the effect of organizational form. These analysts found that privately owned and operated systems were measurably more efficient. They transported more passengers per dollar spent, they collected more revenue, and they required far less in federal subsidies. There was also some reason to believe that the privately owned systems were safer.[47]

But this tendency did not extend to private *management* of publicly owned assets. The researchers found no evidence that private contractors could run public bus systems any better than civil servants could. Management contractors, working for fees rather than for net profits, had only limited stakes in increased efficiency. Most privately run transit systems remain monopolies, with no competition to inspire innovation and efficiency improvements. Finally, Perry and Babitsky found that the provisions built into management contracts generally failed to give private managers adequate incentives to control cost.

WATER AND POWER UTILITIES

The issue of whether civil servants or profit-seekers are better suited to pipe water into urban homes has a long history. Happily, on this question—unlike on the question of the optimal arrangement for collecting garbage or mopping office floors—we have a specific verdict from one of the modern era's intellectual giants, John Stuart Mill.[48] In the mid-nineteenth century, London residents got their water from collected rainfall, from the Thames River, or from one of a handful of companies that pumped in water from outside the city. These private suppliers sometimes engaged in brief spates of competition, featuring price wars and the employment of thugs to sabotage each others' equipment. But more often they colluded to keep prices high. These inadequate water supply arrangements, coupled with a pestilential urban sewage system, produced appalling public health conditions. In the wake of a particularly ghastly season for typhus and cholera, a group of reformers formed the Metropolitan Sanitary Association to petition for state action. They sought the support of the famous philosopher, known for his general adherence to laissez-faire principles.

Mill responded with a February 1851 letter in which he noted that "the policy of depending on individuals for the supply of the markets assumes the existence of competition." He observed that urban water supply has large elements of what modern economists term *natural monopoly*. When the number of firms is small, he went on, their "interest prompts them, except during occasional short periods, not to compete but to combine," charging excessive prices and restricting supply. Despite his principled distaste for collective enterprise, Mill endorsed the creation of a public water authority for London.

The problem of deciding who should pump the water remains with us, though it may be that advances in technology, regulation, and corporate organization would lead a modern-day Mill to alter his judgment. Both public and private water suppliers operate in the United States today, though municipal authorities predominate. The American Water Works Association periodically surveys water utilities and publishes data on costs, returns, and other features. A number of researchers have analyzed samples from these data over the years in efforts to discover which form of organization is more efficient. There has been ample room for ambiguity, since water utilities vary along dimensions aside from organizational form. They differ by factors such as size and dispersion of the population served; in the scale and age of their capital equipment; in costs paid for labor, machinery, water, energy, and finance; in the quality of available water supplies; and in how much they treat the water before pumping it to customers. Since some of these features might differ systematically as between public and private water utilities, it would likely be misleading simply to divide the water suppliers into "public" and "private," to find the two average costs, and to attribute whatever difference there is to ownership effects.

Seven studies have attempted to isolate the significance of public versus private management. Using statistical techniques to estimate the separate effect on the total costs of each variable, researchers have set up models of the water supply process that incorporate scale, water quality coming in and going out, input costs, and other factors (including ownership). The researchers have varied somewhat in terms of the factors they included, in the ways they modeled cost structures, and in their strategies for extracting real economic information from the often arbitrary accounting data that utilities report. Table 4.3 summarizes the results of the major studies on the issue.[49]

TABLE 4.3
Water Utility Cost Studies: A Summary

Study	Conclusion
Mann and Mikesell, 1976	Public more efficient
Crain and Zardkoohi, 1978	Private more efficient
Bruggink, 1982	Public more efficient
Feigenbaum and Teeples, 1983*	No significant difference
Feigenbaum, Teeples, and Glyer, 1986*	No significant difference
Byrners, Grosskopf, and Hayes, 1986†	No significant difference
Teeples and Glyer, 1987	No significant difference

*Feigenbaum and Teeples, and Feigenbaum, Teeples, and Glyer controlled for differences in output quality and distribution, as well as for scale, water sources, and other input variables.
†While the other studies used multiple regression to estimate cost functions, Byrners, Grosskopf, and Hayes used linear programming to estimate a frontier of technological (not necessarily economic) efficiency and tested to see if public and private utilities differed significantly in the degree of departure from this frontier; they did not.

All of these studies used the same basic data set (although different parts of it and for different years); all were serious analyses published in reputable journals; and all but one used similar analytic approaches. The later studies responded to potential problems in the earlier ones and were based on more elaborate models incorporating a large number of variables. The weight of the evidence, then, favors the conclusion that there is no tendency for private water utilities to be any more productive.

Two scholars have protested against the fundamental premise of these studies, arguing that the burden of proof should be on the proposition that public water utilities are *not* inferior to private utilities.[50] But these inconclusive studies did not find evidence of lower private costs that somehow falls just short of a fastidious analyst's standard of significance. The results are quite persuasive: Despite the presumptively superior incentives of the profit-seeking form of organization, private water utilities, on average, are no cheaper than public ones. Before considering why this should be so, and the implications for other public services, it is worth briefly examining some related evidence on electric utilities.[51]

Both governmental and profit-seeking enterprises sell electricity in the United States. Many researchers have looked to the power industry to assess differences between public and private management. (In this section, "public" refers to utilities owned and run by some form of government; both public and private electric utilities are "public utilities" in the usual sense of the term.) The evidence broadly contradicts the common presumption that private utilities will operate more efficiently than their public counterparts. Table 4.4 displays the findings of six major studies, all of which used Federal Power Commission data for various years, and all of which attempted to explain the costs of electricity generation or distribution or both in terms of an array of variables, including organizational form.[52]

TABLE 4.4
Electric Utility Cost Studies:
A Summary

Study	Conclusions
Meyer, 1975	Public more efficient
Yonker, 1975	No significant difference
Neuberg, 1977	Public more efficient
Pescatrice and Trapani, 1980	Public more efficient
Fare, Grosskopf, and Logan, 1985	No significant difference
Atkinson and Halvorsen, 1986	No significant difference

No study even hints at superior private efficiency.[53] The results of Yonker, as well as those of Fare, Grosskopf, and Logan, leaned toward lower costs for public utilities but fell short of statistical significance.[54] Those studies that did find significant differences identified extra costs for private utilities that are big enough—in the range of 24 to 33 percent—to worry about.

These results do not necessarily prove that public utilities are more efficient. One reason for caution is the very care the researchers took to isolate the effect of organizational form. Suppose municipal utilities are inefficient *because* they are too small (serving a single city and losing economies of scale) or because political sensitivities lead them to use too much labor or to pay workers too much. Then studies that control for differences of scale, or factor mix, or wage costs and *then* test for the effect of a separate ownership variable will miss the point. But the pattern is consistent enough, across a wide enough range of alternative specifications, to make this explanation unlikely. What *does* explain the results? The researchers suggested reasons ranging from errors in measurement, or lower capital costs for public utilities;[55] to superior managers lured to public utilities by the prospect of a steadier job;[56] and the eagerness of public utility personnel to prove themselves the equal of private workers.[57]

But the most promising explanation starts from the observation that these studies, and those of water utilities as well, compare public and private management not generically, but in a specific context: that of a "natural monopoly." It is difficult, if not strictly speaking impossible, for utilities to compete for customers in a given area. Utilities are local monopolies, and if unconstrained, monopolies tend to charge too much and produce too little. Thus utilities are usually *regulated*. The studies cited here compared public management with private management facing a particular set of incentives and constraints imposed by regulation.

Utility regulators normally manipulate allowable prices to ensure that profits will not exceed (and, in practice, cannot fall much below) a mandated rate of return on invested capital. Averch and Johnson argued that this form of regulation imposes incentives to invest too much in capital equipment.[58] Comparisons between the efficiency of public and private electric utilities, then, may be distorted by the tendency of private firms to have needlessly high capital costs because of the way in which their profit ceilings are calculated. The Averch-Johnson hypothesis has been much-cited, much-tested, and generally confirmed,[59] and several of the studies cited in this section attributed the cost differences they found partly or primarily to this perverse feature of regulated private monopolies.[60] Two other scholars suggested a further complexity: The inability of government to commit itself to allowing private utilities a fair long-term return may force managers to choose technologies the cost of which can be recouped relatively quickly. Large-scale, long-lived investments may be most efficient. But if managers suspect that regulators will bend to consumer pressure once the capital is in place and set rates too low to compensate investors, then managers will opt for less vulnerable, albeit less efficient, technologies.[61] The basic story is the same: In the complex relationships among utility managers, investors, regulators, and consumers, contractual structures that give the right signals and incentives are difficult, and sometimes impossible, to fashion.

IMPLICATIONS

What are we to make of all this? The evidence confirms two powerful principles. First, the profit-seeking private firm is *potentially* a far superior institution for efficient production. Second, that productive potential can be tapped only under certain circumstances. *Public versus private* matters, but *competitive versus noncompetitive* usually matters more.[62] Without a credible prospect of replacement, it is hard to harness private capabilities to public purposes. And meaningful competition is often far easier to praise than to arrange. This discussion of transit system management contracts, open competition in garbage collecting, Pentagon support-service contracts, and electric and water utilities illustrates some of the ways in which competition can break down, as well as some of the consequences.

Private contractors may control land, machinery, or other assets that are essential to providing some service. Or *intangible* proprietary assets—inside information, specific expertise, or even camaraderie with their government counterparts—can give incumbent contractors advantages that entrench them against replacement. Or performance may not be sufficiently measurable to inspire real competition on the basis of value for money.[63] Finally, corruption, cronyism, indolence, or incompetence on the part of government officials could mean that competition will not exist even when it is technically practicable.

In sum, when a well-specified contract in a competitive context can enforce accountability, the presumption of superior private efficiency in delivering public services holds true. Applying private means to public ends can at once lighten the burden on taxpayers, generate more information to inform public choice, and conserve public managerial attention for other duties that *can't* be delegated. Yet it is just as true, unfortunately, that half of a market system—profit drive without meaningful specifications or competitive discipline—can be worse than none.

CHAPTER 5

THE TERMS OF THE
PRIVATIZATION DECISION

THE ROOT human problem of accountability takes on a special form and a heightened intensity in the public realm. Collective spending decisions are ineradicably prone to error. When resources flow to an undertaking according to some criterion other than individual judgments of value, as chapter 2 argued, a shadow of uncertainty surrounds the worth of the project. Spectacular efficiency does not ensure expansion, nor does utter failure to create value guarantee extinction. The *performance* of public functions is similarly problematic. Chapter 3 surveyed the perils plaguing the implementation of public tasks and posited three levels of breakdown in the relationship between the public and its agents: inefficiency, opportunism, and self-seeking political activism.

But suppose, for the moment, that our public and private organizations mirrored the cheeriest of primers on free enterprise and public administration. Government employees—although pledged to purposes other than strict cost control—faithfully obey mandates and follow prescribed procedures. Private firms carrying out government contracts—while willing to earn what profit they can—bid competitively and seek to deliver as promised. What considerations should govern choices between profit-seekers and civil servants in this simpler world? In other words, for which kinds of tasks does it make sense to *contract for results*, and for which to *contract for allegiance*?

The concepts and evidence presented in earlier chapters invite a few generalizations. *The more precisely a task can be specified in advance and its performance evaluated after the fact, the more certainly contractors can be made to compete; the more readily disappointing contractors can be replaced (or otherwise penalized); and the more narrowly government cares about* ends *to the exclusion of* means, *the stronger becomes the case for employing profit-seekers rather than civil servants.*

Among these criteria, pride of place goes to *competition*. Indeed, the others mostly concern the conditions that make real competition possible. Consider each in turn: The task must be defined—in detail and in advance—so that potential contractors can make their plans and submit their bids accordingly. Only if performance will be properly evaluated and contractual terms enforced does competitive bidding have much meaning. If profit-seekers fear no penalties for incompetence, negligence, or other failures to deliver as promised, then the bid process becomes a contest in fabricating extravagant claims. And the less the government knows or cares about the means by which the public's business is accomplished, the looser the rein that can be granted to profit-seekers to devise efficient and innovative ways of delivering specified results. Conversely, the more uncertain a task is, the harder it is to measure results, the less the task allows for ongoing competition, then the less there is to gain by turning to profit-seekers, and the more there is to lose.

When a task is subject to redefinition, then contracts—the codes that delimit a profit-seeker's responsibility—may have to be periodically cancelled or renegotiated. Employing civil servants preserves for government the valuable right to modify mandates. Contracting for results, in other words, is hard to do well if results cannot be measured. Such conditions, of course, are notoriously common in governmental undertakings.[1] When selecting among competing agents is impractical or impossible—either because technical reasons preclude competition or because organizational imperatives dictate continuity—market discipline evaporates, and other structures of accountability are required. Finally, if means matter as much as do ends, then the profit-seeker's characteristic advantage in technical innovation may lose much of its appeal.[2]

In this hypothetical world in which both markets and bureaucracies work well, in sum, what the public *loses* by choosing a bureaucratic over a profit-seeking agent are the cost discipline of competition and the benefits of accelerated innovation. What the public *gains* are control over methods, and the right to change mandates as circumstances require. Civil servants are seldom inspired or authorized to place top priority on cost control. Profit-seekers cannot be expected to limit prices unless competition requires them to do so, nor to attend—at any significant cost—to dimensions of value other than those specified in the contract.

Consider one particular public task—applying a fresh coat of white paint to the White House. Suppose that the building manager can specify the scope and durability required of the painting project and can verify by personal inspection the quality of the job. Suppose that several contractors submit sealed, final bids, and that the contract leaves the building manager the right to replace incompetent contractors in midproject. Finally, imagine that the manager has no special insights into the best way to paint the White House, and does not care whether the contractor uses brushes, rollers, or spray guns, ladders, scaffolds, or hydraulic lifts, big crews or small crews, union or nonunion labor, so long as the job is done well and on time. In these circumstances, it makes sense to write up specifications, to solicit bids from profit-seekers, and to select the lowest-bidding contractor and let her figure out the best way to paint the White House, pocketing the profit if she does it efficiently.

Consider another public task, protecting the president from aspiring assassins. Suppose that the presidential schedule is contingent on events and thus frequently revised, so that neither the amount of protection required nor the conditions of the task can be specified in advance. Suppose that it is impossible (because of the variability of the task) or unwise (for security reasons) to distribute bid specifications for a month's worth of bodyguarding; or that only a few firms are equipped for a job of that scale and sensitivity; or that it would be difficult to switch security firms after an incumbent contractor masters routines and develops relationships with the president and his staff. Suppose too that it is hard to gauge different degrees of risk short of an actual attack, or to count the number of assassination plots deterred, but relatively easy to tell if an alert bodyguard is on the scene. Suppose further that experience has demonstrated the effectiveness of certain procedures, the departure from which is far more likely to degrade security than to enhance it. Finally, suppose that it matters *how* the president is protected, and many conceivable tactics—keeping all crowds one-half mile away, transporting the president in an armored car or in disguise, opening fire on all shady looking characters—are unacceptable.[3] Under such circumstances, the potential gains from competitive contracting are swamped by the potential losses. It makes sense to set up a governmental security organization, to establish rules and standard operating procedures for it, and to evaluate agents largely by their fidelity to routine.[4]

So long as our painting and presidential protection examples remain hypothetical, we may as well proceed to imagine the results of alternative choices. Suppose that the building manager at the White House insists upon civil servants to do the paint job. With a typical governmental organization, oriented to process rather than product, the cost would very likely be somewhat higher than with a contractor selected through competitive bidding. If the building manager hoped to retain civil service arrangements *without* sacrificing cost control—and if he were authorized to use *any* form of contracting—he might set up a new bureaucracy along these lines: The painting staff is unconstrained by routine. Workers are urged to experiment with new methods for painting the White House. Each worker can propose an approach and each submits a budget. The building manager selects the most attractive proposal and appoints its author as leader of the painting team. If expertise and innovations enable it to do the job for less than the budgeted sum, the team gets to keep any excess, with the leader to decide how it will be shared among the members.[5]

Analogously, if the presidential security director strongly prefers private sector protection services he could, in principle, write a contract enumerating the job requirements in full. Since the output (protection from a range of imperfectly observable risks) cannot be completely defined or measured, payment would have to be based in large part on activity rather than on results. The security firm would provide bodyguards to accompany the president as needed—using an agreed upon set of acceptable security tactics—and would be paid for the time and materials spent on the job.[6]

But in the case of the White House paint job, the result is a bureaucracy that mimics private contracting, and in the case of the presidential protection arrangements, a private contractor comes to resemble a public bureaucracy. The civil service painting contract (as incentives are arranged to achieve low costs and innovation) surrenders control over means. The private sector security arrangement (as the contract dictates protocol and specifies activity rather than results) will lose the virtues of cost-based competition and innovation.

In other words, *the fundamental distinction is between competitive output-based relationships and noncompetitive input-based relationships rather than between profit-seekers and civil servants per se.*

The efficiency gains of competition usually come at the expense of full control over means and the right to revise mandates without recontracting—and vice versa. There is an inherent tension, that is, between paying for activity and paying for results. To the extent that civil servants hew to output-based contracts, they will tend to shed both the virtues and the defects of bureaucracy and to take on the virtues and defects of profit-seekers. To the extent that profit-seekers contract to accept instructions, rather than to deliver a specified result, they will tend to assume certain fundamental characteristics of civil servants.

If the White House building manager insists on the option to change in midstream the specifications on the paint job, or reserves the right to suspend work during unanticipated state functions, or requires that the paint be American made, or that the workers be unionized, or Republican, or that they be subjected to security checks, or that specified numbers be minorities or women, then each of these process specifications will tend to erode the efficiency advantages of outside contracting. The rationale for privatization is that competition among contractors will inspire more efficient procedures; as their discretion to innovate is restricted, the benefits of competition are lost. Similarly, if the security director seeks to cut the costs of protecting the president by cutting back on monitoring, eliminating standard procedures, and offering bonuses to agents who experiment with ways to foil assassins more cheaply, breakdowns are as likely as breakthroughs. The issue, in both cases, is how much cost minimization *matters* and how well quality can be *measured*. The rationale for bureaucracy is control over means, either when means are more definable or observable than ends, or when means are important ends in themselves.

The point here is to caution against undiscriminating enthusiasm for hybrid organizations that promise all the virtues of both public and private forms and none of the defects of either—"public-private partnerships" or nonprofit organizations that suffer neither the narrowness and vulnerability of contracts with profit-seekers nor the clumsiness and diluted accountability of civil-service arrangements. There *are* often major advantages to such hybrids, and it would be wrong to suggest there is no place for evaluation by results in public organizations, or for specifying inputs and monitoring the activity of private contractors. Nor do I seek here to pronounce on the proper social role of nonprofit organizations, a major topic outside the scope of this book.[7]

My argument, rather, is that if a task allows for clear evaluation by results, then the bias should be toward turning that task over to profit-seekers, instead of structuring elaborate performance incentives for civil servants. And if a task is so delicate and so difficult to evaluate that the contracts that govern it must be layered with constraints and specified procedures, it may be better to abandon outside contracts and to set up a bureaucracy. The Michigan state government rewards its pension fund managers according to how well their portfolios perform, and rightly so: Their relative performance is readily measured.[8] But when the Veterans' Administration sought to spur the efficiency of its appeals board by offering bonuses pegged to rapid job performance, some officials took to spending less than ten minutes on the average case, raising questions about due process and the quality of appraisal.[9] When the federal government launched a program to offer some two million government workers compensation based in part on efficient performance, a senior official declared: "It works with the private sector, so why not the government?"[10] If performance were as readily evaluated in government as in business, such a program *might* make sense. But quality in public service tends to be a complex matter. In 1986, *Wall Street Journal* editorial writers hailed performance-based federal pay as a way to "encourage government employees to do their best." Six weeks later, concerned about due process, they denounced as "turning the IRS loose as bounty hunters" a Senate bill that would give civil servants incentives to pursue delinquent taxes aggressively.[11]

A focus on procedure, rather than on product, is not a remediable *defect* of bureaucracy, but a *description* of input-based contracts. An exclusive devotion to measured costs and revenues is not a failing unique to profit-seekers, but is rather the predictable result of output-based contracts. This is not to say that bureaucracies cannot be made more efficient, or that profit-seeking firms cannot be made more broadly accountable, through carefully balanced contracts that tailor the mix of incentives to the task at hand. But it does suggest caution in efforts to make public agencies more businesslike, or to make private suppliers more responsive to considerations that are not covered in the contract. Isadora Duncan once suggested to George Bernard Shaw that the two of them owed it to humanity to have a child who would combine her beauty with his brains. Shaw declined, horrified at the prospect that their joint effort could instead produce the opposite combination—her intellect and his looks.[12] A comparable wariness should inform efforts to blend public and private styles of organization.

The choice between profit-seekers and civil servants to perform public duties hinges on two sets of concerns. The first set is strictly task-specific. Is the product definable? Can performance be evaluated? Is competition feasible? Can unsatisfactory contractors be replaced? Are *means* important—beyond the broad constraints of law and morality—or can agents be left to choose the cheapest methods? To ask whether bureaucrats or private contractors perform better *in general* is as meaningless as asking whether, *in general*, an ax or a shovel is the better tool. It depends on the job.

But it also depends, of course, on the *quality* of each alternative. "Which type?" matters, but "How good?" matters, too; in some cases, it might matter more. A sharp, sturdy ax might do better for digging a hole than a bent and flimsy shovel. The second set of issues governing the privatization decision concerns how closely each organizational alternative can be expected to approximate its ideal. This chapter has dealt thus far with idealized scenarios in order to isolate questions about the respective advantages of well-functioning contracts and bureaucracies from questions about the tendencies of each to break down. (The two issues are too frequently confused in policy debates.) But in the real world, civil servants do not reliably defer to authority or subordinate their own interests to organizational mandates. Profit-seekers do not always submit to the discipline of competition or dedicate their ingenuity solely to cutting costs and improving quality. And neither civil servants nor profit-seekers can be expected to adapt passively to public spending decisions without exercising—in their roles as political principals—their power to shape collective choices.

EFFICIENCY, UNCERTAINTY, AND DISCRETION

When citizens express their priorities through the political process, information about interests is aggregated, imprecise, and only indirectly conveyed to the people—whether civil servants or profit-seekers—who do the work. The mandates assigned to either type of agent will be based, at best, on honest but error-prone definitions of the public good. Public officials will tend to specify goals with less precision, monitor work in progress less vigilantly, evaluate less rigorously, and sanction poor performance less sternly than would the owner of a closely held firm. These are problems of collective action, not of any particular organizational instrument.

But basic accountability problems manifest themselves in different ways depending on which organizational form is chosen. These distinctions are explored here along two dimensions of efficiency. The first concerns getting the right things done (where civil servants may have an advantage). The other concerns getting them done at minimum cost (where the advantage is to the profit-seeker).

Inefficiency in public spending is sometimes rooted in vague mandates that fail to concentrate resources on the most promising sources of social value. When vagueness results solely from political officials' negligence or failure of nerve, shifting from civil servants to profit-seekers may offer a partial remedy. Writing contracts with profit-seeking agents requires devising specifications by which performance will be evaluated. Basing contracts on inputs rather than outputs, conversely, can leave goals obscure. When political officials find it tedious or politically distasteful to spell out the purposes of public endeavors, there is much to be said for the discipline imposed by output-based contracts.[13]

But what if neither valuable results nor value-creating procedures *can* be spelled out in advance? The dilemma presents a choice between two risky options. Public officials can specify mandates on the basis of incomplete information, which will frequently result in the wrong thing getting done—profit-seekers assigned to produce the wrong outputs, or civil servants assigned to follow wasteful or perverse procedures. Or they can leave mandates open-ended, granting agents some measure of discretion. The relative risks of inefficiency due to *vaguely* defined mandates versus inefficiency due to *badly* defined mandates depends on what happens at lower levels when goals or procedures are left imprecise. When are agents *able* to fill in the details correctly—that is, to select from within loose mandates those options promising the highest social value? And when, assuming that they are able, are they *motivated* to do so?

Agents are *able* to refine ambiguous mandates if they appreciate the ultimate goals to be served and if they command either technical expertise, or insight into context, which their principals lack. A National Park Service wildlife specialist probably knows more than do congressmen about how to encourage a proper balance of species within a park; a Federal Aviation Administration engineer knows more about the technical arcana of air-traffic control. Similarly, a schoolteacher gains valuable information about context as he becomes familiar with the strengths and weaknesses of individual students, as does an infantry officer in the field as he gathers information about terrain and enemy positions that his rear-echelon superiors lack. In each case, agents are well positioned to efficiently fill in the details of vague mandates such as "maintain ecological balance," "ensure air safety," "teach the children," or "contain the enemy."[14]

Suppose the public's agents are equipped to efficiently fill in the details of loosely defined mandates. Under what circumstances will they act on that ability? One seemingly obvious expedient is to build into their contracts both rewards for efficient interpretation and penalties for bad choices. But the notion of contractual incentives to correctly interpret a vague commission seems to contain an element of paradox. If good performance can be defined, why leave mandates vague in the first place? And if good performance cannot be defined, how can there be any sensible basis for rewarding and penalizing agents? This seeming paradox in fact defines cases in which requirements cannot be specified in advance but results *can* be judged in retrospect. These features, of course, describe much of the work to be done in the world. They describe a particularly large fraction of public tasks, where multiple goals and contextual uncertainties combine to make advance prescriptions far more difficult than judgments after the fact.

When John Jay embarked for Europe in 1779 to negotiate an end to the War of Independence, his instructions from Congress were a mixture of the vague and the unachievable. During the subsequent four years of wrangling with the British, French, and Spanish over the terms of America's separation from Great Britain,

Jay gained a vast amount of information that a distant and preoccupied Congress lacked. He exercised considerable discretion in adjusting the details of the American position; indeed, he ignored explicit instructions when he judged that Congress, had it been privy to the details of the negotiations, would have instructed him otherwise. The Treaty of 1783 was declared a triumph for America on Jay's return—when the motives and machinations of the foreign interests became known—and his shrewd exercise of discretion earned him acclaim.[15] One could argue that Jay, as the agent of the American people, was "contractually" motivated to harness his judgment to the public interest, and was duly rewarded for good performance. But it was an odd sort of contract, feasible only because of Jay's intrinsic desire to secure the best deal for America. Had he been motivated by self-interest alone, he would likely have balked at the implicit contract of "use your judgment, and accept evaluation by criteria to be determined later."

In circumstances in which good performance can be defined only in retrospect, an agent faces the risk that circumstances beyond his control (including incoherent or inconsistent goals) will lead to unfavorable evaluation. Prudent profit-seekers may well shun endeavors in which their compensation depends so heavily on chance. It may be possible to write conditional contracts that take into account unfolding events and assess agents' judgments in light of the information available at each stage. But such contracts are likely to be cumbersome, expensive to adjudicate, and open to interpretive disputes. These problems help to explain the immense value of an *intrinsic* motivation on the part of agents. To the extent that higher-level officials can rely on civil servants to exercise discretion in the public interest, based upon the latter's special training or privileged grasp of circumstances, mandates can be left open, projects can be adapted as context requires; and monitoring costs can be spared. The public's business becomes much easier to accomplish if agents display a combination of informed fidelity to the public interest, initiative, and integrity that can be summarized by the word *honor*, a term that is admittedly complex, but is also too important to neglect.[16]

Some observers, and especially adherents of the "public choice" school, contend that the motives of government workers are uniformly selfish and almost uniformly material. This view is demonstrably false—fortunately so, since the problem of implementing public policy would be immeasurably more difficult if it were not.[17] Anthony Downs, in his book *Inside Bureaucracy*, has written that the range of motives animating civil servants includes not only power, money, security, and convenience, but also "loyalty to an idea, an institution, or the nation, pride in excellent work, and desire to serve the public interest."[18] Max Weber gave "social honor" equal weight with "material reward" in motivating bureaucrats.[19] By *honor* I mean that intrinsic sympathy between a civil servant and the goals of his organization, and the propensity to advance these goals without compulsion or certainty of material reward. In a soldier or a diplomat honor involves patriotism, in a teacher love of learning, in a judge a devotion to justice, and so on. It is particularly valuable when limited information at the policy-setting level requires that agents exercise discretion, and when extrinsic motivations are difficult to arrange.

But even if bureaucratic honor is often useful and sometimes essential, some complications remain. First, a civil servant may be motivated—however sincerely—by a view of the public good at odds with that of elected officials and of the citizenry. Rather than supplementing an incompletely specified mission, then, discretion informed by an idiosyncratic sense of honor may undercut it. Few people would deny that Oliver North and John Poindexter *felt* themselves to be acting honorably when they arranged for secret arms sales to Iran, for example, but still fewer would argue that the project advanced the national interest.

One might ask why honor should be counted valuable for civil servants but not for profit-seekers. Clearly, we are better off when both sorts of agents display integrity. If profit-seekers were *uniformly* honest and public-spirited—as indeed most of them are—many objections to privatization would disappear. But if profit-seekers *differ* in their devotion to the common good, the more public-spirited of them tend, by the logic of cost-based bidding, to lose contract competitions. If the honor-bound profit-seeker anticipates spending extra resources to produce value in excess of what the literal provisions of a contract require, his costs and hence his bids will exceed those of less ambitious competitors. If his bids do not reflect such costs, he will steadily lose money and eventually go out of business. (If the superiority of his performance can be accurately measured after the fact, he may develop a reputational advantage that will counter this cost disadvantage in a *series* of contracts. When regulations require public officials to accept the lowest qualified bid, however—as is generally the case, and for good reasons—reputation cannot be taken so fully into account.)[20]

Finally, it is easy but unhelpful to observe that honor among civil servants is a good thing. A consensus on distributive justice would be a good thing, too, but it nonetheless remains elusive. To conclude that it helps if bureaucrats are honorable does not make them so. Everyone has encountered some civil servants strongly devoted to the public interest and others conspicuously free of any such motive. While it is wasteful to ignore bureaucratic honor where it exists, it may well be worse to rely upon it where it does not exist. The potential for honor to bind civil servants depends in part on the nature of the task and in part on broader cultural factors. Intrinsic commitment is more likely to arise for tasks that are clearly important, or surrounded by professional tradition, or charged with moral or emotional significance. Civil servants performing military and diplomatic functions, or involved in teaching, research, social work, medicine, and law enforcement may be highly motivated by honor, as well as the opinions of their colleagues and the public. Functions with little visibility, prestige, or autonomy are less likely to summon such motives. The power of professional honor as a bureaucratic motivation also depends on the cultural standing of bureaucrats. In many nations civil servants enjoy a good deal of status. Carrying out official duties faithfully and efficiently earns high social regard and reinforces self-esteem. But when the civil service commands little prestige—as is generally true in the United States today—there is less scope for honor and status as bureaucratic incentives.[21] This point argues for caution in relying on bureaucratic honor to buttress weak formal devices of accountability in this country. At the same time, it suggests that the opprobrium heaped upon civil servants in recent years—further reducing the potential for honor as a hallmark of public service—erodes our culture's ability to accomplish these public tasks for which close monitoring and extrinsic motivations are difficult to arrange.

The relative advantages of civil servants and profit-seekers along the first dimension of efficiency—getting the right things done—depend crucially on whether public officials are technically able to specify mandates in detail and in advance. If mandates *can* be specified, but tend not to be, writing contracts with profit-seekers is likely to be a useful discipline. But if officials are *not* equipped to draft detailed goals, the advantage may shift to civil servants. And in cases where agents can neither be motivated extrinsically nor trusted to choose efficiently, we must either abandon the undertaking or resign ourselves to a measure of inefficiency in its performance. In sum, *profit-seekers cannot be expected to exceed the literal specifications of a contract. The less completely can duties be defined in advance, the more valuable is bureaucratic honor.*

THE VIRTUES OF OWNERSHIP

The past several pages have dealt with the efficient *specification* of public tasks. The second dimension of efficiency concerns *performance*. This issue is considerably simpler, and the key proposition can be summarized in a sentence: *The more*

*complete and more fully asserted are ownership rights, the less an organization will suffer
from simple waste.*

When those who control the productive organization are *owners* (or are strictly
answerable to owners), the exercise of ownership rights will tend to limit random
inefficiency. By "random" I refer to waste, muddle, and correctible error, as
distinct from breakdowns rooted in the conflicting interests of principals and
agents. This tendency of profit-seeking organizations holds true—albeit with different implications—*whether or not* contracts are competitive and well enforced.
Owners take up economic slack and convert it into lower prices or higher quality
(if competition and official vigilance bridle contractors' profit ambitions) or else
into elevated profits (if they do not). Virtually every proposal urging a greater
role for profit-seeking agents in the public realm turns on this point and
rightly so.

In private firms, a layer of managers attuned to profitability has considerable
influence over the behavior of lower-level employees. When a firm is commissioned to undertake a public task, the owners (or their agents) translate the *external*
mandate to produce goods or services into an *internal* mandate to generate revenue
and limit costs. There is no truly equivalent function in a public bureaucracy, no
link in the chain of agency relationships where incentives and authority to press
for efficiency are quite so potently concentrated. Civil servants also much prefer
efficiency to waste, to be sure, but their interest in policing the details of subordinate's performance is usually less tangible and less focused. More importantly,
public managers usually lack the rights to select and direct subordinates that private
owners enjoy. Civil service regulations, established as barriers against favoritism
and corruption, often make it difficult to control public workers through selective
incentives or sanctions.[22] Multiple mandates and constraints on management, even
if imposed in sincere efforts to codify the complex criteria for public action, make
efficiency measures ambiguous and imprecise.

Profit-seekers are generally more motivated to eliminate random inefficiency,
then, and less constrained than civil servants in their capacity to do so. Three
points qualifying this celebration of the virtues of ownership deserve emphasis,
however. First, if the managers of a private contractor are not themselves owners
and are weakly accountable to owners, there is room for the same kind of slack
that saps the efficiency of governmental agencies. Second, profit-seekers may
perceive as slack *any* use of resources that does not boost net revenue, whether
it is simple waste or attention to some precious public goal that has not been
made contractually explicit. Third, *random* inefficiency is not the only, nor necessarily the most damaging, defect to which the collective agenda is subject.

Breakdowns of accountability can involve not merely wasteful or rigid or inept performance, but also politically corrosive opportunism.

CIVIL SERVANTS, PROFIT-SEEKERS, AND RENTS

The same impediments to enforcing the public interest that allow random inefficiency also invite public servants to benefit themselves at their fellow citizens' expense. To use the economist's terminology introduced in chapter 3, agents collect *rents* when they are paid more than the public should have to spend to get its business accomplished. Civil servants and profit-seekers differ in the types of rents they typically collect and in the manner in which they seek them. These differences matter enough to warrant some discussion.

Civil Servants' Rents

A near-universal feature of bureaucracy is limits on pay. Even if the relevant legislators were sufficiently broad-minded, incompetent, or corrupt to accede to his demands, a deputy assistant secretary in the Department of Agriculture would be hard pressed to have his salary increased to $1 million per year. In the federal government, and in most state and local governments, many salaries are set through legislative or administrative guidelines and can only be changed through formal procedures. Indeed, it is unconstitutional to reduce the salary of federal judges, or to raise or to cut the pay of an incumbent president.[23]

Government pay scales are also quite compressed. Lower-level civil servants sometimes earn more than their private sector counterparts, while senior officials generally make less.[24] It is conceivable, though not very likely, that this pattern simply reflects relative worth: The public sector needs and gets better clerks and backhoe operators and worse top managers than the private sector. A more plausible explanation is that political as well as economic considerations affect the compensation of public workers. Employees exercise political influence to push up wages and salaries. Public managers have little reason to resist such pressures and are generally happy to have their subordinates well paid. But government pay scales are constrained to some extent at all levels and are subjected to intense public scrutiny in the cases of top-level officials and legislators. If average government salaries were to exceed average private sector salaries, lawmakers would find it politically expedient to legislate freezes or reductions. And whenever top salaries exceed what the public perceives as reasonable—whatever their relations to top private sector compensation—there is little to lose politically, and much to gain, by initiatives to limit them.

Since cash benefits are limited, civil servants more typically collect rents in the form of fringe benefits, pleasant working conditions, congenial associates, undemanding work loads, security against dismissal, and other types of what economists call "nonpecuniary rents." The spectrum ranges from arguably legitimate workplace amenities to obviously illegitimate fraud and nepotism. (Roughly one out of three phone calls placed by federal workers is personal rather than official. Officials of the Federal Asset Disposition Association apparently made a practice of charging the agency for petty personal expenses. Custodians in New York City public schools routinely hired relatives as assistants, disappeared for long periods, and refused to carry out basic maintenance.)[25]

Profit-Seekers' Rents

Civil servants may reap unfair and inefficient benefits when senior political officials are unable or reluctant to drive a hard bargain with agents on the citizens' behalf. Profit-seekers collect rents for the same reasons, but in a different form. One member of the public choice school, which indicts grasping bureaucracy as the engine of wasteful spending, depicts government agencies as legally sanctioned monopolies that "yield a relatively large fiscal residuum from which bureaucrats can indirectly extract wealth."[26] The real problem is both simpler and broader. Diffused accountability invites agents, however organized, to exploit the public. At about the same time as outrage was mounting over the lavish perquisites and minimal performance of many school custodians in New York City, some four thousand homeless families were housed at public expense in for-profit "welfare hotels." A complex bankruptcy proceeding exposed the finances of one hotel and revealed that the fees charged for its spartan accommodations yielded profit margins of about 50 percent.[27]

Profit-seekers' rents are far more likely than those of civil servants to come in the form of money. They also tend to be highly concentrated, rather than spread throughout the organization as civil servants' rents normally are. The exercise of ownership rights will tend to transform any contractual slack into extra profits and channel it to owners, rather than leaving it as benefits to the employees.[28] This will not be the case, however, when ownership rights are weakly defended. If nonowning managers enjoy substantial autonomy from dispersed shareholders, rents may take the form of inflated salaries and elaborate perquisites rather than higher profits. If the company work force is organized, or if the firm is dependent on a few key subcontractors, then workers or suppliers may be able to lay claim to rents in the form of higher wages or prices.

Profit-seekers' rents can be difficult to identify. A highly profitable government contractor may be earning rich returns because it is innovative and efficient. Or it may be collecting rents because it is unharried by competition and able to raise prices or cut quality with impunity. Private firms that run nuclear-weapons plants for the Energy Department are paid on a cost-plus basis, with biannual evaluations and the opportunity to get bonuses for cost control, quality, and adherence to environmental, health, and safety standards. Investigations revealed that during the years when an Ohio plant was leaking contaminants into the surrounding area and exposing numbers of workers to radiation, the contractors received more than three-quarters of the maximum possible incentive bonus. Shortly after Rockwell International received ratings of "very good" to "excellent" on health, safety, and environmental scales (and correspondingly high performance bonuses) for the Rocky Flats weapons plant it managed, the plant was shut down when a series of mishaps culminated in the plutonium contamination of three workers.[29]

To gather together this section's arguments: *The attenuated accountability of public undertakings invites both civil servants and profit-seekers to press for excessive benefits. Civil servants' rents are generally dispersed and largely nonpecuniary. Private contractors' rents usually come in the form of elevated profits. Ownership incentives that encourage efficiency also concentrate incentives for rent-seeking.*

The potential for self-serving agents to exploit the public, absent well-crafted structures of accountability, has one particularly distressing implication. Suppose collective duties *differ* in their suitability for civil service or profit-seeking delivery: Public officials can more readily monitor and control profit-seekers in certain tasks, while for others it is easier to manage civil servants. If rents are richer where oversight is weaker, then each type of agent will *prefer* employment in the tasks for which it is less suited. Civil servants will find the richest rents in undertakings in which it is difficult to hold them to account. The stronger or more cynical the public employees' organization, and the less a task allows for effective public management, the more tenaciously will civil servants defend their functions. Profit-seekers will find the richest rents where competition and evaluation tend to be weakest. The less scope there is for effective competition in a given function, the more pressure we should expect from aspiring profit-seeking agents to shift that function from public to private supply. In the case-by-case choice between forms of organization, in short, the material interests of agents run counter to those of the public at large.

AGENTS' INTERESTS AND THE POLITICS
OF PUBLIC SPENDING

In earlier chapters, it was emphasized that the public spending agenda is inescapably political and hence vulnerable to manipulation. A citizen's status as a supplier to some collective endeavor is likely to affect his preferences about public spending and his propensity to act on those preferences. Along with his assessment of the project's *social* value, he may take his private benefits (as an agent) into account as he exercises his rights (as a principal) to shape the common agenda.

The owner of a construction company will consider her prospects for contracts, as well as her convictions on crime and punishment, as she reflects on a proposal to build new prisons. An official of the Drug Enforcement Administration will likely think differently about an antinarcotics initiative than will his neighbor, even if both are equally appalled by drug abuse. A scientist's sense of national research priorities will generally have something to do with her own area of expertise. If citizens' personal interests as agents govern their political preferences, and if such interests are more politically potent—because more concentrated and better organized—than other interests, they may seriously distort public spending decisions. Self-seeking suppliers (often in coalition with other groups that benefit disproportionately from public undertakings) may seize control of the spending agenda to the detriment of the dispersed and unorganized majority.

Of course, the mere fact that an agent's employment interests coincide with her policy preferences does not mean that the former governs the latter. A citizen's choice of occupation and budget priorities may reflect the same underlying values. A teacher's support for spending on education does not necessarily signal opportunism, nor does that of a doctor for public health care. The National Aeronautics and Space Administration worker whose vote goes to the candidate most committed to the space program probably cannot himself say how much his position originates in his own enthusiasm for space exploration, and how much in his eagerness to keep the job that his enthusiasm led him to select.

A related point is less obvious, but no less important. Incentives to manipulate the spending agenda arise *not* from simple involvement in some public undertaking, but from the promise of benefits exceeding those otherwise obtainable. If a laser technician can choose among a number of equally attractive private sector jobs, he has little stake—as a worker—in public spending on antimissile defense systems. If the construction industry is booming and government contracts are no more lucrative than private projects, the building contractor has no material motive to push for more low-income housing. If a Securities and Exchange Commission lawyer knows that he can easily find a comparable job in the private sector, his vote may probably not depend on candidate proposals concerning securities law enforcement. In practice, of course, nearly everyone would rather not lose his job, and nearly every contractor would prefer more business to less. But it is important to recognize that involvement in public projects does not imply any uniform degree of self-interested support for the budget behind the project.

A citizen usually takes several factors into account as she decides how, and how actively, to seek to affect public budgeting. She considers her personal interests as a beneficiary of public programs. She considers how varying uses of public funds promise to reflect and to advance her moral and philosophical values. She examines her tax position to estimate how heavily the burden of public spending falls on her. She considers as well the likelihood that her political efforts will have any effect on spending decisions. These factors, along with her own taste or distaste for politics, determine how politically well informed and active she will be. In general, her interests as an agent will weigh more heavily, relative to other factors, the larger are the rents at stake and the greater is the probability that her reasonable efforts can influence spending decisions. If economic and institutional factors in the health care industry are such that doctors make large rents and nurses do not, for example, we should expect to see doctors, and not nurses, pushing for looser reimbursement rules and generous government spending on health care.

An agent's rent (and thus, her incentives for political activism) will be large if her situation as a public supplier is especially favorable, or if her other options are especially bleak. If National Park Service maintenance workers are paid double the going wage, they will be inclined to resist proposals to shrink the park system or to contract out maintenance work to private firms. A technician who is highly specialized in designing nuclear warheads would find few alternative uses for his skills so that, even if his salary is not particularly high, he would have a lively interest in maintaining military spending and in opposing disarmament.

There is one qualification to the argument linking the level of political activism to the level of rents. Folk wisdom, confirmed by evidence from psychology and from economics, holds that people regret the loss of a benefit more intensely than they relish an equivalent gain. This suggests that *protecting* existing rents will be a more potent political motive than *seeking* prospective rents. Suppliers facing a spending cutback will react more vigorously than will suppliers aspiring to a spending increase. The threshold level of rents triggering political activism will be lower. Moreover, the beneficiaries of existing spending will be more readily identifiable, and thus more easily organized, than will be the beneficiaries of prospective spending.[30]

The likelihood that political influence will be *effective* depends on the solidarity and organization of interested agents (and their potential allies) and on the instruments of influence to be employed. One obvious way that citizens affect spending is through their *votes*. A supplier may vote for the candidate promising the largest (or most recklessly disbursed) budget for the program from which he benefits. Whether he uses his ballot in this way depends both on the benefits at stake and on the candidate's capacity to effect the relevant budget if elected.

The greater is the propensity of suppliers to vote their interests, and the more suppliers there are in the electorate, the more heavily will their votes weigh on budgetary politics. I have argued that profit-seekers' rents tend to be concentrated, while civil servants' rents are dispersed. In the case of the civil service, then, *many* people will have *some* motivation to influence spending decisions. In the case of a profit-seeking organization, *a few* people will have *strong* motives to defend their benefits with their votes. If all the rents available in some public budget go to the owners of the profit-seeking contractor, lower-level workers will have little passion for voting to preserve or to increase the budget. Some military bases have replaced their canteens with private fast-food franchises. If the workers in those franchises are paid no more than they could get in comparable jobs off the base, they will have little financial stake in the size of the defense budget—although the franchise owners would.

Another instrument of political influence is *campaign support*. Suppliers can attempt to influence the spending positions of public officials, or to affect the electoral prospects of sympathetic candidates, through donations of time or money or other resources. Campaign support, unlike voting, can be calibrated to match the intensity of a donor's interest in an election. A citizen with a moderate preference for one candidate can wear a lapel pin or display a bumper sticker. As the intensity of her preference rises, she can attempt to influence the votes of her friends and relatives, work on phone banks at campaign headquarters, and canvass door to door. Financial contributions can be varied with even greater precision. Interested civil servants, while numerous, will each be willing to make only relatively small contributions. There will be *fewer* ready contributors with profit-seeking suppliers, but each contribution is likely to be larger, in line with the rents at stake. Since there are physical limits on the time any one person can donate to a campaign, and since the owners of firms involved in government contracts may tend to place relatively high values on their time, contributions from profit-seekers will usually be in the form of money.

The Hatch Act, as well as comparable state and local laws barring federal workers from most partisan activities, forbids or strictly limits civil servants' donations of their time to campaigns. Campaign finance laws limit the levels of financial contributions by profit-seekers. The influence that agents can exert on spending decisions through campaign support depends on the relative effectiveness of these constraints, as well as on the willingness of politicians to tailor their spending proposals in order to obtain campaign support, and—not least importantly—on the political potency of the campaign resources each type of agent can deliver. One particularly interesting question is how politicians value *votes* (which civil servants can more readily supply) relative to *money* to use in search of votes (which profit-seekers can more readily supply).

Finally, suppliers can seek to shape public spending through bribery or other illegitimate forms of influence. Civil servants and profit-seekers will differ in their propensity to bribe officials in the same way as they differ in their propensity to donate money to campaigns. If a profit-seeker has large rents at stake, and if he is undeterred by moral scruples or the threat of discovery, he may be inclined to devote significant sums to induce officials to boost spending, to increase available rents through looser management, or to steer a contract away from more efficient or more qualified competitors. Individual civil servants, with smaller rents at stake, should be willing to spend correspondingly less to defend or to expand them—probably too little to corrupt a politician. Civil servants may have reason to attempt to pool their resources into a more impressive bribe, but such an arrangement would be difficult to organize and to enforce in secret.[31]

Thus, task by task, and jurisdiction by jurisdiction, the privatization decision should be biased against contracting when campaign contributions are important factors in budgetary politics, or where corruption is difficult to detect or deter. Where corruption is uncommon and campaign finance laws limit the political potency of monetary contributions, on the other hand, the votes of civil servants may present a greater threat to the integrity of public spending decisions and privatization is correspondingly more promising.

To summarize this chapter's main arguments: The more precisely a task can be *specified* in advance, and its performance *evaluated* after the fact, the more certainly contractors can be made to *compete*; the more readily disappointing contractors can be *replaced* (or otherwise penalized); and the more narrowly government cares about *ends* to the exclusion of *means*, the stronger the case for employing profit-seekers rather than civil servants. The fundamental distinction, however, is between competitive, output-based relationships and noncompetitive, input-based relationships rather than between profit-seekers and civil servants *per se*.

Profit-seekers cannot be expected to exceed the literal specifications of a contract. Thus, the more difficult it is to define mandates in advance, the more valuable becomes bureaucratic honor.

The more complete and more fully asserted are ownership rights, the less an organization will suffer from simple waste. But the attenuated accountability of public undertakings invites both civil servants and profit-seekers to press for excessive benefits. Civil servants' rents are generally dispersed and largely nonpecuniary. Private contractors' rents usually come in the form of elevated profits. The ownership incentives that encourage efficiency also concentrate incentives for rent-seeking. And suppliers' motivation for political opportunism depends on the rents at stake. The more important are *votes* compared to other instruments of political influence, the greater becomes the capacity of civil servants to warp spending decisions. The more important are *campaign donations* and *bribes*, the greater becomes the capacity of profit-seekers to distort the budget process.

PART THREE

CASES AND CAUTIONARY TALES

CHAPTER 6

LESSONS FROM THE PENTAGON

MILITARY PROCUREMENT constitutes, by a wide margin, the largest category of government purchases from the private sector. The modern U.S. armed forces are as much a network of contracts with private suppliers of hardware, logistical support, and advanced research as they are a corps of uniformed men and women. Consider: In 1987, total U.S. defense spending came to $295 billion. But only about one-third of this sum went to pay the wages of soldiers, sailors, marines, airmen, and civil servants in the Defense Department. The rest, some $186 billion, was spent to buy goods and services from private suppliers.[1] (For a sense of scale, note that corporate income tax receipts that year came to about $84 billion.)[2] While the largest share went for goods procurement, the tab for purchased services—including research and development, administrative support and base management, and transportation—amounted to $79 billion, more than the entire payroll for the armed forces' uniformed personnel, and well over twice what was spent to pay civil-service defense workers. Defense-related purchases from the private sector account for over 4 percent of America's gross national product.

Military contracting merits attention here not just because it is *important*, but also because it is widely seen as a *problem*. No discussion of the private sector's role in the public's business can ignore the chronic troublesomeness of this particular relationship. Throughout the 1980s, virtually every year saw the eruption of a defense procurement scandal. A large fraction of the Pentagon's major contractors are usually under investigation for some sort of abuse, and each of the top twelve contractors had its turn in the headlines during the past decade facing charges of excessive prices, poor quality, improper billing, and other misdeeds.[3] Soon after the Reagan military buildup got under way, revelations of what seemed to be ludicrous and larcenous overpricing for such mundane items as coffeemakers, hammers, and toilet assemblies sparked outrage and ridicule. The merits of several expensive weapons were called into question, notably the B-1 bomber, the Aegis shipboard air defense system, the Bradley fighting vehicle, and the Sergeant York antiaircraft system. (The defects of the Sergeant York, or Divad, were so profound that it was actually canceled well into production.) In the mid-1980s, investigations uncovered pervasive corruption at the Defense Personnel Support Center in Philadelphia and at several other acquisition centers. The official in charge of buying most of the military's clothing pleaded guilty to racketeering charges after some $400,000 in cash and gold were found in his home. A contract officer at the Yokosuka Navy Supply depot was sentenced to prison in 1985 for steering contracts to Japanese ship repair companies that plied him with money, trips, and geisha girls.[4] The most spectacularly disheartening scandal emerged in mid-1988, as dozens of subpoenas were served against contractors, consultants, and Pentagon officials, while allegations of fraud tainted many billions of dollars in contracts. One veteran observer has estimated that procurement waste and fraud cost the government about $40 billion a year—a sum equivalent to about a quarter of all discretionary domestic spending.[5] Inevitably, the recurring reports of incompetence and corruption sapped public support for military spending, and by the end of the decade nearly half of all Americans felt the government was spending "too much" on defense.[6]

Editorial page complaints, official inquisitions, and academic diagnoses alike center on three broad indictments of the military procurement process: The system costs too much, delivers too little, and fails to enforce accountability. Weapons procurement is seen as too costly, in the simplest sense, as a blunt consequence of fraud and profiteering. This is the major theme in the typical kitchen table discussion of the procurement problem: Unscrupulous contractors dupe or corrupt government officials and then rake in rich profits at public expense. They submit meaningless bids to lure Congress into funding programs, then brazenly pump up the price when it's too late for the government to back out. A somewhat subtler theme points to incompetence rather than greed as the cause of excess costs: Defense contractors—unharried by competition, complacent, old-fashioned, and perhaps rather dim—are simply unable to run their factories with any degree of efficiency. By this view, cost overruns originate less in cynical stratagems than in manufacturing ineptness and in a witless incapacity to predict the expense of developing new systems.

The second broad indictment—the system delivers too little—calls attention to chronic delays in weapons development and production; to performance specifications that steadily erode as a system moves from proposal through development and on to full-scale production; and to recurring reports of dismal quality once the weapons reach the field. More fundamentally, some observers feel that decisions about which weapons to produce seldom fit real military requirements—that we are equipping ourselves to fight the wrong battles, in the wrong places, on the wrong scale. Particularly as defense spending slowed in the late 1980s, many observers feared that the system was delivering too little in the most literal sense of inadequate quantities of tanks, planes, and especially spare parts, ammunition, and other less glamorous goods.

The third indictment—that the system lacks accountability—refers to the routineness with which costs escalate, schedules lengthen, and standards collapse as a system moves from the drawing boards to the arsenals; to the Pentagon's apparent unwillingness or inability to sanction erring contractors; and to the perception that politics, not technological capacity or military need, determine the pattern of contracting. "Iron triangles" of military organizations, private contractors, and legislators playing pork-barrel politics triumph over the broader public interest, forming what Eisenhower termed a "military-industrial complex" impervious to reform.

While the speed and scale of the Reagan military buildup multiplied opportunities for breakdown, these problems are by no means unique to the 1980s. Both world wars witnessed plagues of profiteering, and cycles of scandal and reform have run through the entire postwar era. The United States has had military procurement problems almost as long as it has had a military. In the 1790s, the new country's navy contracted with private shipyards to build six frigates for $690,000; it ended up getting only three frigates and paying $945,000. (The frigates, while unexpectedly expensive, *were* of good quality; one of them, the *Constitution*, became famous as "Old Ironsides" and remains in service today.) The government commissioned Eli Whitney to deliver ten thousand muskets in two and one-half years but, in part due to problems with the experimental technology of mass production using standardized parts, the contract took ten years to fulfill. Quality problems also have a long history in military procurement; indeed, the very word "shoddy" originally referred to a type of wool bought for the use of the Union Army in the Civil War.[7]

Street corner wisdom attributes these problems to simple greed and stupidity. If the terms are defined broadly enough—if we take greed to mean an interest in the good of one's business or congressional district, and take stupidity to mean a failure to anticipate every contingency—then the charges may be accurate. But they remain imprecise guides to reform. Some Americans are especially inclined to find base motives at work in military procurement since, for the healthiest of reasons, the whole topic of modern weaponry repels them. But facile indictments dangerously obscure the blunt fact that weapons acquisition is a complex undertaking in which the best efforts of even honorable and able people can produce unhappy results.

Defense procurement involves the fundamental challenges that complicate governmental contracting with the private sector. This most expensive of experiments in public reliance on outside suppliers offers a rich source of illustrations, lessons, and cautionary tales to inform the rest of this book.

THE DEFENSE CONTRACTING PROBLEM

Consider the textbook scenario for procuring weapons. One of the armed forces, after establishing the need for some particular system, promulgates detailed requirements and solicits bids from industry. Potential contractors compete to fill the requirement. The lowest-bidding qualified supplier is chosen and, once final specifications, delivery schedules, and other housekeeping matters are worked out, a contract is signed. The contractor then goes to work, seeking to produce at a cost below the price it bid. Any excess of the bid price over costs is the contractor's profit, its reward for productive efficiency. If costs *exceed* the price, the consequent losses justly penalize the contractor for inefficient production or sloppy cost estimates. Should the supplier fail to meet the terms of the contract—if it falls behind schedule, or if its product is of poor quality, or if it attempts to boost its price over what it bid—the buyer simply exercises its right to replace the supplier with a competitor.

Things seldom work out this way. There are several impediments to straightforward contracting that bedevil the acquisition of all but the most standardized military goods. First, when there is uncertainty over the mission a weapon is to fulfill, or over the technology involved, the government enters into contracts that are incompletely specified and subject to revision. Second, because contracts are incomplete and changeable, competitive bids are, at best, tentative and, at worst, meaningless. Third, once the government has selected a supplier, it has only the feeblest sanctions to deter poor performance, since there are usually formidable barriers against replacing contractors.[8]

Incomplete Contracts

At least since the longbow gave the English a deciding edge at Crécy in 1346, technological superiority has been a central desideratum of weaponry.[9] This means that defense contractors typically operate at the technical frontier, where uncertainty—about both cost and performance—is pervasive. The mission that a system is meant to support, moreover, may remain ill-defined well into a development program. It is thus difficult or impossible to specify in advance precisely what is required. The more uncertainty surrounds a system's technology or mission at the start, the more there is to be worked out in the course of the project.

One obvious and important consequence of such uncertainty is that firm, fixed price contracts can become impractical. Suppliers are justifiably reluctant to bear the risks associated with design changes and technical uncertainties that they cannot control or even predict. Thus military contracts often base payments to suppliers on the cost of *inputs* as well as, or even instead of, the unknown value of outputs. Contracts reimburse suppliers for what they spend to develop or produce a weapon. They also include a fee that may be fixed or may vary so as to encourage cost control. The proportion of such input-based defense contracts tripled during the 1950s, as weapons systems became more complex.[10] There is a sizeable literature on how these kinds of contractual arrangements are supposed to work, and an equally large literature on how they do not work very well.[11] It is extremely difficult to shield contractors from risks they cannot control, while at the same time motivating them to minimize those costs they *can* control.

While a large fraction of weapons contracts are still, formally, on a fixed-price basis, the prevalence of midcontract changes and repeated renegotiations, as well as the reluctance of the armed forces to let major suppliers go bankrupt, have combined to make "fixed" bids quite flexible. Recurrent campaigns to hold suppliers to firm fixed prices run up against a fundamental characteristic of the procurement relationship. When uncertainty surrounds real requirements and the real costs of meeting them, then budgetary politics, contractors' competitive tactics, and the enduring hopefulness of human nature all encourage optimistic initial cost estimates, followed by cost growth beyond the budget limits. Once a project is under way, there are formidable pressures for cost to increase and few effective counterpressures. The interests that rapidly grow up around any major spending program, meanwhile, protect even the most ill-starred weapons from cancellation. Thus costs grow by about one-third or more in the course of a typical defense contract.[12]

Fragmented Competition

Such unbridled cost growth is rare in commercial contracts, leading many observers to conclude that the solution to defense contracting problems is to make the process more "businesslike" and, in particular, to require more competition.[13] There is much to be said for this sentiment. But for major weapons systems, the situation is more complex than those who call for renouncing monopoly and simply embracing competition acknowledge.

The competitive ideal of the economics textbook envisages *several* equally able suppliers among whom a buyer can choose at virtually any point in a project. For sophisticated defense systems, there are several impediments to this kind of competition. First, there are usually only a handful of companies qualified to submit a bid in the first place. Second, while *development* contracts are formally distinct from *production* contracts, in practice the developer of a system usually receives much of the production work.[14] Third, design specifications and cost estimates tend to change over time, making a mockery of the initial bidding process. The contract for the F-16 fighter airframe underwent 518 design changes in the first two years; eighty of these individual changes were significant enough to add over $2 million each to the cost of the contract.[15]

While the proportion of total contracts awarded competitively varies with the prevailing fashion in procurement reform, all but a few major acquisitions *do* involve some sort of competition. The issue, however, is the precise form that the competition should take. For reasons that may be highly resistant to reform, competition in weapons procurement tends to be fragmented. Some phases of the process are quite competitive; others are not. Unfortunately, the points at which competition would be most beneficial are frequently those where it is rarest. The armed forces have long mounted elaborately structured contests among corporations seeking the right to develop major weapons systems. Aspiring contractors devote considerable resources to crafting and presenting their designs. Since the mid-1980s, these competitions have become more costly and risky for companies. (For example, two rival teams spent over a billion dollars in the 1987 competition for the Air Forces advanced tactical fighter.)[16] The problems with these arrangements are twofold. First, contests turn mostly on the technological potential of competing designs, with little weight given to cost. Precisely because cost projections are notoriously unreliable, the armed forces tend to underweight them in source selection decisions.[17] Second, the winner of the development contract has been able to count on getting most or all of the subsequent production work, thus recouping the losses incurred in the design competition. Since initial bids are subject to renegotiation, pledges made in the development phase seldom bar contractors from increasing prices once rivals are out of the picture. In other words, at the point where the process is highly competitive, there is no serious assessment of cost. At the point of production, where cost *is* supposed to matter, there is seldom much competition.

Limited Sanctions

Incomplete contracts and fragmented competition are not necessarily fatal to efficiency if the chosen contractor can be properly motivated and, when necessary, penalized. In Japan, notes one expert, the executives of weapons firms "have been known to commit suicide for failure to deliver on their promises."[18] American executives, by and large, take a more relaxed view of such matters. Government control over contractors, once a project is under way, tends to be severely limited. The uncertainty surrounding cutting-edge defense goods and the inconclusiveness of all tests short of extensive wartime experience mean that evaluations of contractor performance are seldom definitive, or secure against legal or logical challenge. Only good fortune let the Navy discover, before battle damage made the observation inescapable, that inferior armor plate had been fraudulently installed on the battleship *New Jersey* and several other ships in the early 1980s.[19] Where standards are more subtle and lapses less egregious, it will often be harder to detect contractor failures, and harder still to establish contract breach clearly enough to satisfy regulations and, if necessary, a judge.

Even if competition *does* constrain the chosen supplier as a new system gets under way, there will often be no good alternative to an incumbent contractor five or ten years later. Responding to protests over the mildness of the penalties invoked against General Dynamics for rather serious transgressions, one officer explained, "It would be swell if I could say, 'you're a naughty boy and I'm going to cast you into oblivion.' But if I do, where am I going to buy the submarines and tanks and planes that I need?"[20] The incumbent producer gains experience, acquires specialized equipment, and develops valuable channels of communication that no challenger can instantly replicate. Performance can slip or prices can rise considerably before the government finds it worthwhile to seek alternatives.[21]

Sanctioning contractors is apt to be organizationally and politically painful at best and impossible at worst. The mere mention of excess costs or flawed performance attracts the scrutiny of the press and invites lawmakers to savage procurement budgets. Attempts to challenge or replace contractors will usually cause embarrassing delays in weapons programs that are uniformly seen as urgent and are, almost as uniformly, already plagued by schedule slippage. Lawsuits between military buyers and contractors tend to turn out badly for the government side when claims and obligations are at all ambiguous.[22] Major contractors are well connected in the Pentagon and on Capitol Hill, and for a midlevel procurement officer to take a hard line with suppliers will often be at once futile and damaging to his career. Finally, military procurement personnel are simply reluctant to antagonize contractors who are close working associates and often friends, as well as sources of much-needed new weapons systems, and even potential future employers. (This last factor probably gets more attention than it merits, the others, less.) Procurement officers are keenly interested in getting systems fielded quickly, are only indirectly interested in reining in the military budget, and honestly do believe that a flawed, expensive system that meets a pressing military need is better than no system at all. For all of these reasons—most of which have little to do with venality or stupidity—the government tends not to penalize contractors that fail to deliver as promised, even when sanctions are technically at hand.[23]

THE COSTS OF CONTRACTING

Every procurement fiasco seems avoidable in retrospect. There are almost no weapons acquisition problems that cannot be overcome by better procedures, closer oversight, and more complete evaluation. But the indignant calls for procedural reform that follow every scandal miss the point that contracting *itself* is costly.[24] The more completely rules, obligations, and procedures are defined in order to enforce accountability, the higher the price in time, money, and flexibility. Herein lies one of the Pentagon's most important, and most poignant, lessons for advocates of expanding the private sector's role in the public's business.

The armed forces devote considerable resources to drafting specifications for goods and services from the simplest of supplies to the most sophisticated missile systems. Requirements need to be spelled out as fully as possible, both to set the terms for competitive bidding and to codify the obligations of the winning bidder. But the effort spent writing and enforcing such requirements often looks like pettifogging bureaucratic waste. Examples like the sixteen pages of "mil-specs" for a metal whistle, or equally elaborate contractual requirements for oatmeal cookie mix, are regularly held up to ridicule.[25] Legislators, Pentagon officials, and contractors can all be counted upon to denounce the burden and complexity of military specifications. But they are equally quick to demand still more precise guidelines when ambiguities or omissions lead to disputes. "Mil-specs are the sum total of all our past mistakes," an Air Force procurement official has explained. "They are lists of lessons learned."[26] Lamenting "oversight overkill," the Mc-Donnell-Douglas director of aerospace management complained about the twenty-four thousand documents embodying government specifications for military goods. Meanwhile, other McDonnell-Douglas employees were insisting that quality lapses "resulted from written instructions that were incomplete or unclear."[27]

The regulations setting the basic ground rules for procurement contracting take up some twelve hundred pages in several volumes. One expert writes that "many of the existing [procurement] laws and regulations are not readily understood, even," he adds chillingly, "by lawyers."[28] With the wave of procurement scandals in the first Reagan term, these regulations proliferated and were more vigorously enforced. This led to increasingly bitter protest from contractors without preventing (and arguably even inviting) the yet more lamentable scandals of the second Reagan term. Even before the rules were stiffened, two experts estimated that contracting, evaluation, and enforcement absorbed from 20 to 40 percent of all procurement spending.[29]

Competition, however welcome for other reasons, substantially increases contracting costs. Full sets of plans, specifications, and sometimes prototypes must be distributed. Oversight and enforcement staffs must be expanded. Requests for proposals may be thousands of pages long; bid submissions, including technical appendices, arrive at the Pentagon by the truckload. One study found that the competitive source selection process claimed 5 to 10 percent of total program costs before any metal is bent.[30] Circulating technical information to prospective bidders for the Nike Ajax missile system cost $23 million (in late 1950s dollars) while yielding less than $5 million in savings.[31] While competition *can* lead to very large gains in efficiency, it is an empirical question, case by case, as to whether the savings exceed the increased costs.

It is easy to think of refinements in the procurement process to remedy the problems discussed in this chapter. But it is not easy to come up with *simple* improvements. For example, standard incentive-fee contracts—where suppliers earn a higher fee if they manage to hold down cost—are obviously less than ideal since the contractor is rewarded for performance in only one dimension, cost. Other dimensions, such as performance quality and scheduling, are treated in the contract as simple thresholds; if the contractor exceeds the standard, he gains no extra reward, while if he falls below it, there is no penalty short of disruptively reopening the entire contract. This is wasteful if the contractor could be otherwise motivated to find cheap ways to increase performance or to accelerate completion. One seemingly sensible improvement is to set up a scale of rewards and penalties along *several* dimensions—such as cost, performance, and scheduling. Contracts with these sorts of multiple incentive provisions have in fact been used, for example, in the development of the Air Force B-58 bomber and the Navy A2F attack plane. But at a level of detail well short of the theoretical ideal, multidimensional incentive contracts become mind-numbingly complicated.[32]

One of the most treacherous aspects of contracting for major weapons systems is the need to select suppliers before requirements are fully worked out. The government is thus fated to negotiate the details at a distinct disadvantage with an incumbent contractor. One Rand Corporation analyst has proposed a remedy to this, a system of *contingent* contracts, whereby "contract work begins with the firm's knowing only that one of several possible reimbursement schedules will be in effect, depending upon which design specification is finally selected when uncertainty is reduced sufficiently to make the determination." If at some point *new* design possibilities arise, then "contingent sets of contract terms associated with these new designs should be negotiated as soon as they become viable possibilities" but, of course, before they become final designs. This makes a great deal of sense in principle, and would be a legal and organizational nightmare in practice. Imagine the paper flow, in any moderately complex project. Imagine the lawsuits, should large sums come to hinge on some ambiguous provisions.[33]

Most other refinements, in place or proposed, have costs that are incompletely acknowledged by proponents. "Revolving door" rules that restrict defense officials' movement into lucrative jobs with contractors, while important to prevent conflicts of interest and subtle bribery, impede the flow of valuable expertise between business and government. Ceilings on the overall profit rate contractors can earn from government business—which are immensely appealing to legislators—tend to undercut the effectiveness of incentive contracts, since what performance incentives give, profit ceilings take away. Similarly, provisions allowing the government to renegotiate contracts if profits turn out to be excessive discourage innovation and cost control.[34] In fact, the acceptable range of defense contractor profits seems to be something of a political constant, as officials and legislators step in to adjust the profit rate if it gets either too high *or* too low. Lockheed's air cargo transport business offers an illustration. In the 1960s, Lockheed entered what was formally a fixed-price contract to produce C-5A transports for the military, but cost overruns that threatened the company's survival led to a government bailout involving a sharp increase in payments for the planes. In the 1980s, Lockheed entered what was formally a fixed-price contract to produce

C-5B transports, but cost-*under*runs and embarrassingly high profits led to several rounds of renegotiation and a sharp *decrease* in payments for the planes.[35] Symbolically potent norms of after-the-fact fairness that are wholly alien to optimal-contract theory pervade the acquisition system.

CYCLES OF REFORM

Incomplete contracts, fragmented competition, and limited government leverage over major suppliers tend to boost costs and to undercut governmental control. While most individual breakdowns of the procurement system seem remediable, every remedy—each incremental safeguard, refinement, or level of oversight in the contracting process—comes at a cost, and fixing one problem is apt to exacerbate others. Buying advanced weapons is an inescapably complex and vulnerable contractual chore. While this does not mean improvement is impossible, it does suggest that reform efforts are likely to be incompletely analyzed and ultimately imperfect.

Since 1960, there have been fourteen major analyses of the acquisition system, including four commissioned by presidents. Each has posed extensive recommendations for reform and most have, directly or indirectly, spawned significant changes.[36] The broad evolution of national defense policies, the winds of ideological fashion, the political pressures imposed by scandal, the prescriptions of academics and blue-ribbon panels together set in motion what look like long waves of procurement reform. The wave in the past quarter-century has gone from centralization and formal procedures under Kennedy and Johnson, to decentralization under Nixon and Ford, to centralization under Carter, and then (for the most part) back to decentralization under Reagan and Bush. Robert S. McNamara set out to completely make over procurement policy in the 1960s. He ordained a sharp move away from cost-plus contracts, and crafted an elaborate structure of analytic procedures and monitoring bureaus to keep contractors in line.[37] By the time the McNamara reign came to an end, however, many of his reforms were seen as impractical. Even if they were conceptually sound, the quantity and quality of organizational effort required to carry out McNamara's innovations frequently exceeded the Pentagon's capacity, as well as its will.

McNamara tried making procurement more "businesslike" by applying the scientific management techniques he had exercised in his previous position at the head of the Ford Motor Company. Deputy Secretary David Packard, who headed procurement under Defense Secretary Melvin Laird in the Nixon administration, came from a different corporate culture. One of the founders of Hewlett-Packard (a hugely successful electronics firm that made famous the principle of "management by wandering around"), Packard sought to decentralize procurement by selecting first-rate acquisition officials, setting up a few broad guidelines, and giving them relatively free rein to manage acquisition on their own.[38] Terming the procurement system "a real mess" as he took on the job, Packard set out to move authority out from his office to the individual services, to eliminate much of the paperwork associated with contractor oversight, and to encourage greater efficiency and innovation by liberating private contractors from several layers of bureaucracy. To his dismay, however, Packard found that when specifications were not made explicit or rigidly enforced, they often were not met. Packard reluctantly concluded that "contractors who accept contracts must be willing to accept detailed management."[39] After three years of struggling to find some arrangement of contractual rules and relationships that would "stop this problem of people playing games with each other," this justly celebrated manager resigned in frustration.[40] During the Carter administration, Defense Secretary Harold Brown sought to limit procurement spending without weakening the military by instituting a package of efficiency measures but, like Packard, ended his tenure dissatisfied with the results of his procurement reform efforts.

The Reagan administration, entering with ambitious plans for procurement spending, charged Deputy Secretary of Defense Frank Carlucci with devising reforms to ensure that the cresting flood of money would be spent to good effect. Within months thirty-two procedural reforms—known as the "Carlucci initiatives"—had been drafted. Virtually all of the initiatives made economic sense—such as requiring more competition, insisting on firmer prices, and using longer planning horizons to allow for more stable production—but tended to fail in implementation. One high-ranking procurement officer, characterizing the Carlucci initiatives as an oversold statement of good intentions, concluded that "not much really changed."[41] The first of the Reagan-era procurement scandals erupted soon after the adoption of these reforms.

Fueled by indignation, legislators introduced nearly four hundred procurement reform proposals between 1984 and 1986.[42] The fiscal 1983 and 1984 defense appropriation bills imposed warranty requirements on contractors.[43] The 1984 Competition in Contracting Act emphasized legislative distaste for sole-source procurement, and mandated the deployment of thousands of "competition advocates" throughout the procurement bureaucracy.[44] The fiscal 1986 defense appropriation bill bolstered provisions encouraging competition and declared a broad range of contractor costs—such as lobbying, public relations, and entertainment—out of bounds for billing to the government.[45] The fiscal 1987 appropriations bill reduced allowable profit margins, slowed payments to defense contractors, and required suppliers to bear more of the costs for the special tooling required for weapons production.[46]

Alarmed at the eroding political support for his military buildup, Reagan named a blue-ribbon commission on procurement reform led by the same electronics industry executive who thirteen years previously had taken on the system and retreated wearily back to private business. The Packard Commission recommendations reflected David Packard's core convictions. Its report expressed impatience with politics and formalized procedures, charging that "defense acquisition has become ever more bureaucratic and encumbered by unproductive layers of management."[47] It called for changes that concentrated accountability, streamlined procedures, and encouraged flexibility. Safeguards meant to deter fraud and corruption were stifling a system made up of mostly honest people, the commission felt. It recommended dismantling part of the massive Pentagon oversight and monitoring apparatus while encouraging "improvements in contractor self-governance" and voluntary adherence to a code of business ethics.[48] "The nation's defense programs lose far more to inefficient procedures than to fraud and dishonesty," the report pronounced. "The truly costly problems are those of overcomplicated organization and rigid procedure, not avarice or connivance."[49] In mid-1986, as many of the Packard Commission recommendations moved toward implementation, Justice Department officials were accumulating evidence in the investigations that would explode two years later into the largest corruption scandal in many decades.

The uproar following the late 1980s revelations of influence peddling and bribery distracted attention from the fact that recent reforms—mandating more competition, tougher contracts featuring fixed prices, and stiffer warranties—*were* having some effect. Many of the changes had to do more with form than with substance, and a few bordered on silliness. (For instance, the Navy commissioned the composition of a "Navy Competition March" to be played at a "competition symposium" for Navy suppliers. The music was meant to "inspire sentiments of competition and free enterprise," according to its composer, a former Navy secretary.)[50] But the percentage of Navy purchases made through competitive bidding did rise from around 30 percent in 1983 to 45 percent in 1985.[51] By 1987, roughly 60 percent of all Pentagon contracts (on a dollar basis) were awarded competitively, up from just over one-third in 1983.[52] Rigorous scrutiny and tougher enforcement by the once-passive Defense Contract Audit Agency was saving the government money. And—as a direct result of the Packard Commission report—the position of undersecretary of defense for acquisition, or of "procurement czar," as it was widely termed, was created in 1986.

Yet, from the start, there was widespread dissatisfaction with the mid-1980s reforms. Many observers in the press, in academia, and in government charged that a hidebound Pentagon bureaucracy, in league with powerful contractors, had blunted the reform drive. Some large, secrecy-shrouded programs, such as the B-2 Stealth bomber being developed by Northrop, were exempted from many of the new rules for security reasons, and in other instances second-sourcing was judged too expensive and troublesome.[53] The first "procurement czar" resigned in frustration, complaining that his authority was inadequate.[54]

While these voices complained that the reforms did not go far enough, the defense industry protested that they went entirely too far. While competition and tougher profit guidelines cut returns, stricter warranties and fixed prices substantially increased risk. A study sponsored by a consortium of defense contractors warned that the changes would erode industry viability, stifle product development and process innovation, and—as fewer firms found the defense game worthwhile—lead to *reduced* competition.[55] The study was thoroughly one-sided (most large weapons makers remained quite profitable), but there *were* signs that squeezing contractors could have disturbing consequences. A study by Arthur D. Little found that warranty requirements meant that, in some contracts, "bidders must in effect bet their equity that products will perform."[56] A securities analyst noted "reluctance on the part of managements to commit resources to risky R&D programs" when multiple-sourcing rules let other firms "come in and pick off half their production."[57] While fixed-price contracting policy improved cost projections, the president of one top contractor, Martin Marietta, warned that "the chickens will come home to roost" when it became apparent that firms could not complete contracts and survive, and he predicted that the government would eventually relent as key suppliers faced bankruptcy.[58] By early 1988, three major companies, after losing make-or-break contracts, had dropped out of the military aircraft business, and the president of still another warned, "We'll play the game for a while, until the price of the next card goes too high."[59]

SOURCES OF CONTRACTUAL COMPLEXITY

The Packard Commission report opened with a ringing declaration that weapons procurement requires "a sense of shared purpose . . . between government and the defense industry."[60] The sentiment is admirable, but it amounts to wishing away the basic problem. The interests of government and of its contractors simply diverge on some fundamental points. The government would like to pay as little as possible for the weapons it needs, while suppliers would like to earn as much as possible. Each party prefers stability and would rather shift risk to the other. Each wants the other to fulfill commitments precisely, while retaining flexibility for itself. The craft of contracting is to devise covenants that bring divergent purposes into something approaching alignment. Good contracting assigns tasks to those most competent to carry them out, defines expectations clearly, rewards efficiency and penalizes waste, and allocates risks to the party best able to limit or cope with them. As the decade's events so generously illustrate, writing good procurement contracts is hard to do. The sources and consequences of this difficulty illuminate the broader issues surrounding government contracts with private firms.

Ambiguous Measures of Value

Perhaps the most basic impediment to good contracting is ambiguity as to the worth of what's being acquired. Weapons procurement involves profound uncertainties about value. If the human race is fortunate, the tools of destruction that are the system's purpose will rust away without ever being used. Most of the time, blessedly, we never know for sure whether weapons budgets have been well-spent. Consider the history of Fort Jefferson. In 1846, anxious about plausible threats from England and Mexico, America launched an expensive effort to fortify a small Caribbean islet off Key West. Fifty years later the locale had lost its strategic cachet; advances in naval armor made the fort's smoothbore guns useless; the coral islet itself was crumbling under the weight of the massive walls and armaments, and the War Department turned the property over to the Agriculture Department for use as a bird sanctuary.[61] Weapons constantly come and go without any definitive test of their worth. The U.S. spent $700 million in the decade following World War II to develop and produce the Snark surface-to-surface missile, only to cancel it before full deployment when ballistic missiles made it obsolete.[62] Over eighty major weapons systems were scrapped between 1957 and 1970.[63] Only lunatics lament America's lack of regular occasions to

put its arsenal to the test. But this inherent ambiguity about both the need for
any given weapons system and its efficacy greatly complicates the drafting and
administration of contracts.

Gauging the value of defense goods requires examining both our military
requirements and the capacity of a particular weapon to fulfill them. The first
issue—what do we need?—engages quite basic questions about what our military
is *for*.[64] If we intend only to defend our borders and those of our NATO allies,
we don't need materiel for fighting jungle battles, as we might if our commitments
extend to Central America or to Southeast Asia. The decision whether to acquire
chemical weapons, or first-strike nuclear weapons, implies a whole series of prior
decisions about what we aim to accomplish or to forestall, and about the ethical
boundaries we acknowledge. Defining the requirements for weapons systems depends both upon political values and upon pragmatic doctrinal judgments over
which people may honestly differ. It also involves uncertainties over potential
enemies—their intentions, capabilities, and even their identities. The world is a
dangerous place; our knowledge of those who might threaten us is incomplete;
often, those whom we fear most we comprehend least. Thus, virtually no
imaginable conflict can be ruled out, no response capability judged useless, and
no proposed weapon system deemed dispensable.[65]

Nearly a decade before he became defense secretary, Caspar Weinberger wrote
that procurement requirements can only be defined by reference to "the threats
and opportunities we see in the world at large and to the number and capabilities
of our allies—in short, to our total foreign policy."[66] Room enough already for
ambiguity about value—but consider how history revealed the elasticity of Weinberger's view of "threats and opportunities." In the hectic early weeks of the
Reagan administration, a budget writer's error in calculation led to a budgeted
defense spending increase *double* that which candidate Reagan had promised and
which Weinberger had accepted as adequate. But, seizing the opportunity, Weinberger and his subordinates embraced the erroneous figures, enshrining them in
defense doctrine as a bare minimum that could not be pared without imperiling
the republic's security.[67] Similarly, a $27 billion windfall, collected by the Pen-
tagon when inflation plummeted from the rate built into budget increases, was
instantly earmarked for suddenly indispensable new weapons.

Beyond assessing military requirements, fixing the value of weapons systems
obviously calls for some sense of whether they work. Sometimes this implies a
straightforward, strictly technical test; frequently it does not. The same political
and doctrinal disputes that bedevil definitions of need can complicate performance
testing. If a new fighter-bomber ends up being a pretty good bomber but a terrible

fighter, its measured worth depends on how the evaluation is structured; the test design hence becomes deeply political. Since major weapons can take ten to twenty years to develop, and may be in use for at least that long, evaluations must take into account hypothetical missions and the hypothetical aims and capacities of hypothetical adversaries several decades into the future.[68] Consider these complexities. Consider the prevailing instincts within any organization to embroider or bury bad news. Consider, finally, the political imperatives that block the elimination of any enterprise on which large constituencies depend. It becomes more understandable, if no less lamentable, why the system fails to signal when weapons don't work.

Insurance and Secrecy

Two other issues further complicate the measurement of value in defense procurement. One involves what is variously termed "surge capacity," "mobilization preparedness," or "preserving the industrial base." The idea is that, even if some weapon system is not required *now*, and even if it will not *necessarily* be required in the future, should certain types of conflicts happen to occur it will be so urgently needed that it is worth considerable expense to keep in readiness the equipment and business organizations required to produce it.[69] Thus the perceived value of a weapon includes an insurance component—a premium paid against the risk of a war that escalates too quickly to build new capacity in time.

While this kind of reasoning can be used disingenuously, even cynically— beleaguered makers of textiles and footwear, when seeking government help, often imply that to allow them to fail would be to condemn American soldiers to fighting barefoot and unclad—there are defensible arguments at its core. It is likely that a full-scale conventional war would use up prodigious quantities of materiel. It is true that modern weaponry is so complex and specialized that it would take a good deal of time to begin production, from a cold start, in wartime. The problem is that proponents can use such arguments to justify buying practically any weapon that might conceivably be of use in some conflict. Evaluating requirements for military goods becomes a series of Pascal's wagers—multiplying very low probabilities of use by very large prospective payoffs in the event of use, and coming up with whatever estimates of worth are needed to warrant production. At some hard-to-pin-down point this sort of reasoning crosses the line from military prudence to economic lunacy.

The other complicating issue involves secrecy. A good contracting system ultimately depends upon sound decisions about public spending, and this requires equipping the public with accurate, comprehensible information about what is being done in its name. But large parts—roughly one-tenth—of the military budget are "black," that is, hidden from the view of all but a few officials. In the waning days of the Reagan military buildup, "black" programs continued to grow, and fully one-third of fiscal 1988 Air Force research and development spending—$17 billion worth—was kept secret, either unreported or carrying cryptic labels like "Selected Actions" ($700 million), "Other Production Charges" ($3.1 billion), or "Special Programs" ($2.3 billion).[70] Procurement programs are kept secret in part because some weapons involve technical approaches that should not be revealed; in part because of the strategic advantage of keeping potential adversaries uncertain as to the precise nature and extent of our arsenals; and in part because the armed forces find it politically expedient to limit political scrutiny of certain programs. The problem with the secrecy issue, as with the mobilization capacity issue, is that of discriminating between legitimate and illegitimate recourse to such arguments. While there are, no doubt, some acquisitions items that should be kept secret, one would expect "black" programs to feature more inefficiency and possibly more fraud than other weapons programs.[71]

In sum, uncertainties about both *mission* and *performance* make it difficult to assess the worth of military goods. This means that we risk spending either too much or too little on materiel in general, and are almost certain to misallocate our spending relative to the pattern that would prevail with accurate measures of real value. More insidiously, this uncertainty makes procurement decisions vulnerable to the stratagems of those seeking to manipulate perceptions of value.

SUPPLIERS' STAKES IN DEFENSE SPENDING

Chapter 5 argued that it is chiefly the prospect of earnings *beyond* those offered by other lines of work that motivates producers to influence public spending. If government work yielded mediocre returns, there would be little incentive to lobby. An obviously germane question, then, concerns the rewards that defense contracting offers. While some of the finer points on this matter remain in dispute, the balance of the evidence affirms that producing weapons for the American government tends to be quite remunerative.

The profitability of defense contractors is a perennial (and politically electric) issue. While pointing to the same set of transactions, legislators can be counted upon to denounce excessive profits, and weapons makers to plead starvation.

Profit is an imprecise word with several significantly different meanings.[72] There have been a number of academic and official attempts to come to terms with the issue, employing different definitions and measurements of profitability.

The late 1960s, like the late 1980s, witnessed a running debate as to just how lucrative was military contracting. A 1969 Pentagon-sponsored study found that defense contractor profits (defined as net earnings as a percentage of net worth) were in fact *lower* than those of commercially oriented manufacturers. The General Accounting Office, skeptical of Pentagon motives and critical of its sampling method, concluded four years later that there was no significant difference in profitability between defense and nondefense firms.[73] But Murray Weidenbaum, who would later become President Reagan's first chief economist, found in 1968 that defense work was significantly *more* profitable than commercial business, though he conceded that his small sample rendered his results tentative.[74] Another academic, using a sample that was at once larger than Weidenbaum's and more systematic than that of the Pentagon study, found that the return on net worth of thirty-six major defense contractors tended to be higher than the 1960s norm for the Fortune 500, but that this tendency was too weak to count as scientific proof.[75] A well-structured study by economists George Stigler and Claire Friedland found that major weapons makers were measurably more profitable than industry in general in the 1950s, but not in the 1960s.[76]

The first round of Reagan-era procurement scandals inspired renewed attention to contractor profits. A lengthy Pentagon study released in 1985 aimed to demonstrate that defense contracting had not been unduly profitable for most of the 1970–83 period.[77] But the General Accounting Office took the Pentagon to task once again for biased sampling (essentially, the Pentagon let contractors decide whether or not they wanted to be studied) and for an unconventional and probably illusory method of measuring profits. Using audited data on sales, assets, and earnings of eighty-four major contractors, and comparing those data to corresponding figures on several hundred other firms, the General Accounting Office found that by any measure of profitability—return on sales, return on assets, or return on equity, either before or after taxes—defense business was distinctly more remunerative than nondefense business over the entire 1975–83 period studied, with the gap widening sharply once the Reagan defense buildup got under way.[78] The Navy commissioned its own analysis, comparing the profits thirty-three major contractors earned on their government work with their profits on commercial activities. The study found that contractor return on assets for defense work as roughly twice that earned on nongovernmental contracts between 1977 and 1985.[79] In sum, the financial stakes can be high enough to warrant significant efforts to affect the government's procurement decisions.

Ultimately, of course, it is not profits that motivate political action, but rather payments to people—the investors, managers, and workers who have claims on firms doing business with the government. Consider first the payoff to investors. It is a complex matter to define *normal* returns to equity holders. But even after adjusting for risk and for movements in the market as a whole, investors who bought into defense stocks early in the Reagan era did exceptionally well. The Standard & Poor index of aerospace and defense stocks resoundingly outperformed the overall industrials index through the mid-1980s. Of course, as shrinking procurement budgets and acquisition reforms cut earnings, defense stocks lost their luster. The Reagan buildup offered rich returns to investors, but timing and luck determined precisely *which* investors collected them.[80]

Now consider employees. There is a good deal of evidence that defense workers tend to be exceptionally well paid. The Congressional Budget Office calculated that hourly earnings of aircraft and missiles production workers were nearly 50 percent higher than the economywide average in 1983. Total compensation per employee, including fringe benefits as well as pay, showed an even bigger disparity, with aircraft and missile workers collecting about 75 percent more than the norm.[81] These figures, to be fair, fail to take into account differences in experience, training, and other characteristics that may justify higher wages. But even after careful statistical measures to control for such differences, aerospace workers earn wage premiums on the order of 20 percent. The pattern holds at higher levels as well. When the General Accounting Office analyzed the accounts of twelve aerospace contractors in 1984, it found that top executives collected salaries and bonuses averaging 42 percent over those paid by comparable firms.[82]

Political uncertainty over the worth of weapons systems gives producers the opportunity to shape spending decisions. The rewards typical of defense contracting provide the motive. And producers have ample means to affect public deliberations over the size and allocation of procurement budgets.

Weapons makers may try to shift public opinion to favor the selection of their wares. Given the range of defensible views about U.S. military missions, virtually any weapon system can attract some degree of popular support. And given most citizens' ill-formed views about defense requirements, a fairly broad segment of public opinion—often one large enough to affect a weapon system's political prospects—is open to persuasion. The payoff to public relations campaigns can thus be quite high. When President Carter sought to cancel the B-1 bomber, prime contractor Rockwell International joined forces with the American Legion and the Veterans of Foreign Wars in a crusade to save the project. Rockwell also commissioned a series of advertisements, films, and publications to stir up sentiment for the B-1; urged its stockholders to make their voices heard; and encouraged its workers to write their legislators (even providing stationery, stamps, and suggested wording).[83]

Boeing and Lockheed (backed by their respective governmental champions) squared off in a 1982 lobbying battle to determine whether the Pentagon would buy a new batch of C-5 cargo transport planes, or switch instead to modified 747s. Each corporation's strategy included newspaper advertisements celebrating the virtues of its cargo plane, carefully coordinated letter-writing campaigns, and other tactics. Lockheed won with the assistance of Air Force officials who favored its C-5 and who, according to the General Accounting Office, "initiated and directed" the campaign.[84]

All major defense contractors have at least one political action committee for channeling contributions to legislators, and the weapons industry is one of the biggest players in campaign money politics. The contractors use their resources strategically, focusing on the roughly one hundred lawmakers who sit on defense-related committees. General Dynamics' political action committee contributed to all but six of the forty-seven members of the Housed Armed Services Committee in the 1986 election cycle.[85]

While money matters greatly, it is not the only instrument for cultivating legislative support. The Rockwell campaign to salvage the B-1 bomber included entertaining key lawmakers and procurement officials at corporate fishing and hunting retreats.[86] When the Army decided to cut back on its purchases of Apache helicopters, the McDonnell Douglas efforts to reverse the decision included taking legislators for joy rides in the impressively menacing aircraft.[87]

The least eyebrow-raising inducement to congressional support for weapons programs is also the most important: the provision of good jobs for constituents. While groups ranging from Common Cause to the Grace Commission have denounced legislators' habit of fighting for any system produced in their states or districts, no experienced observer can expect representatives to behave any other way. Recall the uncertainty surrounding the value of weapons systems, and the consequent ease of making a plausible military case for anything considered essential to a town's payroll or tax base. Consider, too, the reelection prospects of a representative or senator who, in effect, votes to shut a local factory. Contractors and the armed services are skillful at tapping this reliable font of political support, siting plants in key lawmakers' districts and dispersing production strategically in order to broaden their constituencies.

A third, more direct means of shaping procurement decisions involves contractor links with the armed services. While press reports of incestuous ties between the various services and their suppliers sometimes give an excessively unsavory cast to their relationships, it is true that weapons makers often exercise considerable influence over their military customers. Defense firms are not only the source of needed equipment, but also a key locus of technological expertise. Through the drawn-out process of setting requirements for a major weapons system, the Pentagon must tap industry knowledge about the boundaries of the possible. Subtly but powerfully, this tends to shape Pentagon views of what is desirable. Sometimes this involves soliciting advance proposals from contractors that will give form to vague requirements. Sometimes corporate officials or their consultants take the initiative in proposing new or modified weapons systems. And sometimes the exchange of information is embodied in the actual flow of personnel between industry and the armed forces.

A fourth tactic for influencing procurement spending, and perhaps the simplest, is to corrupt government officials. History, especially recent history, offers a depressing surfeit of examples. Recall the pervasive bribery at the Philadelphia Personnel Support Center. Recall the Japanese ship repair firms that employed prostitutes and cash to influence Navy repair contracts. Recall the contracts steered to the Wedtech Corporation that sent Mario Biaggi from Congress to prison and added their own whiff to the bad odor with which Ed Meese left office.[88] When the average American thinks of Pentagon contracting problems, she thinks of raw corruption. This is unfortunate. While bribery *does* chip away at the system's integrity, and periodically threatens to cause major breakdowns, in general it usually inflicts less damage than subtler, more insidious contracting problems.

SHOULD PROCUREMENT BE LESS PRIVATE?

In 1974, veteran procurement scholar J. Ronald Fox critiqued the report of President Nixon's blue-ribbon panel on acquisition reform. "While the panel successfully identified several problem areas in the procurement process," Fox wrote, its report "did not explain why previous recommendations along the same lines have never been successfully implemented."[89] Nearly fifteen years later, after several more rounds of procurement reform and just prior to the late 1980s scandals, Fox concluded in a new study that the situation was "worse in 1988 than it was in 1973 or in 1969."[90]

Current blueprints for reform, which closely resemble the remedies prescribed throughout the postwar years, usually feature three themes. The first, and by far the most common, is a call for some combination of reinforced procedures and restored morality to elevate integrity within the acquisition system. Queried by congressmen on the causes of the 1988 bidding-system breakdowns, then Defense Undersecretary for Acquisition Robert B. Costello (who should have known better) replied with one word: "Greed."[91] Defense Secretary Carlucci, at about the same time and in much the same spirit, sent letters to the two hundred biggest Pentagon contractors exhorting them to "honesty and integrity."[92]

Most citizens, as well as most legislators and journalists, endorse both ethical uplift to diminish the incidence of crookedness, and stricter rules and safeguards to catch the crooks that remain. More integrity *would* help; it almost always does. But managing the defense procurement system would be impossible (rather than just difficult) if prevailing standards of probity were not *already* high. Exceptional venality is not the central problem, and there is little reason for confidence that ethical exhortations will fix it.

A second type of proposal, sometimes made in the same speech as the first, calls for loosening the straitjacket of rules that burdens hundreds of thousands of honest souls in an effort to deter the immoral minority. Critics charge that elaborate bureaucratic procedures sap efficiency, block the flow of information, and quash entrepreneurial spirit. Meanwhile, the dilution of accountability and the profusion of procedural ambiguity paradoxically allow corruption to flourish.[93]

A third theme points to *politics* as the core problem—both the habitual intervention of Congress in the procurement process and the internal armed forces politics that blur the responsibilities and undercut the authority of acquisition officers. Following this diagnosis come prescriptions for a professionalized procurement system run by an elite staff insulated from political interference. As the nation's top procurement official and later, as a distinguished outside commentator, David Packard has consistently recommended hiring first-rate acquisition officers, training them well, and letting them do their jobs without undue meddling.[94] Admirers of the French acquisition system suggest emulating its limits on legislative authority over arms purchases, and its concentration of control within a high-level corps of career procurement officers.[95]

While these views warrant respectful attention, they are not new, and they have informed repeated rounds of mostly disappointing reform. It is worth at least considering an alternative diagnosis: paring the role of the private sector. Contracting for the delivery of tentatively defined, highly sophisticated, urgently needed weapons systems may be impossible to do well. It is simply hard to arrange for technological audacity, precise scheduling, high quality, scrupulous honesty, and rigorous cost control by means of a package of contractual provisions bridging the boundary between a government agency and a private firm. Rather than struggling to devise some ultimate contracting system that will end the cycles of reform, it may make sense to rethink the division between public and private roles in arming America.

In light of the criteria developed in chapter 5, the task of developing new weapons systems does not seem to be especially well suited to private contracting. Product requirements are often vague; evaluation is seldom definitive; competition is limited at early stages and nonexistent later; government frequently cares about the means by which weapons are produced; and profit-seeking suppliers have both the opportunity and the motive to influence collective spending. Should the government itself take a larger role in the weapons-making system?

Even at the crest of the popular indignation over Reagan-era procurement debacles, public sector arms production had little political appeal. Just as some people object to the idea of mingling the profit motive with education or corrections, others no doubt find symbolically repugnant the prospect of facing down communism with weapons made in state-owned factories. There are a number of pragmatic drawbacks to public sector weapons production, and nobody would endorse a wholesale shift away from private involvement. Yet it is intriguing to speculate on the potential for moving into the government those parts of the process that are most difficult to contractually define and enforce.

There are plenty of precedents. Until quite recently, much of America's weaponry originated in government arsenals. It was only during World War II that surging production requirements and the new importance of technologically advanced aircraft led to private sector dominance in arms production. Even in the early postwar era, much research and development continued to be carried out in federal arsenals, with private contractors taking over once a design was embodied in a "technical data package" giving detailed blueprints for mass production.[96]

Robert S. McNamara, temperamentally receptive to arguments of public ineptness and private efficiency, hastened the decline of the arsenal network during his tenure as defense secretary.[97] But—leaving aside subsequent disappointments with contract-based weapons development—experience fails to confirm that government organizations are weak on innovation. Researchers at both the Naval Research Laboratories and the Army Signal Corps did much of the development work on radar. The Redstone Arsenal made basic breakthroughs in ballistic missiles, and key advances in metallurgy have come from the Watertown Arsenal. Public sector engineers at the Naval Weapons Center at China Lake, California, invented the classic Sidewinder air-to-air missile, then contracted with various private firms to produce it.[98]

The possibilities for a more public arms-making system range from a full-scale resurrection of the arsenal network to nationalizing major weapons firms to (more realistically) bolstering the public role in integrating the efforts of private contractors. One particularly appealing reform would be to separate design contracts from production contracts. This relatively modest shift still implies fortifying the public sector's technological capacity to judge and to adjust design alternatives. The government would commission ideas from private labs and universities, select and refine them into a well-specified design, and then solicit fixed-price bids for shares of the production work.[99]

There is much to be said for putting the profit motive at some remove from politically charged, technologically complex, and economically fateful decisions about what kinds of weapons America needs. Government professionals, with no financial stakes in any particular design, would be better able to apply valid military and economic criteria to the selection of basic alternatives and to the refinement of the chosen design. As the government's technological capacity grew, it would be better equipped to select and monitor the private firms who bid on production contracts.

There are also, obviously, major drawbacks to fragmenting the process this way. One problem concerns staffing. To hire and to retain technicians and designers of the same caliber as those in private firms, the government would have to offer pay and benefits approaching private sector levels. F. M. Scherer termed recruitment "the Achilles' heel" of the arsenal system a quarter-century ago, and limits on top-level technical and managerial compensation would certainly hamper any effort to upgrade the government's technical capacity.[100] And while economists are often too quick to dismiss professional honor and ego as spurs to creativity, there *is* a risk that disconnecting development from lucrative production contracts might slacken the pace of technological innovation. Perhaps most seriously, separating design from production implies formidable transition and coordination problems.

Would the defects of a more public arrangement be more, or less, daunting than the problems we have so unsatisfyingly sought to conquer in our present system? The question requires its own forum, as well as the application of more specialized expertise. But it is by no means obvious that America's current, overwhelmingly private system strikes the perfect balance.

WEAPONS PROCUREMENT AND THE PRIVATIZATION DEBATE

It is beyond the scope of this book to draft any sweeping conclusions about the weapons acquisition process and its reform. But a few basic observations apply to the larger issues of building accountability into collective undertakings, and of choices about harnessing private energies to the public purpose.

The Elusive Ideal of Competition

Between 1964 and 1986, eleven major Pentagon or congressional reports identified *more competition* as a key to better procurement. Eternally hopeful calls for competition spring from the powerful intellectual aesthetic of economic theory, from a deep and almost mythic American faith in the benign effects of the competitive rough-and-tumble, and from repeated instances in which opening up a previously sole-source contract to new bids has led as promised to dramatic price drops. Yet the healthy conviction that competition is desirable is too often linked with the unwarranted inference that it is easy to arrange.

Competition *does* tend to boost efficiency. But competition is costly. Specifications must be drawn up and circulated; bids must be solicited and evaluated; systems for monitoring and verification must be replicated for each source. Sometimes, when secrecy calls for close control over technical data, or when economies of scale dictate a single producer, competition is simply not feasible. More often, the best that can be arranged is an awkward, stunted form of competition among a handful of established producers. Even when impediments to competition are not so imposing as to mandate monopoly or oligopoly, the balance between the costs of competition and its payoff is an empirical question.

In economic theory (and in real world markets for most things we buy), competition is a matter of steady pressures to cut waste, to innovate, and to refine product quality. The threat of bankruptcy as inefficiency's final penalty is always in the background. But the chief function of competition is to set the pace for a pack of rival producers, not to annihilate the slackers. Consider, in this light, the structure of some of the "competitive" programs set up for major weapon systems. Only a few firms have the expertise, equipment, and capital to even contemplate bidding. The terms of competition are unclear and may be open to manipulation by means legal or otherwise. Winners will flourish; losers may perish. This cataclysmic kind of competition is quite unlike the textbook ideal, and it is not surprising that it invites political gamesmanship, corruption, and

reckless promises. The markets for managing prisons, running wastewater treatment facilities, and many other candidates for privatization may have more in
common with the market for advanced tactical fighters than with the market for
chocolate-chip cookies.

Even when buying low-technology goods in a market in which there *are* many
qualified contenders, it is often far easier for the acquiring organization to deal
with one or two suppliers than to manage a process of wide-open competition.
To the officials who must actually come up with the materiel, cost savings often
matters less than does keeping supply lines simple. It is this, as much as the
accumulation of special equipment or knowledge (and much more than corruption) that explains the regularity with which incumbent suppliers win contract
renewals. In the late 1960s, during one of the episodic campaigns for more
competition, the Air Force accepted a bid for some aircraft wheel components
from a small supplier; a few big firms had controlled the market before. But as
political pressures for competition ebbed, the Air Force reverted to dividing the
business among large, familiar firms. Even as competition once more neared the
height of fashion in 1986, the Air Force set a policy of allowing four years of
monopoly on spare parts when a new plane is introduced, and only then orches-
trating a transition to competition. The deputy secretary of the Air Force responsible for the policy worried that, without the monopoly period, big companies might drop out of the industry, leaving the Air Force reliant on less robust
suppliers.[101]

Not only advanced weaponry, but also a host of other government goods and
services present impediments to lively competition. Not only military, but also
civilian bureaucracies see advantages to sticking with familiar suppliers. Perhaps
the first question about privatizing some government function should be, "Is
competition possible?" The second should be, "Will officials be willing and able
to maintain competition over the long term?" These issues matter at least as much
as any simple technical advantage the private sector enjoys. Without competition,
the gains of greater efficiency will seldom be passed on to the public sector
customer. And as military procurement so amply demonstrates, effective competition is far easier to celebrate in the abstract than to put into practice.

The Split Loyalties of Contracting Officials

Procurement reformers report with dismay on the armed forces' lack of enthusiasm for schemes to limit contractor profits. Dismay may be warranted;
surprise is not. The military priorities are to get the best possible equipment as
quickly as possible and to ensure that the capacity to develop the *next* generation

of equipment remains intact. While the armed forces would by and large rather pay less than more, they are not preoccupied with minimizing the procurement budget. Economy is not their cardinal value; readiness is. Many commentators are quick to infer cooptation or corruption from the armed forces' concern for their suppliers. But for wholly understandable, even healthy, reasons they see contractors as vital partners in their mission of defending America.

The role that reform periodically imposes on the armed forces—that of penny-pinching guardians of the public fisc—remains a thin veneer. To a procurement officer, the consequences of too much emphasis on economy may include skimping on features that turn out to be essential on the battlefield, or causing the collapse of a crucial supplier. Too *little* emphasis on economy means only a distant and relatively minor rise in government spending. Contracting officers in health care, education, corrections, or training are likely to feel comparable priorities.

Links that begin as arm's-length transactions tend to evolve into closer relationships. Public officials who work daily with private suppliers, and who rely on these suppliers to accomplish their missions, come to care greatly about keeping contractors healthy and helpful. Budget officials elsewhere in government must rein in not only contractors, but also the civil servants who work closely with them. The detailed rules that govern public contracts are meant not just to deter corruption, but also, at least as importantly, to bridle this natural sympathy between suppliers and line officials.[102] If an organizational budget can be increased through political maneuvering (and especially if costs can be shifted to other jurisdictions or future generations), there will be little enthusiasm for driving hard bargains with suppliers. In any contractual relationship between government and private business, a key question becomes who is representing the broader public interests. Unless there are sturdy provisions to prevent it—and even if all parties are immune to corruption—the natural outcome is an alliance between private sector suppliers and government officials at the taxpayers' expense.

The Burden of Process

Privatization's appeal owes much to the dream of stripping away the red tape that festoons bureaucratic undertakings. Contemplating the military procurement system, however, might give pause on this score. Believers in the private sector's instinct for streamlined efficiency hold that it is government that infects an enterprise with procedural excess. But administrative complexity inheres in public *tasks*, not in public *organizations*. Collective purchases are different from private purchases. Collective interests must be codified as a set of requirements. Institutions must carry out the monitoring and feedback functions that decentralized individual decisions perform so elegantly in commercial markets. Complex purchases carry an especially heavy burden of process. But even for simple standardized goods, contracts with private firms are apt to involve painstaking requirements and provisions for evaluation. (Recall the sixteen pages of specifications for oatmeal cookie mix.) Hopes that privatization will free government from the straitjacket of bureaucratic rules and regulations are due to be dashed. The *type* of rules will differ, but the total burden is unlikely to lighten. Indeed, operating across organizational boundaries may turn out to require *more* process, not less. In particular, as private firms are called on to perform tasks that cannot be defined in straightforward output-based contracts, *input* specifications proliferate.[103]

When bureaucracies perform tasks that *can* be covered by output-based contracts, to be sure, privatization may shrink the burden of process. But when complexity and contingency are fundamental characteristics of the task, privatization's promise of simplicity will turn out to be illusory. Recall the procurement officer who described detailed military specifications as the "sum total of our past mistakes." Comparably painful learning processes will no doubt accompany each experiment in privatization; this ought to be anticipated as the wisdom of each initiative is assessed. Contracts may start out simple. But over time, the defects of the original, blessedly straightforward contracts—ambiguities, omissions, unforeseen eventualities—will become apparent, sometimes with expensive or embarrassing consequences. In the next round, rights and duties across various contingencies will be spelled out explicitly. Rules will be codified. Monitoring provisions, safeguards, formal qualifications, and dispute-resolution procedures will be layered on. And new wrappings of red tape—perhaps of a somewhat different shade than before—will surround the task.

The Spending Agenda's Vulnerability

One of the oldest and most constant complaints about defense procurement concerns the intensely political nature of the process. Average citizens, as well as a number of supposedly more sophisticated observers, assume the problem originates with the special political clout of weapons company executives, or the special capacity of admirals and generals to get their way whatever the cost. This view suggests, erroneously and perhaps dangerously, that politicized spending decisions are a peculiar problem of weapons acquisition from which other areas of public-private contracting will be immune. But the real causes are distressingly general. Politically effective actors—the managers, employees, shareholders, and other constituents of profit-seeking suppliers—have major stakes in procurement decisions. Uncertainty over the real value of spending alternatives allows commercially congenial arguments to be advanced and defended with the appearance, and even the subjective reality, of conviction on the merits.

The lessons on this score for those contemplating a shift to private delivery for other public goods and services are three. First, the more uncertainty there is about *value*, and the more debatable are requirements, the more opportunity exists for interested parties to manipulate perceptions of common need. Second, the richer are the potential rewards—whether in the form of high profits, high wages, desirable working conditions, or security against displacement—the fiercer are the incentives to politicize spending decisions. Third, the more politically effective are private interests, relative to public workers and organizations, the more privatization imperils the integrity of the spending agenda.

CHAPTER 7

LOCAL SERVICE CONTRACTING

W HILE the federal government allocates only 14 percent of its budget to pay public workers, at the state and local level the payroll claims more than 53 percent of total spending. The federal government already spends $3 on outside suppliers for every $2 it spends on its own workforce; at the state and local levels, the ratio is reversed.[1] The federal government had roughly three million civilian workers on its payroll in the mid-1980s, while state and local governments employed nearly fourteen million.[2] In short, there is simply more *room* to contemplate shifts toward private suppliers at lower levels of government. Hence it is at the state and, especially the county and municipal levels, that privatization has gained the most attention in recent years.[3]

Contracting out for state and local services is nothing new. Nor, for that matter, is privatization as a distinct policy theme an especially recent phenomenon. The Committee for Economic Development declared in 1971 that the public sector "seems likely to function best as a market creator, systems manager, and contractor of social tasks rather than as an actual operator of every kind of public service."[4] But local officials—and the staffers, consultants, and academics who advise them—became increasingly interested in outside contracting in the late 1970s and through the 1980s as shrinking federal help and a wave of tax protests tightened local finances. Officials became squeezed between escalating demands by constituents—coupled with rising claims by public employees' unions—and the reality of fixed or declining budgets. "Communities that are to survive and thrive in the uncertain economic conditions of the 1980s must be alert to new solutions," declared *American City and County* magazine in 1984. "Privatization is one such solution."[5] While federal privatization initiatives have been driven largely by ideology, at the state and local levels they have more often been spurred by expediency. New York Governor Mario Cuomo, no prophet of the minimal

TABLE 7.1

Privatization of Selected Local Services

Service	Share of localities contracting out for the service (in percent)*
Car towing and storage	57.8
Legal services	44.3
Vehicle maintenance	30.0
Streetlight operation	28.1
Refuse collection	27.3
Tree trimming and planting	25.3
Street repair	24.9
Traffic signal maintenance	22.9
Labor relations	19.6
Solid waste disposal	19.2
Data processing	18.9
Ambulance service	17.0

SOURCE: Data for table 7.1 are originally from Carl Valente and Lydia Manchester, *Rethinking Local Services: Examining Alternative Delivery* (Washington: International City Management Association, 1984), p. xv, table B, reprinted in "Privatization in the U.S.: Cities and Counties," NCPA Policy Report 116, National Center for Policy Analysis, pp. 4–6, table 1.
*Services for which 5 to 10 percent of localities contract out: payroll preparation, utility billing, park landscaping and maintenance, animal shelter operation, day-care center operation, pest control, building inspection, bus operation and maintenance, airport operation, meter reading, parking lot operation, hospital management, operation or maintenance of recreational facilities, tax billing, tax collection, tax assessment, public relations, building security, and animal control.

state, has said that "it is not government's obligation to provide services, but to see that they're provided."[6]

Private businesses working for local governments carry out over one hundred functions, from car towing, tree trimming, and streetlight maintenance (which are commonly handled by private suppliers) to fire fighting and drug counseling (which are only rarely delegated). Table 7.1 shows the proportion of the 1,780 cities and counties surveyed in 1982 that contracted with for-profit firms for various public services. (Only functions delegated by more than 10 percent of the cities surveyed are included.)

There is a good deal of impressionistic evidence to suggest that privatization has been on the increase. For example, while only 3 percent of the localities surveyed in 1973 reported hiring for-profit firms to repair streets, the 1982 survey found an increase to 27 percent; the use of private law firms increased from 8 percent in 1973 to 44 percent in 1982; use of private data processing rose from .5 percent in 1973 to roughly 10 percent in 1982. Yet, in fact, the private sector has *lost* ground in recent years. The share of state and local budgets that went to buy goods and services from outside suppliers actually *fell* measurably between

1978 and 1987, from over 40 percent to around 36 percent. At the federal level, the opposite pattern prevailed.[7]

"On the average," a 1985 study bluntly declared, "city governments can cut in half the cost of city services by contracting with private firms."[8] The reasons put forward for the private sector efficiency edge are essentially the same as discussed in previous chapters: Private ownership allows the concentration of interest in efficiency; public ownership does not. Public management is constrained by layered authority, mandatory reviews, civil service rules, formal bid procedures, and so on; private management is not. Public organizations usually are secure against competition; private organizations frequently are not. Private firms that fail to deliver face bankruptcy; public agencies that fail to deliver do not.

The conceptual case for superior private performance is well developed and fairly persuasive. Yet many of the studies invoked in support of such claims are based on small and unsystematic sets of observations and on relatively primitive methodologies. Such studies invite ideological rivals to brandish equally dubious statistical studies demonstrating the opposite point.[9] Argument by anecdote, and by the selective statistics that amount to anecdotes on stilts, is doomed to inconclusiveness. Consider two New York City incidents from 1986.

The Wollman Memorial Skating Rink in Central Park was badly in need of repair in the late 1970s. After several years of preparation and planning, the New York City Parks and Recreation Department closed down the rink in 1980 for a rebuilding project scheduled to take two years and to cost just under $5 million. Technologically, the undertaking was simple. It involved dismantling the old surface, then installing a new network of coolant pipes and pouring concrete over them. But for reasons that two subsequent studies failed to fully explain, the work went badly. Midproject delays left the coolant pipes exposed to the elements for a year. When the concrete was finally poured there was not quite enough, and the last batch was diluted to finish the job. The coolant system, once it was hooked up, developed leaks—possibly because of the long exposure to frost and floods, possibly because of cracks in the watered-down cement, possibly because of damage as the cement was being poured, and possibly because the freon-based cooling technology, chosen because it used slightly less energy than the traditional technology, still had some basic technical flaws. In any event, after spending six years and $12 million on the job, the city found that the work to date was essentially worthless and that the rebuilding would have to be started again from the beginning.[10]

Donald J. Trump, a well-known New York developer, wrote to Mayor Ed Koch in May 1986 to express his "amazement" at the city's failure to accomplish so simple a task during six years in which Trump had built several major Manhattan projects (including the ornate Fifth Avenue tower bearing his name). Trump offered to rebuild Wollman Rink himself, at no profit, as a good-will gesture to the city and, he added, so that his young son could ice-skate in the park before he grew up. The capital projects director of the Parks and Recreation Department conceded that Trump possessed advantages over his own agency, which was "bound by the city's rules and regulations and checks and balances." The city had to follow stipulated procedures for selecting contractors; Trump could choose on the basis of reputation. The city had to take the lowest bidder that met the literal terms of the contract; Trump could consider aspects of quality beyond contractual specifications. If a city contractor performed superbly the city would reward him with the agreed-upon fee and nothing more, beyond polite thanks; Trump could offer bonuses pegged to fine gradations of performance and promptness. If a contractor failed utterly to deliver, the city could suspend the contract and threaten, not too convincingly, to sue for the return of progress payments already made; Trump could make it clear that any firm hoping for future work with his far-flung organization had better deliver on the Wollman job. "I'm going to get good contractors and push the hell out of them," Trump declared. And he did.

The Wollman rink reopened, with a gala ceremony, months ahead of schedule and 25 percent under budget. What the city had been unable to do with six years and $12 million, Trump did in three months for $2.3 million.

In the mid-1970s, at the same time the Wollman rink was beginning to show its age, a surfeit of unpaid parking tickets coupled with a shortage of funds led New York City to step up its collection practices. Municipal workers were expensive and their deployment was restricted by intricate labor agreements. The Parking Violations Bureau staked its hopes on the flexibility and efficiency of for-profit organizations, opting to contract with private firms to identify and track down scofflaws. Ten years later several city contractors were bringing in $46 million a year, keeping a third of the take as their fee and passing the rest to the city. At some point along the way, city officials began accepting bribes for awarding rich collection contracts without competitive bidding. Collection companies hired former city officials to lobby the Parking Violations Bureau and, on occasion, to pass cash and securities to officials able to influence contract awards.[11]

Donald Manes had become one of the most powerful politicians in New York during his fourteen years as borough president in Queens, wielding considerable influence over the Parking Violations Bureau and other city agencies. In early 1986, a quiet investigation by a U.S. attorney led to the first tentative press reports of a corruption scandal. On March 10, Geoffrey Lindenauer, a close associate of Manes and deputy director of the Parking Violations Bureau, confessed to taking bribes from contractors for himself and Manes, and agreed to cooperate with authorities. Three days later, Manes escaped indictment by running a kitchen knife through his heart. Federal officials quickly issued over a dozen indictments, and several conspirators were convicted and imprisoned.

Should cities and states contract out for public services? These two cases, both from one city in one year, illustrate the perils of any simple answer to that question. (Most cities in most years offer similarly conflicting evidence, though seldom in quite so dramatic a form.) This chapter attempts to go beyond the standard catalogues of triumphs and horror stories to explore the sources and size of the gains from privatization; to examine how the private sector's appeal varies depending on the service; and to note the broader implications of delegating municipal tasks to outside organizations.

As of mid-1987, there were some twenty-eight thousand recorded instances of public services being provided by private firms under contract to local governments.[12] Virtually every function of local government has been delegated to the private sector at some time, in some city. Shasta County in California contracts with a local law firm to provide legal counsel to the indigent while, to the south of the state, Rancho Palos Verdes contracts out for a local prosecutor. Florida and Kentucky, among other states, have private mental hospitals. The privately owned Detroit-Windsor Tunnel links Canada and the United States, while a for-profit company has been authorized to build a toll road to Dulles airport. Nearly forty jurisdictions use profit-seeking fire protection companies, and a private company runs the air-traffic control tower in Farmington, New Mexico. Until tax reform cut into the implicit federal subsidies for such endeavors, dozens of communities were contemplating for-profit water or sewage treatment facilities; a few already have them.[13] La Mirada, California, a city of some forty thousand, contracts out for more than sixty services and has a municipal work force of only fifty-five. Lakewood, California (population sixty thousand), a pioneer in contracting for services, has eight city workers, and one Dallas suburb with twenty-five hundred citizens has no city workforce at all aside from a single secretary to handle the paperwork knitting together the nexus of contracts that constitutes the town's public sector.

STRATEGIC VERSUS TACTICAL PRIVATIZATION

The private role in public services could expand for at least three reasons. First, local officials opting for private rather than public providers could simply be making a big mistake. Critics of privatization, notably the American Federation of State, County, and Municipal Employees, suggest as much. "Public service, provided directly by government, is a distinguishing hallmark of a civilized society. It is also an American tradition that deserves the best protection and safeguards we can give it."[14]

Second, localities could replace public workers with private contractors for reasons other than simple efficiency gains. The privatization movement coincided with two closely related but distinguishable trends: eroding faith in governmental competence and a diminished willingness to fund common endeavors. Privatization could be driven more by the second motive than by the first. If city officials are forced by tax resistance and shrinking federal help to cut back public services, but feel political pressure to avoid the appearance of doing any such thing, privatization could offer an attractively confusing way to impose austerity without acknowledging the intent. When Phoenix first switched to private sector trash collection for a part of that city, it coupled the change with a deliberately lowered level of service.[15] A more open decision to cut services may have invited unhappy citizens to make common cause with sanitation workers fearful of potential lay-offs. *Strategic* privatization (aimed at shrinking the collective realm), as distinct from *tactical* privatization (aimed at cutting costs for the same level of government services), has been a major theme at the federal level.[16] One critic has contended that the "first thing that happens when a city sells or leases a hospital to the private sector is that they reduce care for the poor."[17] To the extent that his charge is true—and that it holds true for other services—privatization may be a maneuver by city officials seeking to substitute a cheaper package of services for the fuller package that had previously been provided by civil servants. Contracting out may offer insulation against political pressures and may thus serve as a stratagem to achieve otherwise unfeasible austerity measures.

The privatization of local services, then, might be a blunder, or it might be a gambit for easing back on city services that citizens simultaneously insist upon and refuse to pay for. But let us grant, provisionally, that most of the time it is meant to be precisely what its proponents claim—an organizational reform promising more value for the taxpayer's dollar. The issue then becomes how reliably contracting out for public services works as advertised.

What we would like to turn to, ideally, is a set of meticulous studies covering many different services in many different cities, comparing cost and quality for public and private delivery, and controlling for factors *other* than public or private management. But for a number of reasons—including the expense and trouble involved in large-scale field studies, the methodological difficulty of isolating the effect of organizational form from a host of other determinants of cost or quality, the demonstrated readiness of both advocates and opponents of privatization to make claims and make policy without waiting for empirical validation, and, perhaps, the issue's general lack of glamour—few researchers have investigated whether, in what circumstances, or by what means contracting out secures more value for the taxpayers' money. The data we have to draw on fall far short of the ideal, as is generally the case. There *is*, however, some evidence that merits attention.

The Touche Ross Survey

Touche Ross and Co. conducted a major survey on privatization, cosponsored by the International City Management Association and by the Privatization Coun cil, a trade association that Touche Ross helped to found.[18] Questionnaires were sent out to all but the smallest U.S. cities and counties, eliciting the views and experiences of officials. About one-fifth of the surveys were returned, giving a sample that may or may not be fully representative (depending on whether the communities that responded differed in any systematic way from those that did not) but was in any case quite extensive, including over one thousand respondents.[19]

The survey resoundingly confirmed that what public managers want from privatization is lower costs. The chief motives for considering contracting out—in fact, the only reasons cited by as many as one-half of all respondents—were citizen demands for services and objections to taxes, along with the curtailment of federal revenue sharing. Those who had already experimented with for-profit service delivery reported saving money as the major advantage.[20] (When city officials were asked about privatizing physical facilities—switching from public to private buildings, dumps, sewage treatment plants, and so on—cost saving was also the motive cited most often. A close second was "cutting risk," an aspiration that Touche Ross noted "bears further study, since the risk often stays with the government.")

Respondents ranked their motives for contracting out eighteen different local services, from snow removal and streetlight maintenance to running day-care centers and homeless shelters. "Cost savings" was the most-cited motive for eleven of the eighteen services, and was first or second for all but one. "Better quality" was the *least* important of four possible motives for nearly one-half of the services, and was last or next to last on all but three. In general, the respondents got what they were after: Most reported cost savings in the range of 10 to 20 percent. Two-fifths of the respondents reported savings in excess of 20 percent, while one-tenth of the respondents reported savings of 40 percent or more.[21]

The Stevens Analysis

A research team commissioned by the Department of Housing and Urban Development, and led by economist Barbara J. Stevens, undertook by far the most ambitious statistical appraisal to date of the relative efficiency of governmental and private organizations in delivering municipal services.[22] This study is the source of the much-repeated finding that municipal agencies are 50 percent less efficient than private contractors. One enthusiast hailed Stevens for providing proof that, through privatization, "without any change in service, the average city could cut its budget for these services in half."[23] Indeed, the Stevens study has been cited in virtually every subsequent book and article on the privatization of public services. Both because of its impact on policy debates, and because it offers systematically collected and processed data on an issue more often characterized by guesswork and anecdote, this study warrants some discussion.

Stevens surveyed every community in the five counties making up the Los Angeles metropolitan area, seeking out examples of public services delivered by *both* contractors and city agencies. Among these 121 cities, local governments paid for or delivered thirty-eight different services. Since not every city offered every service, Stevens selected eight functions—street cleaning, janitorial services, residential trash collection, payroll preparation, traffic signal maintenance, asphalt laying, turf maintenance, and tree maintenance—which at least ten cities performed themselves, and which ten other cities paid for-profit firms to deliver. The overall sample, then, consisted of 160 observations—eight services, in twenty cities each.

For each function in each city, on-site research yielded data on the total cost, scale, quality, and other characteristics of the service, as well as the organizational form for delivering it. Mindful that municipal accounting methods often fail to reflect real costs, Stevens attempted to measure directly the cost of the resources used—including the costs of administrative, maintenance, and support functions usually reported on separate budgets—rather than to rely on city budget numbers to estimate municipal costs. Similarly, the cost of contracting out was defined to include municipal expenses for monitoring private suppliers, which average roughly 25 percent of the overall cost.[24]

TABLE 7.2
Estimated Gains from Privatization

Function	Extra cost of municipal service over the cost of contractor service (by percent)
Asphalt overlay construction	96
Janitorial service	73
Traffic signal maintenance	56
Street cleaning	43
Trash collection	42
Turf maintenance	40
Tree maintenance	37
Payroll preparation	0

SOURCE: Barbara J. Stevens, "Comparing Public- and Private-Sector Privatization Efficiency: An Analysis of Eight Activities," *National Productivity Review* (Autumn 1984): 401, table 5.

Stevens used regression analysis to explain the total cost of each service in terms of five types of variables. First is the scale of service (such as tons of asphalt laid, acres of grass mowed, square feet of buildings to be cleaned). Second is the level of service (times per month streets are cleaned, times per year that traffic signals get preventive maintenance). Third is quality, which for most services is measured visually (cleanliness of streets and buildings, health and appearance of turf and trees). Fourth is "physical conditions" (number and nature of businesses on streets to be cleaned, population density of neighborhoods for trash collection). The fifth and final variable is organizational arrangement—whether the service is provided directly by a municipal agency or by a for-profit firm under contract to the city.

The results: For every service except payroll preparation, Stevens found a large and statistically reliable cost advantage for private contractors. The excess cost of municipal delivery, Stevens estimated, ranges from 37 percent for tree maintenance to 96 percent for asphalt overlay application. Table 7.2 summarizes the estimated extra costs of using municipal agencies instead of outside contractors.

SOURCES OF CONTRACTORS' COST ADVANTAGE

Might not the lower costs of contractors simply reflect lower quality? Stevens determined that there was "no statistically significant difference in the quality of service provided by contractors as compared to municipal agencies . . . for any

TABLE 7.3

How Agencies and Contractors Differ

	Cities using contractors (by percent)	Cities using agencies (by percent)
Share of direct labor in total cost	49.0	60.2
Workforce unionized	20.0	48.1
Average age of workers	32.1	36.1
Average job tenure (in years)	5.8	8.1
Vacation days per worker	10.1	14.0
Average absenteeism (all reasons)	8.8	12.9
Management layers above laborers	1.5	1.9
Foremen can fire workers	53.7	16.0
Written worker reprimands used	33.8	72.5
Employee incentive systems	26.9	12.3
Workers maintain own equipment	92.5	48.1
Formal staff meetings held	53.8	81.5

SOURCE: Barbara J. Stevens, ed., *Delivering Municipal Services Efficiently* (Washington: HUD Office of Policy Development and Research, 1984), pp. 18–19, ex. 10.

service studied." In fact, she found that in each case the "quality" variable—cleanliness of buildings and streets; noise and spillage created by trash crews; number of broken traffic signals; cracks in asphalt; errors in paychecks; and health and appearance of trees and turf had *no* statistically detectable effect on costs at all. While quality does vary considerably from city to city, these differences seem to be correlated neither with total cost nor with organizational form. This seems peculiar. But it is unlikely that misestimates of the effect of quality on cost caused Stevens to wrongly attribute efficiency advantages to private contractors, since for six of the eight services whatever (statistically inconclusive) quality differences the team detected go *in favor* of private contractors.[25]   What *does* explain the cost savings? Stevens attributes it primarily to astute management practices and superior technology. The study compares cities using contractors with cities using municipal agencies along twenty dimensions. On twelve of these dimensions, the differences between the two groups are systematic and statistically meaningful. Table 7.3 summarizes the comparisons.

Labor claims a smaller share of total costs in cities that privatize service delivery. In one-half of the cities using municipal agencies the workers are unionized, versus one-fifth for cities using contractors. Several other points of difference are traditionally linked with unionization: Workers tend to be older, to have been on the job longer, and to enjoy more vacation days. Public sector wages are quite similar across functions, while private sector wages vary substantially. For contractors, workers in the highest-paid service make 2.8 times as much as workers in the lowest-paid service; for municipal agencies, workers in the highest-paid service make only 1.4 times as much as workers in the lowest-paid service. Municipal agencies are more structured and rule-bound. Foremen can seldom fire workers, and discipline involves formal reprimand procedures. Incentive systems are less common. Specialized departments handle equipment maintenance and repair, instead of the employees who work with the equipment.

In short, private contractors improve efficiency through more flexible use of labor, a richer array of incentives and penalties, and, often, a more precise allocation of accountability. Just as one would expect, they are less constrained by process; just as one would hope, they seem to be more tightly focused on results. Municipal street-sweeping crews do a better job each time they clean a street— that is, they faithfully adhere to input specifications. But they do not score so well on the *output* criterion of keeping the streets reasonably clean most of the time. Private crews sweep less thoroughly but more frequently, and, at least in the cities Stevens studied, this turns out to be the better way to keep streets looking good.[26] Private trash collection firms suffer less down-time from equipment failures; the municipal practice of having central motor pools handle maintenance seems to dilute accountability for keeping vehicles in working order. (This problem appears in several other services as well.) Contractors also improve efficiency by paying workers on the basis of routes covered rather than hours worked.

Contracting and Scale Economies

Cities take on a physical layout for complex reasons of history and politics. Only by the least likely of historical accidents will this *administrative* unit turn out to be of the ideal *economic* scale for delivering public services. A farm too small for efficient mechanization will have higher than average costs no matter how hard the farmer works; similarly, a city that must maintain its own fleet of garbage trucks, street-sweepers, and asphalt trucks is likely to be battling against the economics of scale efficiency. (The Touche Ross survey found that smaller cities were more likely than larger cities to report extremely high savings from contracting out.)[27]

Contractors may enjoy three distinguishable advantages rooted in their freedom to let technical efficiency govern the size of their operations. The first pertains to simple scale economies: Contractors can spread the costs of capital and overhead across several cities. Stevens found ample evidence of differences on this score. The public works agencies she studied tended to lack the specialized tools and labor needed for rapid traffic signal repairs, for example. For several other services, individual cities are too small to afford an adequate inventory of spare parts, and hence suffer from too much down-time. In the case of tree care and pruning, few cities have enough trees to keep a specialized crew busy year-round, and contractors that handle several cities get more value out of dedicated labor and equipment. Stevens and her associates found evidence that municipal agencies use capital equipment that is outmoded, too small, or otherwise wrong for the job. (Since these agencies pay more for labor, to minimize costs they should use *more* capital than contractors do. But the same pressures that keep wages relatively high may limit efforts to substitute capital for labor.)

The second scale-related advantage concerns incentives to innovate. Developing more efficient ways to deliver public services can be very costly, in terms of money, time, and specialized labor, and in terms of the public disgruntlement caused by failed experiments. For a municipal agency, the potential *payoff* for innovation is limited to whatever lower costs or higher quality can be achieved within the city limits. Except in the biggest cities, it seldom makes sense for public works departments to make large investments in innovation. A private contractor, however, can claim proprietary rights to innovations, diffuse new methods throughout its operations, and use technological advances as a competitive edge to expand its market. For example, the leading for-profit fire company, Rural Metro, devotes 3 percent of its gross revenues to research and development. Rural-Metro innovations include fast "attack trucks" for handling small blazes, a double-hose pumper truck to deliver twice the normal volume of water to a fire, variable-pressure hoses, and a remote-controlled fire-fighting robot to spare human fire-fighters from the most dangerous tasks.[28] Private garbage collection companies continually improve on truck design and seek competitive advantages in equipment. ServiceMaster Industries, Inc., an Illinois-based company that manages custodial services for hospitals, schools, and other institutions, spends considerable sums on improving janitorial technology, and has developed light battery-powered vacuum cleaners, ergonomically advanced mops and brooms, and other new tools and methods.[29] This is not to say that *all* innovation comes from the private sector; there are plenty of public works departments displaying initiative and ingenuity. Civil servants in Phoenix, for example, have used technical and procedural innovation to win bid competitions with private rivals.[30] And well-entrenched contractors may disdain research and development. But, on balance, contractors have more potent incentives for innovation.

The final scale advantage concerns management. Many things may motivate workers to exert their best efforts, including pleasure in the work, commitment to organizational goals, intimidation, self-esteem, and financial incentives. One particularly powerful inducement is the opportunity for advancement within the organization. In a municipal department, advancement usually depends in large part on seniority. Moreover, the top jobs are generally reserved for elected officials or their appointees. And room for advancement is limited by the size of the department. Private contractors, on the other hand, may be able to offer a long and flexible career ladder. Top-performing employees can be promoted upward in the hierarchy at a single site, or can be offered advancement to a larger and more challenging client city, or can rise to management jobs at divisional or corporate headquarters. Of course, if promotion decisions are seen as capricious, career mobility will do little to promote enterprise. But contractors who fail to reward good performance will be at a competitive disadvantage to those who offer attractive career ladders.

Losses to Labor

Many analysts, including Stevens, are utterly disingenuous on one key point. In the less technical, more widely circulated summary of her report, Stevens writes that "on average"—that is, bundling together all the services she analyzes—the "contractors paid workers a monthly salary averaging $1,521 while municipal agencies paid their workers an average monthly salary of $1,442."[31]

The implication that labor cost is not the issue has invited others to brandish her study as proof that politically neutral managerial strategies are all that distinguish private from municipal suppliers, and that labor has nothing to lose from privatization. One proponent declared that "Stevens found that most of the cost differences can be explained by the use of technology and management practices."[32] Another said the study "demolished the notion that lower private-sector salaries account for the cost differences."[33] The idea that labor costs do not matter rings false because of the labor-intensive nature of the services; because municipal jobs are well known to offer relatively good pay and benefits; and because the vigor with which public employee unions resist privatization suggests that they come to a different conclusion.

In fact, for six of the seven services for which Stevens collected usable wage data, contractor employees are paid less than are municipal workers. For those functions that are more labor-intensive, or are major components of city budgets, or both, municipal wages tend to be well in excess of contractor wages, as table 7.4 shows.[34]

Stevens's finding that contractors pay no less on average than municipal departments is an artifact of aggregating (without weighting) the wage data for all services. The one service where contractors pay more is asphalt overlay construction, a fiscally unimportant and highly capital-intensive service. For many services

TABLE 7.4
Labor Costs and Privatization

Service	Average labor cost for this service as a share of city budgets (by percent)	Municipal wages for this service relative to contractor wages (by percent)
Trash collection	1.89	115
Turf maintenance	1.40	129
Tree maintenance	0.91	106
Traffic signal maintenance	0.46	115
Street cleaning	0.41	103
Janitorial services	0.33	140
Asphalt laying	0.26	63

SOURCE: Derived from Barbara J. Stevens, ed., *Delivering Municipal Services Efficiently* (Washington: HUD Office of Policy Development and Research, 1984), p. 3, ex. 1, p. 11, ex. 6.

for which wage bills weigh heavily on municipal budgets—collecting the garbage, cutting the grass, tending the trees—city workers earn a good deal more than do contractor employees. Still more puzzling is Stevens's claim that "the average difference in fringe benefits paid does not account for cost differences between contractors and municipal agencies."[35] The data presented in the Stevens study indicate that monthly benefits costs for municipal employees average $553, as compared to $368 for contractors.[36]

For most services, in fact, lower labor costs—both wages and benefits—are a major part of the contractor cost edge. Consider turf maintenance, a labor-intensive service that claims a relatively large share of the typical city budget. Stevens's regressions show that mowing an acre of grass costs a municipal agency $81, on average, and costs a contractor $58—about $41 for labor, and about $17 for other resources.[37] City grounds-crew workers cost $1,737 a month, counting wages and benefits; private contractors pay their workers $1,141.[38] If contractors paid the same wages and benefits as did city agencies, it would cost them about $73 to mow an acre of grass.[39] To put this another way, Stevens estimates that it costs city agencies 40 percent more than it does contractors to cut the grass. If cities made no changes in their turf-maintenance practices *except* for paring pay and benefits to private sector levels, the cost gap would shrink to 10 percent. Aside from asphalt laying (where contractors actually pay more for labor), this pattern holds for the other municipal services. Higher wages and benefits alone account for a large part—from one-fifth to three-quarters—of the extra costs estimated for municipal agencies, as table 7.5 shows.

Moreover, the *management* differences between city agencies and contractors summarized in table 7.3 are by no means neutral. Public sector organizations are

TABLE 7.5
Wages and the Public Sector's Cost Disadvantage

Service	Percentage of public sector's extra costs due to higher pay and benefits
Asphalt laying	0
Janitorial service	48
Traffic signal maintenance	18
Street cleaning	21
Trash collection	29
Turf maintenance	75
Tree maintenance	22

SOURCE: Derived from Barbara J. Stevens, ed., *Delivering Municipal Services Efficiently* (Washington: HUD Office of Policy Development and Research, 1984), p. 11, ex. 6.

more unionized, have older workers with longer average tenure, offer more vacation time, spare workers from the chore of maintaining their own equipment, and require more due process before a worker can be disciplined. These differences exist *not* due to accident or collective absent-mindedness on the part of public managers, but because city workers prefer things this way. In short, a good deal of what taxpayers stand to gain from privatization comes at the expense of municipal employees.

Stevens downplays the tougher private sector stance toward labor, perhaps because the Reagan administration officials who commissioned her study preferred not to antagonize municipal labor groups. But public employees are unlikely to be misled, and it seems pointless to mislead the rest of us. Two facts are equally evident: Delegating certain functions to private firms usually saves tax dollars, and much of these savings comes at the expense of public employees. What remains to be done is to weigh the joint implication of these two facts. A proponent of aggressive contracting out declares that "the purpose of local government is not to provide jobs; it is to deliver services to people."[40] A critic insists upon government's "socially important role of providing good jobs to people who might otherwise not get them."[41] Is local service privatization a good thing, or not? The question is as political as a question can be.

On the one hand, municipal patronage jobs have been the gateway to the mainstream economy for several waves of immigrants and minorities. City governments still employ disproportionate numbers of women and minorities, and pay them unusually well. Government work offers job security and employee rights that are uncommon in the private sector. To insist that nothing matters in public service delivery but the raw dollar cost is to adopt a needlessly narrow view of government.

On the other hand, it is hard to discern any democratic mandate for redistribution through the municipal payroll. There is also a certain arbitrariness to making worker interests a trump argument in the privatization debate. If street-sweeping should be public so that street-sweepers will be well-paid, why not barbering, or plumbing, or flower arranging? Equally troubling is the fact that city workers are frequently better off than many of the taxpayers who pay their salaries. And even those who endorse the distributional effects of extra municipal employment might lament its inefficiency, since it usually costs taxpayers well over a dollar to deliver an additional dollar into a city worker's pocket.

REWARDS AND RISKS

The evidence and assessments in this chapter boil down to a cautious, conditional endorsement of expanding the private role in public service delivery. While there are many governmental functions that can never be delegated, a substantial portion of state and local services meet the criteria set forth in chapter 5—they can be specified in advance, subjected to competition, and monitored throughout. The studies surveyed in this chapter, and in chapter 4, illustrate the private sector capacity for superior productivity when its energies can be properly harnessed.

The *potential* for efficiency gains is enormous. If selective privatization could pare as little as 15 percent from the cost of functions now carried out by state and local workers, the overall savings would come to nearly $50 billion, or roughly 1 percent of America's gross national product. At the same time, public officials could concentrate their energies on tasks that cannot be delegated.

Some reservations remain, however. First, the losses to labor present a real problem that is too often ignored or submerged in rhetoric. On a technical economic level, the tendency of contractors to offer lower wages and benefits means that the *efficiency* advantage of privatization is usually overstated, since some of the cost difference is simply money that stays in taxpayer pockets instead of going to city workers. More generally, municipal employees have pride in their work, mortgages to pay, and a set of expectations formed before contracting out emerged as a major cost-control strategy. It is perfectly understandable that these citizens resist bearing so much of the burden of municipal austerity. Even if taxpayers' stake in efficiency takes precedence over workers' claims to their jobs, taking steps to cushion privatization's shock to municipal workers—while it will likely cut savings considerably—is both politically prudent and commendably humane.

Corruption is a second problem that is typically debated in shrill ideological terms, but that nonetheless remains a cause for concern. The trick is to determine just how big an issue it is. Public employee unions like the American Federation of State, County, and Municipal Employees suggest that bribery and kickbacks are routine in municipal contracting; privatization enthusiasts insist that they are rare. It is certainly true that illegal or unsavory dealings between municipal contractors and public officials occur.[42] Unfortunately, there are no statistical compilations of corrupt municipal contracts by which we can calculate the respective proportions of clean and of tainted transactions. But in an environment of rampant corruption, contracting out obviously makes less sense than in a well-governed town.

The third caveat concerns competition. The good news is that there is considerable evidence that carefully structured competition with for-profit rivals can dramatically boost the efficiency of *public* organizations. The bad news is that the absence of competition can just as dramatically stifle any benefits that privatization would otherwise offer. Throughout this book, I have argued, first, that efficiency springs primarily from competition, not from privateness *per se*, and second, that competition is often difficult to arrange. The cost comparisons discussed in chapter 4 and the troubled history of Pentagon procurement reviewed in chapter 6 amply illustrate these points. And it is on this issue that the limited scope of the Stevens study—the small number of services appraised, and the narrow geographic boundaries of the study—warrants concern. Municipal contracting is common enough in the Los Angeles area that the cities opting for private delivery can expect a fair degree of potential competition to discipline contractors. When services are relatively simple and observable, there is little risk that incumbent contractors will gain special advantages that protect them against challenge should their prices get out of line or their service quality erode. But if competition is lacking for any reason—and potential reasons are legion, including technical barriers to entry, corruption, mob intimidation, and such simple failings as the disinclination of public officials to keep contractors feeling appropriately insecure—there will be far less to gain from contracting out.

The final note of caution starts from the fact that the potential benefits of contracting out *vary* from service to service. The problem is that there is little reason for confidence that local government will privatize the right services in the right order. There are many instances of unwise privatization. A California state college canceled a contract to run its computer center when costs ballooned.[43] Shrewsbury, Massachusetts returned to civil service custodians after a disappointing foray into contracting out.[44] In one of the less astute experiments on record,

TABLE 7.6
Contracting Out: Payoff and Prevalence by Service

Service	Estimated municipal cost disadvantage (by percent)	Percent of surveyed cities contracting out (by percent)
Asphalt laying	96	25
Janitorial service	73	19
Traffic signal maintenance	56	23
Street cleaning	43	7
Trash collection	42	27
Turf maintenance	40	19
Tree maintenance	37	25
Payroll preparation	0	10

SOURCE: Barbara J. Stevens, ed., *Delivering Municipal Services Efficiently* (Washington: HUD Office of Policy Development and Research, 1984), p. 13, ex. 7; and author's own calculations.

South San Francisco hired a private consulting firm to handle all of its public works, including engineering, building, and parks and recreation functions. A vice-president of the firm, who retained his corporate role, was named the head of a new "Department of Ecological Development" with sweeping powers over municipal budgets and personnel as well as authority to define new initiatives and to award additional contracts—including contracts to his own firm. As one researcher dryly described the incident, a "basic question arose over accountability," and the arrangement was terminated in less than a year.[45]

More generally, consider the eight services analyzed in the Stevens study in light of the results from a separate but contemporary survey of 1,780 cities (see table 7.6). It would be reassuring to find that municipal choices as to which services to privatize are in line with the payoff from privatization. But the evidence suggests a weak link at best. One-quarter of the cities surveyed have delegated responsibility for asphalt laying, where contractors enjoy a very large cost advantage. The same proportion of cities contract out for tree maintenance, however, when the private sector cost edge is much narrower. Janitorial service and turf maintenance show a similar disjointed pattern. More cities contract out for payroll preparation—where there is no private advantage at all—than for street cleaning, where Stevens reports a 43 percent cost edge for contractors.

This pattern may be partly explained by the facts that the cost data come from the Los Angeles area, and that the service-by-service merits of contracting out could well differ in other regions. But there are more general reasons to worry about bad decisions on privatization. The most basic reason is lack of information. Municipal officials may have only a limited understanding of which public services are being performed efficiently by public workers and which are not, and even less information on the availability and overall cost of private options. While there are a great many publications, seminars, and conferences dealing with the virtues and defects of privatization in general, there are few objective sources of advice on which services are best suited to contracting out, and in what circumstances.

A second reason relates to the exposure of public employees to losses (both financial and nonfinancial) from contracting out. Public workers often are able to block privatization.[46] The relative infrequency of private sector street-cleaning, turf maintenance, and janitorial services may be because janitors, street-sweepers, and lawn workers are much better off in the public sector, know it, and are able to defend their interests.

A third reason is in some ways the mirror image of the second. Private suppliers have political clout, too. They are apt to use it selectively. Firms are unlikely to push hard to wrest some service away from the bureaucracy if they anticipate fierce competition and barely adequate profits following privatization. On the other hand, aspiring contractors might lobby energetically to privatize those public services where they will be the least harried by competition and the least distracted by monitoring—in short, where they will be the least tightly constrained to *deliver* on the promised advantages of the private sector.

CHAPTER 8

THE PRIVATE PRISONS DEBATE

FEW SOCIAL ROLES appear more inherently *public* than those of the cop, the judge, or the jailer. Yet despite the seeming rightness of preserving the justice system as the exclusive province of the state, the private sector already has a hand in each of its three components—police services, the courts, and corrections. There are now a good many more private security guards than public police officers. While criminal courts remain in the public sector, plaintiffs and defendants in civil cases are increasingly abandoning crowded public courtrooms in favor of a variety of private arbitration and mediation services, many of which are operated for profit.[1]

The expansion of the private sector role into the third component of the justice system—corrections—began to generate considerable interest and controversy in the mid-1980s. Nearly all corrections systems already contract with private firms to construct prisons or to provide various support services. Two-thirds of all facilities for juvenile offenders are privately run, though seldom for profit. But delegating the job of incarcerating adult criminals to profit-making firms summons a set of special issues.

THE PUNISHMENT INDUSTRY

The total American corrections budget is roughly $10 billion per year—a bit more than is spent on the courts, about 50 percent of the budget for police services, and well under 1 percent of total government spending. State governments account for about 70 percent of overall corrections spending; cities and counties spend most of the rest, with the federal government accounting for only around 5 percent of the total.[2] There are roughly five thousand institutions in the United States for holding adults in custody, including some thirty-three hundered local and county jails; seven hundred state prisons, work farms, and other secure facilities; and several hundred halfway houses, federal prisons, detention centers for illegal aliens awaiting deportation, and assorted other places of confinement.[3] Only a tiny fraction of these institutions are privately run. In the late 1980s, there were around twenty or thirty private correctional facilities, with the exact number depending on the precise definitions of *private* and of *correctional facility*.

Probably the most prominent company in the incarceration industry is the Nashville-based Corrections Corporation of America, which owns two juvenile detention centers, four county jails, two penal work camps, two alien detention facilities (which it built and runs under contract to the Immigration and Naturalization Service), and two minimum-security state prisons in Texas.[4] (In 1985, the company boosted its visibility in the private corrections market when it made an unsuccessful bid to take over the entire Tennessee state prison system.)[5] The first state prison to go private, the Marion Adjustment Center in Kentucky, is run by the U.S. Corrections Corporation on the campus of a defunct Catholic college. Behavioral Systems Southwest has converted four motels into detention centers for aliens awaiting deportation.[6] Aliens convicted of crimes during their undocumented stays in America serve terms in the 575-bed facility run (for the Federal Bureau of Prisons) by Palo Duro Private Detention Services on the site of a vacant U.S. air base. There are hundreds of nongovernmental juvenile correctional facilities, several of which are prison-like operations run by profit-seeking firms. Eclectic Communications holds young federal criminals in a secure California facility, and since 1975 RCA has operated the Weaverville, Pennsylvania detention facility for underage hard cases. Pricor, another Nashville-based company, runs five correctional facilities and has large ambitions directed chiefly at the juvenile corrections market. Two major corporations entered the corrections industry in the late 1980s when a joint venture of the Wackenhut and Bechtel corporations contracted to build and run two Texas prisons.[7]

The Context

Proposals for expanding the private sector role in corrections have coincided with the confluence of demographic, legal, and political trends that, for the past decade or so, have been termed "the prison crisis."[8] From the mid-1920s through the mid-1970s, the number of state and federal prisoners edged up haltingly and unevenly from around 100,000 to roughly 200,000. But from 1974 on, prison populations began to surge, reaching 300,000 by 1980 and 600,000 by 1988.[9] In 1970, fewer than one out of every 1,000 Americans was serving a term in a state or federal prison; in 1985, it was about one out of every 450.

The surge in imprisonment has several causes, the simplest of which is demographic: The baby boom generation hit its crime-prone years as the American male population ages twenty to twenty-nine peaked. But the increase in crimes and in arrests exceeded what could be explained by demographic trends, and the increase in convictions and imprisonment, in turn, exceeded what could be explained by crime rates. Some might point to a decay of morality and a consequent rise in hard-core delinquency; others cite a growing vindictiveness in public opinion and a readiness to lock up erring citizens. In either event, the fear of crime and the urge to punish seem far more vivid in the public consciousness than the pedestrian fact that imprisonment implies prisons, which somehow must be built, staffed, and maintained. This leads to peculiar strains on the public agenda.

In 1968, when American prisons held fewer than two hundred thousand inmates, 63 percent of the surveyed public said that courts were too lenient with criminals. In 1978, the prison population neared three hundred thousand—and 88 percent of respondents felt that courts should be tougher.[10] Support for vigorous anticrime policies remains high, and public opinion frequently equates tough law-and-order policies with lengthy prison terms for malefactors. In 1985, North Carolinians were surveyed as to the fitting punishment for various crimes. Respondents called for long stretches of hard time for burglary, car theft, and other crimes far short of murder, rape, or major drug dealing. Only 5 percent, for example, thought a year and a half in prison was too stiff a sentence for two teenagers caught breaking into a house to steal a TV and stereo. In only one hypothetical crime-and-sentence combination—a $50 convenience-store armed robbery earning a six-year prison term—did more people feel that the sentence was too long rather than too short. Two-thirds found it about right.[11]

Like other states that have toughened their penal codes in the past decade, Kentucky has a "repeat offender" statute ensuring that the third felony conviction brings a lengthy prison term beyond the penalty the crime would otherwise earn. In the mid-1980s, concerns over prison overcrowding led to proposals for changing the Kentucky statute to apply only to repeat crimes against persons; property crimes would carry only the normal penalty, with no extra term on the third conviction. In an October 1985 survey conducted by the University of Kentucky, a sampling of 743 Kentuckians opposed the proposal by two-to-one, insisting on long prison terms for all repeat offenders. The same sampling of citizens was surveyed on state spending priorities. While over 75 percent favored increased spending on Medicaid, elementary and secondary education, and state roads and highways, fewer than half supported more spending on Kentucky's severely strained prison system.[12]

Similarly, 43 percent of the Floridians polled in 1985 declared themselves "extremely concerned" about crime (nearly all of the rest were at least "concerned") and cited "combating crime" as the most pressing state task. But prison construction was by far the least popular of the twelve alternative uses of state funds rated in the same survey.[13] A 1985 survey of New Mexico voters found that prison construction was less popular than any other uses of state funds except for welfare, state museums, and pay raises for state employees.[14]

These contradictory public sentiments have their effect, through the various mechanisms of democracy, on governmental practice. Elected officials and their appointees push for more arrests, higher bail, and longer prison terms, swelling the ranks of inmates, while bond referendums to build prisons are frequently defeated. The results should be foreseeable by anyone schooled in arithmetic: Prisons get crowded. By 1984, the population of state prisons nationwide averaged 5 to 16 percent over capacity, while federal prisons were overcrowded by 10 to 37 percent.[15] While the American Correctional Association drafts standards for space per inmate and prison cell amenities, only a small percentage of detention facilities meet these standards.[16] "Medical care has been neglected, educational and recreational programs have been ignored, and overcrowding has become the norm rather than the exception," according to a 1986 study. "Even the pretense of rehabilitation is abandoned as prisons are converted into human warehouses."[17] At the Massachusetts Correctional Institution at Concord—where as many as 770 inmates occupy a facility built for 225—recreation rooms, infirmaries, and the corridors of administrative wings have been converted into dormitories, and prisoners sometimes deliberately break rules in search of some privacy in solitary confinement.[18]

The effects of overcrowding include increased tension among inmates, rises in the rate of stress-related and infectious illness, and violence against other prisoners and prison employees.[19] And in an avidly litigious society, in which prisoners have as much right as anyone to take their complaints to court, and rather more time and incentive than average, the effects also include lawsuits. Between June 1983 and June 1984, there were some nineteen thousand lawsuits filed by prisoners claiming violation of their civil rights.[20] Most of these complaints were directly or indirectly related to overcrowding, and virtually all of them were beyond remedy without a major infusion of new funds.

While many prisoner rights cases are dismissed, enough have succeeded so that a randomly selected American jail or prison is likely to be facing a court order to improve conditions, and is almost equally likely to be financially incapable of complying.

This is the backdrop for the debate over expanding the private sector role in corrections. A Pennsylvania state senator justified his sponsorship of a privatization bill in these terms: "I don't think that the private sector can do any worse than what we have now."[21] The *Wall Street Journal* endorsed the idea of prisons for profit, predicting that "faced with swelling inmate populations, riots, court orders to improve prison conditions, and tight budgets, more states may be inclined to find out for themselves whether private prisons work."[22] The inclination is both undeniable and understandable. But the real issue is whether these are the kinds of public problems that private involvement can solve.

THE TERMS OF THE DEBATE

The chairman and cofounder of the Corrections Corporation of America has said that the notion of private corrections is initially "foreign to most people's experience. Their first impulse is to say only the government can do it, because only the government has ever done it. But their second reaction is that the government can't do anything very well. At that point, you just sell it like you were selling cars or real estate or hamburgers."[23] Lucius Burch, another of the company's founders, posed the case for private prisons as a straightforward issue of relative managerial capacity. Public entities, he wrote, "are not managing the prison systems effectively. Private entities can manage correctional facilities more economically and efficiently than the government."[24]

Beyond promising to deliver the same service more efficiently, corrections entrepreneurs have argued that, free of bureaucratic red tape and restrictions, they can also deliver a better, more innovative service. Ted Nissen, the head of Behavioral Systems Southwest, promised that he could outperform governmental competitors on rehabilitation, that once-central but currently distant goal of corrections policy: "We have a national recidivism rate of 50 percent. I offer to forfeit my contracts if the recidivism rate is more than 40 percent."[25]

The American Correctional Association, a quasi-official organization, has cautiously endorsed the "use of profit and nonprofit organizations to develop, fund, build, operate, and/or provide correctional services, programs, and facilities."[26] The President's Commission on Privatization declared in 1988 that "contracting appears to be an effective method for the management and operation of prisons and jails at any level of government."[27] And throughout the 1980s, a small but growing number of corrections officials tacitly signaled their own views on the subject as they signed contracts with private firms to run jails and detention centers.

The opponents of private corrections, meanwhile, are many and vocal. The National Sheriff's Association adopted a resolution strenuously opposing for-profit jails and prisons in 1984, while 75 percent of the correctional agencies polled that same year by the National Institute of Corrections responded that they would not consider contracting out the management of detention facilities.[28] The American Federation of State, County, and Municipal Employees issued a statement that "for the public, for correctional personnel, even for the inmates, contracting out is a terrible idea—it's bad policy, and it's bad government."[29] The American Bar Association adopted a resolution urging that "jurisdictions that are considering the privatization of prisons and jails not proceed to so contract until the complex constitutional, statutory, and contractual issues are satisfactorily developed and resolved."[30] The American Civil Liberties Union (ACLU) also went on record against for-profit corrections, in part because it feared that private facilities would fall short of even the lamentable inmate rights standards set by public prisons. The legal director of the ACLU Pennsylvania branch, testifying before the state legislature, charged that "private prisons by their very nature are time bombs waiting to inflict injury on those detained."[31]

Two prominent liberal intellectuals have considered and condemned private involvement in corrections. Michael Walzer has charged that "the private prison . . . exposes the prisoners to private or corporate purposes, and it sets them at some distance from the protection of the law. . . . For aren't the purposes of their private jailers different from the purposes of the courts that sent them to jail?"[32] Robert Lekachman took a similar stance when he argued that "the most powerful charge against corrections privatization is ethical. Imprisonment punishes its human target. . . . The men and women who administer punishment are state agents, responsible to elected public officials and elected or appointed judges. Private prisons . . . are driven by profit maximization, not sensitivity to the needs or rights of prisoners."[33]

But these arguments on their own are uncompelling briefs against privatization. To insist that everyone involved in a public enterprise be driven by wholly altruistic motives would imply rejecting Medicaid (since it relies on private doctors), food stamps (since collective aid to the hungry is mediated through farmers, processing companies, and grocery stores), and indeed virtually all governmental undertakings. The question is not whether supplier goals are identical with the public purpose; this coincidence of interests, while generally helpful and sometimes essential, is by no means *always* necessary. Neither civil service prison employees nor corrections entrepreneurs can be expected to share in every particular the "purposes of the courts" or to be motivated by a commanding "sensitivity to the needs and rights of prisoners." The question is, What form of relationship between the public and its agents best harnesses the efforts of agents to the common purpose, whether that purpose be tending to the community's dependent members or confining its delinquent members?

The American Bar Association statement in opposition to private corrections stresses the *symbolic* dimension of so central a public function as punishment.

> When it enters a judgment of conviction and imposes a sentence a court exercises its authority, both actually and symbolically. Does it weaken that authority, however—as well as the integrity of a system of *justice*—when an inmate looks at his keeper's uniform and, instead of encountering an emblem that reads "Federal Bureau of Prisons" or "State Department of Corrections" he faces one that says "Acme Corrections Company"? . . .[I]t could be argued that virtually anything that is done in a total, secure institution by the government or its designee is an expression of government policy, and therefore should not be delegated. We cannot help but wonder what Dostoevsky—who wrote that "the degree of civilization in a society can be judged by entering its prisons"—would have thought about privatization of corrections.[34]

Dostoevsky presumably would not have based his judgment on the tags adorning the guards' uniforms. (For that matter, Dostoevsky is a strange authority to invoke here.) Grounding arguments on the unseemliness of private prisons is, for two reasons, a poor tactic for opponents of privatization. First, reasonable people may disagree about the symbolism. Second, the symbolism issue cannot really be determinative. Even if, all other things being equal, we would prefer to keep the profit motive out of the criminal justice system, all other things may not be equal. If a private prison treats inmates humanely, protects them from indignity and assault, endeavors to aid their rehabilitation, and charges the community a fair price, would the fact that its shareholders anticipated a return on their investment make that prison inferior to one in which public employees neglect, humiliate, and abuse prisoners while needlessly straining the public purse? Few critics of privatization, I suspect, would go that far.

The symbolism issue, like the ethical case that Lekachman raised, is a contingent concern. Declaring private prisons to be unethical or symbolically unseemly makes sense only as the culmination of a series of separate arguments showing that the array of checks, pressures, and incentives associated with for-profit corrections is likely to lead to morally inferior results. We have learned that private profit-seeking organizations perform some public functions rather well (for example, producing and delivering sustenance to food-stamp clients) and others rather badly (for example, waging covert warfare). The trick is to determine the category into which corrections properly falls. Ideological critics of privatization are right when they point out that corrections is a particularly important and delicate public task; they err when they conclude from this fact alone that only government can perform it. *Government* is an abstraction. Public acts are carried out by men and women who agree, through various types of organizational and contractual arrangements, to serve their fellows. The particular kind of relationship called civil service has some symbolic and practical properties that are especially valuable for tasks that are difficult to arrange through the market. But whether the warden reports directly to the corrections commissioner or indirectly through a corporate entity is not in itself an ethical issue; what matters are the ethical consequences of each structure of accountability.

What we need, ideally, is evidence. The answer to the accountability question—on which depends the answer to the ethical question—would be much less elusive if we could assign one-tenth or one-half of the jails in America to private control, ensure that public and private operations get comparable burdens and resources, devise clear criteria for evaluating performance, and (after ten or twenty years) compare the results. A senior analyst who appraised private corrections for the Massachusetts legislature argued that both the claims of proponents and the charges of critics will remain inconclusive until the issue gets "the vigorous examination by disinterested parties that is necessary to produce unbiased assessments. Until private prison operators are given an opportunity to succeed or fail in meeting their promises, the debate over private prisons will continue to be based more on hypothesis than fact."[35] It is hard to argue with a call for more data. But while facts are indisputably more convincing than hypotheses, they are also much more expensive. The wisdom of an experimental approach to the private prisons debate depends, first, on how costly—in financial and other terms—the experiment is likely to be and, second, on how conclusive will be the evidence produced. Experiments with private corrections carry the risk of heavy costs. Transfers of control may be difficult to reverse, and the consequences could be severe in the interim. Officials in each state might rationally hope that some other state would undertake a large-scale experiment with private prisons.

The evidence provided by initiatives now under way or envisaged is unlikely to settle the issue. Virtually every state prison system already contracts out for some services—most frequently medical care, food services, maintenance, or transportation. Some officials report that outside suppliers offer higher quality, cost savings, and better accountability. Others, however, report poor quality, inflated costs, and trouble controlling contractors.[36] Without careful studies that control for factors *other* than public versus private organization, the available evidence allows no definitive judgment about contracting out prison services, much less the management of entire prisons.

Worse still, the small sample of detention centers under private control is by no means random with respect either to facilities or inmates. Most private detention centers are low-security operations for juvenile offenders or aliens who have committed no crime aside from unauthorized border crossing. Private firms' performance in these areas—favorable or otherwise—may not say much about how they will handle higher-security operations. All of the private prisons in operation or under construction are minimum-security facilities. (As this is written, Kentucky is considering for-profit medium-security prisons.) *Public* minimum-security prisons have operating costs about 20 percent below those of both medium- and maximum-security facilities; comparing the cost performance of private prisons with *all* public prisons would thus be seriously misleading.[37]

Cost comparisons may be still more distorted if private prisons differ systematically in the characteristics of their inmate populations. For example, the Marion Adjustment Center, run by the U.S. Corrections Corporation, costs Kentucky $25 per inmate per day, or roughly in the middle of the $18 to $31 dollar range of publicly run prisons. But inmates are screened for medical and behavioral problems before they are assigned to Marion. "We don't want to overload them with problem cases," the administrative director of the Kentucky corrections system has explained. "We tend to send them the best in the bunch."[38] Similarly, the Immigration and Naturalization Service rates deportation-bound aliens by the probability of escape attempts, saves its own facilities for the tougher cases, and assigns the more docile aliens to the contract detention centers.[39] Such practices ensure that the evidence yielded by such experiments will remain inconclusive.

Moreover, early experiences with contracting for incarceration may not be representative of what a fully developed private corrections industry would look like. Costs could fall and performance could improve over time as firms gain experience and new entrants heighten competition. Or costs could rise and performance decay as a few dominant firms become entrenched while public corrections departments are dismantled, leaving governments with no alternative to private jails and prisons.

Private hospitals have for decades provided public services of a sort that is at least as delicate as those at stake in incarceration. But the fervor of the ongoing debate over profit-seeking hospitals counsels against any expectation that experience will soon settle the private prison issue. For-profit institutions now account for over 10 percent of all hospitals. Several major statistical studies have attempted to weigh the effect of organizational form on costs, service to the poor, and other dimensions of hospital performance. But there is enough room for variation in the selection of samples, choice of methodologies, and definition of quality and efficiency to assure that consensus remains elusive. It seems likely that even many years' experience with private prisons could still leave us without unassailable evidence on efficiency, cost, or quality.[40] Throughout this chapter, accordingly, I not only employ the available data, but also supplement hard facts with the less satisfying but far cheaper expedient of speculation about the "fit" between profit-seeking organization and the public task of incarceration.

The chief virtues of delegating public tasks to the private sector are the cost discipline inspired by competition, and an institutional setting that affords superior motivation to discover better, cheaper ways to deliver value. The more the technical nature of a public task allows for innovation to improve quality or to lower cost, the greater the potential benefits of contracting out—provided, of course, it is possible to forge a firm contractual link between creating value and collecting profits. This link depends, in turn, on the existence of realistic competition, on how carefully and completely the product can be specified; on the degree to which quality can be monitored; and, finally, on the purchaser's ability and inclination to reward, penalize, or replace contractors on the basis of performance. These considerations apply to nongovernmental deals as well. In *private* transactions where no tight connection can be made between value received and payment rendered, individuals must either put up with perceptibly imperfect market arrangements, or else structure alternative ways—involving family, church, or other nonmarket forms of organization—to carry out exchanges. But *collective* tasks involve further complications—ambiguities about the real dimensions of public value, and the potential for self-interested suppliers to distort the demand for public goods and services.

Assessing the wisdom of greater private involvement in corrections, then, means taking up three sets of questions. The first set concerns the task of incarceration itself, and the scope for innovation and efficiency improvements. The second set involves the measurement of quality and the devices—contractual and otherwise—available for ensuring accountability. The final set concerns the vulnerability to manipulation and distortion of public demand for correctional services.

PRIVATE CORRECTIONS AND EFFICIENCY

Organizations confronting competition will generally be more efficient than organizations secure against challenge. Workers and managers in a position to benefit, directly or indirectly, from efficiency improvements will generally be more energetic in reducing costs than those with no such prospects. And lower costs, in a competitive market, will generally translate into lower prices. Whether and how these broad articles of faith apply to the corrections issue depend, first, on the *technical* scope for efficiency gains in the task at hand, and, second, on the nature and degree of competition in the incarceration industry. The Corrections Corporation of America estimates that private management should lead to costs 10 to 25 percent below those of public corrections bureaucracies. When that company took over the Silverdale Work Farm in Tennessee, it charged the county twenty-one dollars per prisoner per day, a 12.5 percent saving over the cost under prior county management. When Bay County, Florida, solicited proposals from private firms for running its jail, CCA's winning bid was fully 20 percent below the sheriff's proposed budget.[41] Indeed, most of the jurisdictions experimenting with private corrections report either anticipated or achieved cost savings.[42] But one need not credit state and local officials with too much shrewdness to expect that the first few of them to opt for private corrections will have done so in response to a price inducement. But will private management offer *durable* efficiency gains and cost savings? Lacking large-scale, long-term experience with private prisons, we might seek lessons in comparable endeavors with longer histories and richer stores of data. Private organizations—profit, nonprofit, and voluntary— have long been involved in juvenile corrections. Do differences between public and private custodial facilities for juveniles suggest anything about the efficiency of the alternative organizational forms? Table 8.1 summarizes the data. The cost differences are minuscule. The total cost per resident of private facilities is a bare 1 percent higher than that of public centers. But the private juvenile corrections field is growing more quickly, so private centers spend more, on average, for investment. *Operating* costs are lower for private centers—but by only 3 percent. One could argue that merely matching public costs shows that private facilities are more efficient, since they are generally smaller and lack economies of scale. Alternatively, one could argue that public centers are more efficient, since they deal with slightly older and potentially more troublesome residents, have higher turnover, and—with less control over the flow of juvenile delinquents sent to them by courts or social agencies—are more plagued by undercapacity and overcapacity.

TABLE 8.1
Custodial Centers for Juveniles, 1985

	Public	Private
Number of facilities	1040	1996
Average number of residents	48	17
Average age	15.4 years	14.9 years
Less than 70 percent full	35 percent	20 percent
Over 100 percent full	10 percent	1 percent
Total cost per resident*	$22,600	$22,845
Operating cost per resident*	$22,000	$21,300
Growth from 1979 to 1985	14 percent	19 percent

*1982 data
SOURCE: Department of Commerce, *Statistical Abstract of the United States 1987* (Washington: 1987), 171.

Detaining illegal aliens may be a task more closely analogous to that of imprisoning adults. The Immigration and Naturalization Service divides illegal aliens among its own seven detention centers as well as five contract centers run by for-profit firms. What data exist fail to support any claims of private sector superiority. The cost to the INS—per detainee, per day—averaged nearly 20 percent *higher* at contract centers.[43] This does not, of course, prove that private facilities are inefficient. Factors aside from ownership status clearly affect the cost of detaining illegal aliens. For one, centers must be located in the vicinities in which aliens are arrested—such as New York City, Denver, Houston, Los Angeles, and the rural Southwest. Hence geographic variations in land and labor costs may swamp cost differences attributable to management. There may also be economies of scale in running detention centers, or other dimensions of cost that distort the comparison. Analyzing the cost and sizes of the public and private centers is drearily inconclusive. Beyond the fact that private centers are smaller on average, and the very weak suggestion of economies of scale, the data support no confident generalizations. The cheapest center is private—but so is the most expensive. The lower average cost of public centers may be attributable to their larger average size— but two of the public centers are cheaper than a slightly larger private center. In all, the evidence from alien detention centers offers little guidance either way on the overall question of comparative efficiency.

We return, then, to conjecture as to the possible sources of superior private performance. There are three reasons to expect private prison managers to be more concerned than would be their public counterparts over cost control. First, private managers will be spared various procedural requirements that tend to distract public managers from the pursuit of technical efficiency and often mandate practices that (at least in economic terms) are decidedly inferior. Second, the managers of private prisons are often either part-owners themselves or are directly answerable to owners; in either case, they tend to anticipate some degree of personal benefit from increased efficiency. The third reason is organizational. Managers and other employees are motivated not only by simple monetary incentives, but also by the prospect of advancement into higher posts. A private prison corporation, including several separate facilities as well as a central headquarters, may be able to offer a greater number and variety of opportunities for advancement than can a public prison.[44] It thus seems likely that private prison managers will be more highly motivated to efficiency.

The incentive, though, is only part of the requirement. There must also be meaningful *opportunities* for cost control if these superior private incentives are to have any effect. Cost-reducing innovations must represent real efficiency gains, moreover, and not simply the shifting of costs or risks or the debasement of quality. It is easy to imagine perverse ways by which an economy-minded manager could cut the cost of incarceration. He could dispense with expensive walls, bars, gates, and locks by surrounding the jail with a minefield, or by hiring an eager sniper. He could abandon efforts to protect prisoners from their violent or deranged fellow inmates. He could feed the prisoners bread and water, hire them out as slaves to earn their keep, and scrimp on shelter and medical care. A few minutes and a little creativity could provide many more such options. But the question is how costs can be reduced while fulfilling the public mandate to detain prisoners humanely. There are only two ways to cut costs without lowering quality: Using *fewer* resources, or *paying less* for the resources used.

Private firms almost surely *are* better than corrections bureaucracies at economizing on resources. Behavioral Systems Southwest detains illegal aliens in converted motels; the Corrections Corporation of America alien detention center in Houston was designed to be usable as a warehouse if the detention business hit a slump. Using such structures—when they do the job—represents a real efficiency gain over specialized detention buildings that must stand empty when they are not needed to hold prisoners. Better food service practices, such as portion control, can limit waste. There are also opportunities for cutting labor costs through automation. Carefully designed and installed surveillance cameras and electronic security systems can substitute, to some extent, for human guards.

But in general, incarcerating people is an enterprise with relatively little scope for resource-sparing technical progress. There is a range of alternatives to incarceration—including probation, parole, electronically enforced house arrest, community service, execution, forgiveness, and exile. But once the task is defined as imprisonment, the range of alternative technologies is relatively narrow. (Broadening the task to include *rehabilitation* would obviously expand this range, and vastly complicate the definition and measurement of efficiency.) Prisoners must be sheltered, fed, cared for when sick, protected from each other, and prevented from escaping. These do not appear to be tasks that allow for radical innovations in technique. (If this judgment is mistaken—if there is room for significant technical progress in incarceration, if such innovations are the source of the advertised cost advantage of the private sector, and if firms can be constrained to compete on the basis of such innovation—then I am underestimating the potential for efficiency gains through private management.)

With real but limited options for cutting cost through innovation, prison contractors seek to improve on the government's cost performance largely through driving harder bargains with the suppliers of goods and services. Incarceration entrepreneurs point to wasteful and cumbersome government purchasing requirements, and cite bulk purchases of food and other supplies as one of their advantages over the public sector.

A prison's main "supplier," of course, is labor. Both proponents and critics cite lower labor costs as a key feature of private prisons. The payroll accounts for roughly 60 percent of the overall costs of corrections.[45] Corrections firms and some legislators hail private management as a device for breaking the iron grip of public worker unions, bridling unreasonable wage and benefit demands, thus easing the burden on the taxpayers. Those same unions, meanwhile, are the most vigorous and effective opponents of privatization, warning that economizing on labor will victimize workers directly and inmates indirectly. The labor cost question can best be addressed in the terms introduced in earlier chapters: Are corrections workers collecting compensation beyond fair pay for the work required? If so, private management might be a valuable tactic for restoring the balance. If not, private firms will be unable to reduce labor costs without debasing the quality of the work force and, with it, the conditions of confinement.

Guards at the Massachusetts Correctional Institute at Concord start at $22,000 a year.[46] Are they overpaid? On the one hand, this is triple the minimum wage for a job that requires no advanced degrees and no heavy lifting. On the other hand, it involves unedifying working conditions and a great deal of stress. (Prison guards suffer from high rates of alcoholism, domestic problems, and suicide.) Most tellingly, the state has trouble finding people willing to take the jobs at that salary—turnover at Concord is about 40 percent, and there are usually unfilled posts. Prison guard pay and benefits vary widely from jurisdiction to jurisdiction, however, and by carefully selecting examples one could argue that prison guards are grossly overpaid, or the opposite.

What do the national figures show? The most recent aggregate data are from the 1980 census, which included a tally of earnings by occupation, age, and education. Prison work is not particularly lucrative. The hourly pay of male correctional officers—and 86 percent of all guards are male—was a bit less than 80 percent of the average pay for all males.[47] This means little on its own, however. Whether or not there are rents to be pared away by efficiency-minded private operators depends on whether other people would be willing to do the same work more cheaply. Suggestive evidence on this score might be found by comparing the data for public prison workers with data for a related set of workers—security officers who work for private firms. Table 8.2 summarizes the comparison.

TABLE 8.2
Labor Cost and Quality

	Public corrections workers	Private security guards
Average hourly wage	$ 6.80	$ 5.91
Average annual earnings	$13,757	$10,206
Work full-time, full-year	80 percent	55 percent
Ages 25–54	77 percent	49 percent
High school graduates	87 percent	67 percent

Private security guards (representing one of the main labor pools from which private prisons will presumably draw their employees) command about 15 percent lower wages than do public correctional workers. Since payroll costs are about 60 percent of total prison costs, trimming the wage bill by 15 percent would itself offer private corrections firms a 9 percent cost advantage. Cutting corrections budgets nationwide by 9 percent would save taxpayers roughly one billion dollars per year, by no means a negligible sum. But would this represent a real gain in efficiency?

Not necessarily. The costs of the two workforces differ, but so do their characteristics. Public guards are far more likely to be high school graduates, to work full-time and year-round at their jobs, and to be of prime working age. Employers who hire from the private labor pool pay less and get less. If age and experience, education, and full-time status matter for prison workers, lower labor costs simply signal a lower-quality workforce. (The census data show that private workers and public workers are paid roughly the same at each age and education level; indeed, college graduates working full-time as private security guards actually make *more* than their counterparts in the public sector.) While data on private security guards may not fully reflect the characteristics of the people who will become private prison guards—and while the vigor of the guard unions' objections to privatization feeds suspicion that there are at least *some* bonuses to labor at stake—it seems unlikely that private operators can cut labor costs very much without turning to a lower quality workforce, with the likelihood of worsened prison conditions.[48]

Competition and Contracting

Lower costs for prison contractors, however they may be achieved, need not lead to lower costs to government. Without competition or tightly drawn contracts, savings on wages and other inputs increase profits instead of shrinking public spending. Will the incarceration industry, once it matures, be competitive? Perfect competition—many alternative suppliers, ease of entry and exit, full information, and so on—is out of the question here. But what are the prospects for "good enough" competition? Several considerations suggest caution. Even if the number of corrections firms eventually exceeds the current handful, it is unlikely that there will ever be more than a few serious contenders in any given region at any given time.[49] Firms are likely to face substantial costs of entering the incarceration industry, as well as potential *exit* costs (particularly if any entrant must invest in specialized buildings) high enough to deter many firms from experimenting with the business.

Even if there are a number of firms bidding to take over when a city, state, or county first decides to privatize, jurisdictions will probably find it difficult to switch contractors if their incarceration company disappoints them.[50] Private prison operators will face sunk costs of operating in an area, and will accordingly demand multiyear contracts—Corrections Corporation of America contracts, for example, generally run for twenty to thirty years[51]—or else require compensation if contracts are canceled. And even in cases where canceling a contract triggers no formal penalty clause, a change of management in a jurisdiction's corrections system will be awkward at best and more likely seriously disruptive. Nobody expects the prison industry to be competitive in the way that the fast-food industry is competitive. But there is some reason to fear that, instead of being competitive like the trash collection industry, it will be competitive like the nuclear submarine industry—which is to say, not at all. Thus, even if private management does result in greater efficiency, the cost savings may not be passed on to governmental clients.

The Burden of Process

Compared with payroll processing, park maintenance, waste disposal, and other tasks that a city or state might entrust to a private firm, incarceration is a complicated undertaking. The contract regulating the relationship between the jurisdiction and the corrections firm is likely to be correspondingly lengthy, detailed, and tricky to write. An official of the Federal Bureau of Prisons, who broadly favors private prisons, nonetheless laments that the "difficulty is in knowing what to ask for and how to ask for it in the RFP [request for proposals]."[52] Who pays the medical bills when an inmate in a private prison contracts AIDS? Who is liable if he sues, claiming that he was wrongfully exposed to the disease while imprisoned? How are changes in incarceration costs to be shared if the number of convicts rises or falls sharply from year to year? If facilities are destroyed in a riot, who pays to rebuild them? The contract for running the Marion Adjustment Center in Kentucky runs to thirty-five pages of small print.[53] Attempts to exhaustively spell out contingencies and assign rights and duties for each conceivable case will be awkward and burdensome, and will almost surely fail to cover everything. But gaps and ambiguities mean vulnerability.[54]

Hamilton County, Tennessee, operated its new Silverdale Work Farm for less than one year before the Corrections Corporation of America contracted to take it over. The cost per prisoner under county management had been twenty-four dollars per day; the company agreed to charge twenty-one dollars per day, offering the county a significant saving. The twenty-four-dollar baseline, however, had been set while Silverdale held 250 prisoners, or about 75 percent of capacity. In the first year of private management, the number of prisoners sentenced to Silverdale surged, due largely to a tough new drunk-driving law. Fees to the Corrections Corporation of America soon exceeded the original county corrections budget. Officials complained that the per diem had been based on average *total* costs, consisting mostly of fixed costs that did not vary with the number of prisoners. The incremental cost per prisoner—so long as no new construction was needed—was closer to five dollars. The company's marketing chief insisted, "we haven't charged them a dime more than we said we would," which is perfectly true. The problem, from the county's perspective, was that the contract failed to consider cost structures or to anticipate contingencies such as new laws and tougher sentencing.[55] Some jurisdictions will surely write more sophisticated contracts than the one that left Hamilton County disappointed—Bay County, Florida, negotiated a far more favorable rate deal with the Corrections Corporation of America that accounts for falling per-person costs, for example[56]—but, just as surely, others will not.

A contract embodies an allocation of costs and responsibilities. Efficient contracting means finding the right allocation, parceling out duties to the parties most competent to perform them. But, as the Silverdale example illustrates, contracts also allocate risks—in this case, uncertainty as to the demand for incarceration. By privatizing its work farm, Hamilton County shifted risk to the Corrections Corporation of America. Whatever the cost of incarcerating a prisoner should turn out to be, the county locked in its liability by agreeing with CCA on a fixed per diem rate. Had the citizens of Hamilton County suddenly become law abiding, or had a soft-hearted new judge refused to send delinquents to the work farm, corporate earnings would have dropped. As it happened, the incarceration rate rose, and the work farm became a gold mine. One could argue that the county had no more valid grounds for complaint than does the airline passenger who buys flight insurance and subsequently fails to crash. Had he known that he would live through the flight, he could have saved some money; similarly, had Hamilton County known that the average cost per prisoner would drop, it would have held out for a better deal. But uncertainty about the future is the whole rationale of a market for risk.

The issue here is whether it makes sense for governments to pay entrepreneurs to relieve them of the risks associated with running prisons. Privatization has been promoted as a way of avoiding the risk of building too much or too little prison capacity.[57] If the government is very small or very poor, it might prefer to pay a little extra, on average, to eliminate any chance of an unexpected surge in prison costs. But governments are usually better at spreading risks than are private companies, simply because they usually encompass more people. (A $1 million risk borne by Elwood, Indiana, is obviously less diffused than one borne by General Motors, but the basic point holds true.) State and city governments very likely have better information about crime rates and sentencing practices than do private firms, and they probably have some degree of control over the demand for jail space. In general, the party with more information and control is the efficient risk-bearer. And off-loading risk at a reasonable cost requires a contractual sophistication and a concentration of purpose beyond that of many governments.

A related point concerns recent court judgments. Governments, it turns out, generally cannot get rid of perhaps the largest risk of the incarceration business, liability for damages arising from prisoners' rights lawsuits. Most such suits are brought under Section 1983 of the Civil Rights Act, which provides that any "person who, under color of any statute, ordinance, regulation, custom, or usage . . . subjects, or causes to be subjected, any citizen of the United States . . . to the deprivation of any rights, privileges, or immunities secured by the Constitution and laws, shall be liable to the party injured in an action at law, suit in equity, or other proper proceeding for redress."[58]

Courts passing judgment on claims of Eighth Amendment violations under private detention have taken a broad view of this "color of law" criterion. For example, when illegal aliens were discovered stowed away on a ship in an American port in 1981, the Immigration and Naturalization Service arranged for them to be temporarily detained by Danner, Inc., a private security firm. The facilities were neither big enough to hold the stowaways in tolerable conditions nor secure against escape. When some detainees forced the door and attempted to flee, an untrained guard opened fire, killing one alien and seriously hurting another. In the suit that followed, the court found that the Immigration and Naturalization Service, the officials who arranged for private detention, and Danner, Inc., were jointly and severally liable for damages.[59] One scholar asserts that private prisons will be operated under "a scheme which establishes a stronger nexus than that found in *Medina*" (the Danner, Inc., case) and that "both private providers and contracting governments will be subject to Section 1983 liability."[60] Governments are thus likely to end up with little or no relief from liability in prisoners' rights suits, and with a good deal less direct control over the conditions of imprisonment.[61]

Will private operation mean generally lower corrections costs? We cannot know for sure, but the guess is yes—costs will be slightly lower on average, though with considerable variation, and some tendency to rise over time. Much of prison management involves the kinds of straightforward housekeeping functions where private firms generally have an edge, and most examples to date point to limited but real cost savings from prison privatization. On the other hand, the prices prison entrepreneurs charge as they launch their businesses may not be sustainable. The Corrections Corporation of America, for example, is marginally profitable by the most generous measure, nor is there any indication that its smaller competitors are earning adequate revenues at the rates they currently charge.[62] If the private prison industry is to satisfy its investors, either rates will have to climb or new ways of cutting costs will have to be found.

Simply curbing the cost of incarceration, moreover, may not be an achievement beyond public managers' competence. One way of recounting the recent history of corrections costs is to note with alarm that total spending on state prisons surged 74 percent in only four years, rising from $4.5 billion in 1980 to $7.7 billion in 1984. One could argue that *something* must be done to stanch the drain on the public purse, obviously, and privatization is one of the few suggestions on the table. But this argument ignores both inflation and, more significantly, the rise in prison populations. Between 1980 and 1984 the number of state prison inmates rose by 42 percent (from 295,363 to 417,797) while corrections budgets, measured in constant dollars, rose only 33 percent. The real cost per inmate, accordingly, *fell* by around 6 percent. The same numbers, depending on the interpretation, suggest either an insupportable trend of ballooning expenses, or a remarkable feat of cost control on the part of prison officials.[63] Of course, the cost per inmate has been reduced primarily by overcrowding prisons, foregoing maintenance, abandoning rehabilitation, and otherwise degrading the conditions of confinement. It is at least conceivable that corrections entrepreneurs envisage a comparable approach to cost control.

QUALITY CONTROL AND THE CONDITIONS OF INCARCERATION

Will private prisons neglect or abuse inmates in the name of cost control? There are obvious *technical* opportunities to do so. There are also precedents from previous eras. Corrections expert John J. DiIulio has written that

> the history of private sector involvement in corrections is unrelievedly bleak, a well-documented tale of inmate abuse and political corruption. In many instances, private contractors worked inmates to death, beat or killed them for minor rule infractions, or failed to provide inmates with the quantity and quality of life's necessities (food, clothing, shelter, etc.) specified in their often meticulously-drafted contracts.[64]

Indeed, there are scattered incidents of cost-cutting leading to mistreatment in modern-day private detention facilities, despite their generally high quality.[65] But, to repeat, there is no sure way to know whether private prisons will end up more or less humane, on average, than public ones. Every tale of bad conditions or brutality at a private facility can be matched by a story about the horrors of public prisons and the superiority of private prison conditions.[66] The anecdotes cut both ways, and settle nothing.

The Corrections Corporation of America's vice-president for legal affairs protests that "this cutting corners idea attributes to man only the basest of motives. It does not recognize that there are good, responsible, pillars-of-the-community type people who want this concept to work as an industry for the long term."[67]

There is no evidence whatever that the officials of Corrections Corporation of America (and most other private prison entrepreneurs) are anything but decent businesspeople who aim to cut costs through better management, and not through lower quality.

But the real issue is the shape a fully developed incarceration industry is likely to take, and on that score the integrity of the pioneers does not matter much. If the central goal of privatization is saving money, if incarceration contracts are awarded on the basis of cost, and if it is possible to cut costs by lowering standards, then quality control becomes an urgent issue. Are the people now bidding to run prisons entering the industry in order to make money by brutalizing inmates? Almost certainly they are not. Are there within our society people who would be willing to make money by brutalizing inmates? Almost certainly there are. And without robust measures to guarantee the conditions of confinement, the businesspeople least constrained by scruples are likely to enjoy a competitive advantage in the imprisonment industry.

In most businesses, quality is enforced by the customer's grasp of his own preferences and his freedom to abandon suppliers who let standards slip. In a few industries where the immediate consumers are unable to evaluate or respond to quality—such as the nursing home and day-care center industries—there have been periodic scandals over deplorable lapses in performance. But prisoners are conspicuously unable to take their business elsewhere, however dissatisfied they might be.*

The *customer* in this case is not the prisoner, but rather the rest of the citizens who pay to have delinquents locked up. If the community wants the conditions of confinement to be short of luxurious but well this side of cruel and unusual, the issue becomes the standards set for prison operators (public or private) and the community's inclination and ability to monitor conditions and to enforce its standards. "Private management of a facility is under the control of government, which sets the policy," an official of the Corrections Corporation of America has emphasized.[68] If the community wants prisoners to be held in decent, uncrowded conditions, it need only select and reward contractors on that basis. "We won't cut corners to make the bottom line because we wouldn't stay in business," according to another corrections entrepreneur. "It doesn't make business sense

---

*They can sue, however. If Section 1983 civil rights lawsuits, discussed earlier, can be an efficient enforcement device—that is, if high-quality private prisons reliably escape or win lawsuits, and low-quality prisons reliably lose them—quality control will be less of an issue. But the fact that liability will fall on jurisdictions as well, and the likelihood that tort costs will depend as much on the skill and vigor of legal defense and the vagaries of the legal system as on the actual conditions of confinement, undercuts confidence in this mechanism of accountability.

for us not to have clean and humane facilities."[69] A study done for the Massachusetts legislature finds reassurance in the prospect that prison entrepreneurs "will have to balance their desire to cut costs with their need for long-term contracts."[70] This perspective assumes a clear link between financial success in the imprisonment business and the quality of conditions provided, which will only be true if the market for incarceration is competitive, and if humane treatment—and not winning lawsuits, minimizing budgets, or even connections, bribes, and campaign contributions—turns out to be the dominant dimension of competition.

If comprehensive contracts could easily be written, performance could be perfectly monitored, and promises could be enforced without cost, then private prisons would provide exactly the conditions of incarceration that the community desired. There are few objections to private involvement in corrections that cannot be answered by calls for careful contracting and tough performance evaluation. The National Institute of Justice study of prison privatization, for example, is studded with warnings about "judicious contractor selection and monitoring procedures" and "care in defining criteria and restraining the discretion of private providers."[71] But full, effective monitoring is a tall order.

Bentham's Monitoring Proposal

The first proponent of contracting for corrections was Jeremy Bentham, who called for a new approach to imprisonment, organized around an architectural innovation, in his 1791 book *Panopticon*.[72] As the name suggests, the Panopticon was a structure designed for maximum visibility and ease of inspection. The building would be circular, and the central "Inspector's Lodge" would be ringed by individual prisoners' quarters with see-through walls made of metal grillwork. (Bentham's proposal has strongly influenced prison design, and in fact he coined the term "cell" to refer to the rooms within a prison.) Escapes and other infractions would be deterred by "the apparent omnipresence of the Inspector" who could, at least potentially, have any prisoner under observation at any time. Moreover, the Inspector could be confident that his assistants and guards—just as exposed to view as the prisoners—would faithfully follow procedures.

Professing concern for "pecuniary economy," Bentham came out squarely for private management. "I would do the whole thing by contract," he wrote. "I would farm out the profits, the no-profits, or if you please the losses, to him who, being in other respects unexceptionable, offered the best terms." Entrepreneurs would bid to run prisons. The winning bidder would be awarded an open-ended contract that could only be revoked for cause. Privatization had its critics in Bentham's day as well, and he was fully aware that many would object to the idea of consigning a public function and public resources to gain-seeking entrepreneurs. "But contractors, you will say perhaps (or at least if you don't there are enough that will) are a good for nothing set of people, and why should we be fleeced by them?"[73]

To reassure skeptics, Bentham proposed two mechanisms of accountability to limit costs and guarantee performance. First was a short but strict set of specifications on how the contractor could treat inmates: "In the first place, he shall not starve them. . . . In the next place, I don't know that I should be for allowing him the power of beating his boarders, nor in short of punishing them in any shape." Finally, the contractor would be penalized if his charges died at an excessive rate; the contract "would make him pay so much for every one that died, without troubling whether any care of his could have kept the man alive." The penalty would be set at a level that made it worth the contractor's while to refrain from brutalizing inmates. Bentham reasoned that basing the penalty on *all* deaths, rather than on *avoidable* deaths, would save monitoring costs and eliminate disputes over fault.[74] In Bentham's world, both the public and the prison entrepreneur faced simpler goals and constraints than their modern counterparts. But however straightforward the contract, the problem of enforcement remained. How would the public know that prisoners were being fed and kept safe against abuse? Bentham's second device for holding contractors accountable was an extreme version of what would today be called sunshine provisions. While the contractor would be free to manage the prison as he saw fit (short of starving or beating inmates or piling up an inordinate body count), his operations, by explicit contract, would be subject to unlimited scrutiny. "I will require him to disclose, and even to print and publish, his accounts. . . . I will make him examinable and cross-examinable *viva voce* upon oath at any time."[75]

Beyond this open-book policy, the very "panoptic" design that would let an Inspector manage the prison with a minimum of manpower, Bentham suggested, "presents an answer, and that a satisfactory one, to one of the most puzzling of political questions, *quis custodiet ipsos custodes?*" The conditions of confinement could be monitored by simply entering the Panopticon and looking around. Not only would public officials and the families and friends of inmates be allowed to observe conditions, but "the doors of these establishments will be . . . thrown wide open to the body of the curious at large—the great open committee of the tribunal of the world." Under these circumstances, Bentham predicted, any mistreatment of prisoners would quickly be detected, triggering the loss of a lucrative contract.[76]

The requirements of publishing accounts, of admitting all observers, and of entertaining questions from any quarter would not only make it easier to detect breaches of the basic rules against brutality; they would also—by stripping the contractor of trade secrets and other privileged information—ensure the *potential* competition that would keep the contractor on his toes. "Without such publication, who should I have to deal with, besides him? . . . *After* such publication, who should I have then? I should have every body; every body who, by fortune, experience, judgment, disposition, should conceive himself able and find himself inclined to engage in such a business." Bentham felt it prudent, if ungracious, to assume that prison contractors would be motivated by greed and constrained by only the most rudimentary moral scruples. Even so, he argued that competitive bidding, careful provisions to preserve potential competition, simple, unambiguous contracts, and extensive automatic monitoring would ensure accountability. "Gentlemen in the corn trade, or in any other trade, have not commonly quite so many witnesses to their bargains, as my contractor would have to the management of his house."[77]

What does *Panopticon* have to contribute to our modern private prison debate? We recognize a far broader range of prisoners' rights today, and the dimensions of accountability for modern prison contractors would exceed those limited parameters—no starving, no beating, no excess deaths—imposed upon the Panopticon manager. But Bentham's obsessive attention to monitoring remains all the more relevant. Even with so simple a set of contractual provisions, he called for overlapping layers of inspection and evaluation to enforce them—including official visits, constant observation by prisoners' family and friends, doors open to the public at large, and published accounts. As modern expectations are more extensive, modern monitoring provisions should be even more elaborate.

Will private prisons be adequately monitored? Proponents insist that they will be. "The claim that our level of visibility is so low that we will be able to cut corners is ludicrous," according to the president of the Corrections Corporation of America. "We are the highest profile people in corrections today."[78] And in fact this may be true—today. But will the press, the public, and the academics maintain their scrutiny as the incarceration industry matures? Nobody can say for sure. But it seems possible, indeed likely, that as private prisons become less novel, attention will flag.[79] Less visibility would mean less pressure on jurisdictions to hold private prisons accountable, and, correspondingly less vigorous enforcement of cost standards, quality standards, or both.

Even in the present infancy of the private prisons industry, monitoring efforts have sometimes proven inadequate. A study of private prison experiments commissioned by the National Institute of Justice found that "performance criteria were usually vague while procedures for conducting the monitoring were limited."[80] It is instructive to recall that governments frequently underspend on performance evaluation and oversight in areas other than corrections. For example, the Massachusetts legislature voted several million dollars in the 1970s to pay private nursing homes to take care of handicapped children, while allocating no funds at all for monitoring.[81] One might wonder whether a public that has refused to put up the resources to bring public prisons up to minimal standards will resist the temptation to turn a blind eye to the conditions of confinement in bargain-rate private prisons.

THE POTENTIAL FOR WARPING PUBLIC CHOICES

Public purchases differ from private purchases because *value* is a complex notion when preferences are plural and indirectly expressed. Some collective tasks, of course, are more difficult to value than others. Incarcerating malefactors, in the degree of indeterminacy of its real worth, more closely resembles dispatching a naval task force to intimidate potential enemies than it does sweeping city streets. The community demand for imprisonment, like its demand for military power, depends only in part on objective facts about the world, and perhaps in larger part on the shifting hopes and fears of the citizenry. Recall that the American incarceration rate is only loosely linked with the crime rate. Our feelings about crime, and not just the fact that some of us break laws, affect our inclination to lock people up.

Examining the origins of the now routine corrections "crisis"—citizens fear crime, want criminals incarcerated, but refuse to pay for prisons—likewise cautions against an exclusively rational approach to the imprisonment issue. In an area where policy is so heavily shaped by variable perceptions, and where the public capacity for delusion is so thoroughly demonstrated, it is prudent to consider the collective agenda's vulnerability to manipulation if we opt for private corrections. Three issues merit attention.

The first, and probably least disturbing, possibility is that privatization amounts to a fiscal sleight-of-hand that violates sensible procedures for committing public resources. Many jurisdictions are considering private corrections in the wake of bond referendums denying officials the funds to build public prisons in spite of severe undercapacity and even court orders to curb overcrowding.[82] Is this conflict between the imperatives of the ballot box and the imperatives of the judicial bench a problem that privatization can solve? Perhaps—if current capacity requirements are only temporary, if private firms have an edge in adjusting prison capacity, if the contracts are in fact (and not just in form) short-term and revocable, and if this logic is what drives the public's rejection of new construction. But this scenario is implausible on several counts.

Projecting the demand for prison space has proven hazardous. The crime-prone population is shrinking only slightly, the pestilence of drug abuse continues, and public sentiment in favor of tough sentencing shows no signs of abating.[83] Undercapacity thus may not be a transient problem. And unlike detention centers for aliens or juveniles, secure adult prisons require special structures with few alternative uses. If new prisons are built and the need for them subsequently drops, *somebody* gets stuck with the extra cell space. Corrections entrepreneurs—unless they are improbably short-sighted—will accept this risk only for a price, or will ensure that jurisdictions are effectively bound to renew what are technically short-run contracts. It seems unlikely that private firms have any special advantage in bearing the risk of overcapacity, and thus it is equally unlikely that a jurisdiction is better off contracting out for peak capacity than it is building its own facilities.

Budgetary gimmickry is probably a major factor in many privatization decisions. Bonds to build prisons usually must be cleared by referendum, while yearly appropriations to pay a corrections contractor need not. Contracting out, even if it turns out to cost more or deliver less in the long run, offers jurisdictions a way around the public's refusal to pay for the prison cells it insists on filling. Private corrections thus might debase the process of collective choice by obscuring information about the cost of incarceration. But it could also, conceivably, *improve* the flow of information. Several proponents have suggested that, by making more visible the link between costs and prison conditions, private contracting will help remedy the public's self-delusion and demonstrate that locking up criminals without violating their constitutional rights simply requires more money. Private facilities will be better (albeit more expensive) and will set standards to which public prisons (willingly, or under court orders) will aspire.[84] This is an interesting scenario. But the pitch for private prisons to date has generally emphasized lower costs far more than it has improvements in quality. And it seems imprudent to assume that the voters who have steadfastly refused resources to public prisons will suddenly be more forthcoming once the form of management changes.

A second factor concerns prison rules, indeterminate sentencing, and parole. The time a convict serves in prison depends on the crime he committed, the judge he happens to draw, and on sentencing guidelines. But it also depends in large part on his behavior while behind bars. All prisons have rules, and infractions are often punished by what are effectively extra prison terms—the denial of the "good time" that hastens parole. When a corrections contractor makes the rules, reports infractions, and recommends (or does not recommend) prisoners for parole, it takes on a far more central role in the justice system than simply managing the physical facilities. The American Civil Liberties Union bases its opposition to privatization squarely on its distaste for the prospect of mingling the profit motive with decisions about the length of confinement.[85]

The chief of one private detention center, in an effort to reassure critics raising fears of guards' arbitrary authority, said, "I review every disciplinary action. I'm the Supreme Court."[86] This should make us nervous. Will profit-seeking prisons multiply rules during slow periods in order to ensure enough infractions to deny parole to existing inmates until new convicts come to fill the cells? Not necessarily, perhaps not even probably, but it could happen. It is even conceivable that an unscrupulous corrections entrepreneur would perversely rig parole recommendations to release prisoners who are troublesome, dangerous, sickly, or otherwise expensive to detain, while holding on to the more profitable inmates. (By analogy, health maintenance organizations have been known to boost profits by fine-tuning their treatment and fee policies so as to attract more robust patients and discourage frail, elderly, or chronically sick patients.) Public prison officials are at least free of any direct financial temptation to manipulate the prison population.

The profit motive might not push prison operators to such extremes. And there are remedies—such as consigning discipline to a residual staff of civil servants; deputizing private guards; and setting up formal evaluation procedures for parole candidates. But these remedies will likely be incomplete, and they will certainly be costly. The problem of the "internal" justice system may not make the case against private corrections, but it is a major ethical and practical drawback.

A third factor concerns the ability of private corrections companies to influence officials and shape public opinion. There is always the possibility of simple corruption. There are also subtler efforts to sway public officials. "They have salesmen tell you what a great bunch of guys they are," said a Louisiana sheriff of corrections entrepreneurs, "and how they'd love to contribute to your campaign."[87] These are the universal dangers of public sector contracting, but the incarceration area presents a special cause for concern. Since public enthusiasm for imprisoning criminals is demonstrably variable, might it not vary in response to publicity campaigns orchestrated and paid for by firms with a financial interest in locking more people up? "With a 99-year lease, they're going to see to it that people are sentenced," warned an Illinois sheriff. "They're going to lobby against alternative programs, including probationary programs." A former Minnesota commissioner of corrections voiced similar fears: "Private operators whose growth depends upon an expanding prison population may push for ever harsher sentences. With the public's unabating fear of crime, and lawmakers shrinking from any move that appears to be soft on criminals, the developing private prison lobby will be hard to resist."[88] If public fear of crime is truly "unabating," of course, the private prison lobby will be simply redundant. The question is whether and to what extent public opinion on this issue can be altered by outside pressure and persuasion.

A fully developed incarceration industry would doubtless support trade groups with appropriately high-minded–sounding names (they could perhaps borrow "The Committee for Public Safety" from Robespierre) that would publicize crime statistics, contribute to campaigns for tough sentencing laws, and support law-and-order candidates. While "private prison operators will certainly lobby in their own behalf," one study argued, "it does not necessarily follow that they could manipulate public opinion and the law-making process as easily as their opponents suggest."[89] True enough. But the prospect of profit-motivated groups fanning the flames of popular vindictiveness is repulsive enough to make objectionable even a small chance that such lobbying would succeed.

What are the prospects for private prison management? The potential cost savings seem modest. There is little room for radical technical improvements in the business of locking people up. The cost of labor probably cannot be reduced by very much without lowering the quality of the workforce. Even if entrepreneurs succeed in cutting costs through better management, moreover, it is far from clear that there will be enough competition—especially once the first round of contracts is awarded—to ensure that taxpayers reap the savings.

It could be that there *is*, in fact, a good deal more scope for innovations in incarceration than I anticipate. If so, private proposals that turn on sound, verifiable new approaches might have considerable appeal. Another set of circumstances inviting privatization would be a continuing decay of prison conditions coupled with a consensus of despair over any other avenues of improvement. In this case, a fiscal sleight-of-hand involving private ownership could be the last chance for prisoners to be rescued from brutal overcrowding, and the last chance for citizens to be rescued from the self-delusion that allows them to betray constitutional norms. It is to be hoped, however, that we have not reached quite so desperate a pass.

If advocates have oversold the likely benefits of privatization, the worst fears of opponents are also far-fetched. Prison privatization will almost surely not mean a return to the chain-gang era. The extra organizational layer between government and inmates has proven quite permeable to the power of the courts, and there is no reason to expect that private prisons will brutalize inmates with impunity. The prison industry lobby will face resistance on several fronts in any attempts to engineer tougher sentencing laws. Yet the cost and trouble of guarding against these grim scenarios are themselves disadvantages of greater private involvement in corrections. And the risk remains that the worst case will happen after all.

I argued earlier that the symbolic dimension should not determine, on its own, the decision about private prisons. This is not to say, though, that the symbolism does not matter. Incarceration *is* a symbolically potent public function. We should stifle our uneasiness about introducing profits into punishment only for far more compelling reasons than the case for private prisons can summon.

CHAPTER 9

BUSINESS, GOVERNMENT, AND

JOB TRAINING

Late in 1982, Ronald Reagan signed the Job Training Partnership Act (JTPA) into law. "We are eliminating the bureaucratic and administrative waste that has characterized so many so called jobs bills in the past," he declared. The federal government would relinquish most direct responsibility for training, and limit its role to "cooperating and working with the private sector." The legislation signaled a vigorous repudiation of the Comprehensive Employment and Training Act (CETA), which had governed American training policy for a decade. Unlike CETA, JTPA called for the private sector to become heavily involved in designing and carrying out job training programs. Training goals would be precisely specified, closely monitored, and geared to the imperatives of the marketplace.[1]

In an era where better job training is prescribed as the remedy for social ills as fundamental and as diverse as widening class differences and ebbing international competitiveness, JTPA is a financially modest but symbolically significant initiative. (It is also the chief legislative achievement of then Senator Dan Quayle, who cosponsored the JTPA with Senator Edward Kennedy.) The Job Training Partnership Act was by no means so radical a reform of American manpower policy as it was sometimes advertised to be, but it did represent a marked shift from a process-based to a product-based structure of accountability. This chapter explores JTPA's "contractual" approach to subsidized training.

FROM CETA TO JTPA

While federal manpower programs go back at least as far as the New Deal's Works Projects Administration, the direct institutional antecedents of the JTPA first took root in the 1960s. The Area Redevelopment Act of 1961, although chiefly concerned with financing public works projects in depressed regions, included some federal funds for occupational training. The training effort gained both greater prominence and a sharp increase in funding with the Manpower Development and Training Act of 1962. This program was shaped and motivated by concerns that technological change was bringing about a mismatch between the skills of the American workforce and the requirements of industry—a theme that would recur intermittently throughout the next quarter-century. In its early 1960s version the fear was that factory automation would render huge numbers of production workers redundant while straining the supply of technicians to tend the new machines. Federal money would subsidize retraining—both in the class-room and on the job—to restore the balance.

Economic recovery and a shift in national anxieties quickly led to changes in legislative priorities, however. By the mid-1960s, it was clear that the unmanned factory was still some distance in the future, and that the economy could accom-modate displaced employees with no major disruption. Meanwhile, America was discovering poverty. As the War on Poverty got under way, the focus of man-power policy shifted away from workers at risk of displacement from established crafts, and toward Americans who had never found a place within the economic mainstream.[2]

By the early 1970s, there was a bewildering array of training, placement as-sistance, wage subsidy, and public employment programs run by different agen-cies, with different divisions of administrative and fiscal responsibility among the federal, state, and local governments, as well as among private companies. The varying mix of mandates included remedial training for the hardcore unemployed, adjustment assistance for the established worker, and countercyclical public job creation in order to buffer macroeconomic troubles. In 1973, most of these were brought together into the Comprehensive Employment and Training Act, the massive, multititled, and soon to be scorned CETA.

The central enterprise of the first year of CETA was to fund local-level class-room and on-the-job training programs. But in response to the 1974 recession, a new title authorizing expanded public employment was added to CETA, and by May 1975 some 300,000 people were put on city and county payrolls with federal money. Early on in the Carter administration, public employment leaped again, reaching its peak in 1978 at 750,000 workers.[3] Between 1975 and 1980, the federal employment and training budget (consisting mostly of CETA programs) surged from less than $5 billion to over $11 billion.[4] But spending on *training* programs remained relatively constant; the sharp increase in the manpower budget (and its subsequent shrinkage) was mostly a matter of subsidized jobs.[5]

There proved from the start to be a fundamental tension between the interests of the federal government and those of the local governments that were directly or indirectly responsible for hiring CETA workers. The federal government wanted to increase national employment through providing CETA funds to pay for employing workers who would otherwise be jobless. Local governments, conversely, were anxious to fill public jobs with people who would perform well, and were reluctant to take on unskilled, inexperienced, and disaffected workers. They preferred to use CETA funds to hire people very much like those already on the payroll; indeed, they found obvious advantages in using CETA funds to hire precisely the same people who would be hired anyway, thus freeing up local money for other uses.[6]

Congress tightened CETA eligibility standards in 1978, limiting subsidized public jobs to disadvantaged workers. But local governments, eager as they were for federal money to supplement their own strained payrolls, had little stomach for dealing with the problems of the hardcore unemployed. One consequence of the 1978 amendments was to inspire local officials to a surprising adeptness at finding candidates who technically met the eligibility standards but who were free of serious occupational deficiencies. Another result, common in jurisdictions less ingenious at circumventing the spirit of the law, was to relegate CETA employees to undemanding and generally unrewarding tasks. Public service and "work experience" positions increasingly came to be seen as "make work," and citizens generally failed to discriminate between these components (which eventually claimed the majority of CETA spending) and the smaller, less visible and more sensible training components. Public opinion soured on the whole enterprise. *Fortune* magazine declared CETA "a four-letter word."[7] *Reader's Digest*, a considerably more potent arbiter of popular perception, ridiculed CETA expenditures on projects like building an artificial rock for rock climbers to practice on in a park unendowed with natural promontories; a public service job slot for a "communist agitator" to organize "demonstration and confrontation"; and art classes for the blind.[8]

One of the Reagan administration's earliest, biggest, and most-relished budget cuts was the elimination of CETA's public service employment component. As the whole program came up for reauthorization in 1982, there was widespread support for restructuring to enlarge the private sector's role.[9]

The premise that CETA training had been wholly governmental, coupled with the judgment that it had been almost wholly ineffectual, fed support for a restorative shift toward private sector control. The prevailing perception was that manpower policy to date, lamentably, had been a matter of make-work government jobs and pointless classroom courses, all run by bureaucrats and community groups innocent of any labor market expertise. In fact, the private sector had been involved in training programs from the 1960s onward, albeit in different forms and to different degrees over the years. But the Job Training Partnership Act made American manpower policy more consistently and explicitly "businesslike," in three broad ways. First, it stipulated that business representatives would control local training programs. Second, it encouraged more reliance on private sector providers of training, both in the classroom and, especially, on the job. Third, it mandated a far more results-oriented, contractual approach to publicly funded manpower development.[10]

ORGANIZATIONAL STRUCTURE

Under JTPA the federal training budget is allocated among states by a formula based on the number of unemployed and disadvantaged citizens.* Governors, in turn, are expected to allocate most of the money among local programs by the same criteria.[11] While some state governments have sought to tailor JTPA to statewide needs and strategies, most have functioned chiefly as conduits of money to local training programs. In general, that way the real choices are made at the local level.[12]

Private Industry Councils, made up mostly of local business people, had been formed in 1978 to oversee a small business-oriented pilot program within CETA. Under JTPA, these councils took on a central role. The legislation specified that each local training program would establish a governing board with a majority of business members, a private sector chairman, and a minority of representatives

*Unless otherwise noted, references to JTPA budgets or requirements refer only to Title IIA, the main program for the economically disadvantaged (JTPA has a total of three major titles and several subtitles covering summer youth programs, programs for dislocated workers, pilot projects and research, and so on) that accounts for roughly half of all JTPA funding and participants.

from education, labor, community groups, and government agencies. The Private Industry Councils were to "provide policy guidance for, and exercise oversight with respect to, activities under the job training plan . . . in partnership with . . . local government."[13] The precise nature of this "partnership" is left open in the legislation, with the details to be worked out differently in each of the roughly six hundred local JTPA programs.

The Job Training Partnership Act and its accompanying regulations grant local programs wide discretion. The legislation bars virtually no plausible uses of funds and specifically endorses job counseling, placement assistance, remedial education, on-the-job training, literacy and English language training, "employment-generating activities," training programs tailored to specific industries and companies, "vocational awareness," and high school equivalency studies, among other approaches.[14] The definition of "economically disadvantaged" governing eligibility for subsidized training is not particularly restrictive, covering roughly the bottom one-fifth of the national income distribution. There are two main constraints on budget allocations. The first is that at least 40 percent of the money must be spent on training for youths age sixteen to twenty-one.[15] The second (a response to complaints about CETA's administrative costs) is that 70 percent of all funds allocated to local programs be spent on training per se, as opposed to administration, stipends for trainees, and so on.[16] Other legislative criteria are ambiguous, loosely enforced, and sometimes contradictory. Local programs are required to serve "those who can benefit from, and who are most in need of training opportunities."[17] (The law makes no mention of the very real possibility that these two criteria may not neatly coincide.) Congress directs that welfare recipients and high school dropouts "shall be served on a equitable basis," (with no definition of "equitable" offered).[18] Federal funds "shall only be used for activities which are in addition to those which would otherwise be available in the area in the absence of such funds."[19] In short, only *incremental* training should be subsidized.

Local JTPA programs generally do little training themselves, delegating most operations to outside organizations, including local education systems and community-based organizations as well as proprietary schools and private firms. While JTPA has not precipitated a complete transition to for-profit providers of training—public schools and community groups continue to provide classroom training, counseling, work socialization courses, and other services—in most local programs there has been a marked shift toward private suppliers, especially for on-the-job training. According to one study, two-thirds of local programs spent at least one-tenth of their training funds for on-the-job training contracts with private firms, while only one-half spent that much on contracts with public schools.

For-profit suppliers of classroom training are major providers for more local programs (39 percent) than are community colleges, the public employment service, or community-based organizations.[20] More to the point, even public and not-for-profit organizations have been affected by JTPA's sharpest organizational departure from CETA—a legislated, enforced emphasis on output-based measures of performance.

THE CONTRACTUAL APPROACH TO SUBSIDIZED TRAINING

The Job Training Partnership Act represents a shift away from input-based contracting with public organizations and toward output-based contracting with private organizations. This shift was entirely deliberate. During the congressional deliberations over CETA's successor, Senator Paula Hawkins argued that the proper federal role should be "an insistence that job training programs meet performance standards—not to dictate how such results should be accomplished." Another of JTPA's architects, Senator Orrin Hatch, said that "the new system will be based on performance, not process."[21]

The central assumption governing the 1982 JTPA reforms was that bureaucratic, process-oriented manpower policy had failed, and that an outcome-oriented system of accountability would mean better training, delivered more efficiently. This assumption summons the questions that the rest of this chapter attempts to illuminate. Does JTPA's contractual structure embody the social goals that justify public spending on training? Are contracts between the government and training suppliers sufficiently well specified to hold agents closely to account? If the contracts *are* specific enough to be enforceable, are they actually enforced?

The JTPA legislation characterizes job training as "an investment in human capital," and directs the secretary of labor to develop "criteria for measuring the return on this investment" and to translate these criteria into operational standards that local programs must meet.[22] Congress suggested standards based on increased employment, increased earnings, and lessened welfare dependency, and called for "cost-effective methods for obtaining such data as is necessary" to ascertain effectiveness.[23]

This is a deceptively formidable mandate. It is fairly easy to assess employment, earnings, and welfare status at any given point. It is a good deal harder to measure changes over time. And it is impossible, as the next section discusses, to confidently attribute such changes to subsidized occupational training without information systems far more elaborate and intrusive than a program advertised as lean and permissive could support. The performance measures that were actually established are, as they must be, much more limited. The congressional mandate to set standards for measuring the "return on investment in human capital" was translated by the Department of Labor into seven specific performance indicators. Each program year the Department of Labor issues national performance goals. Table 9.1 gives the standards for the first four JTPA program years. (A program year runs from July through the following June.)

TABLE 9.1
National Standards for JTPA Programs

Performance Indicator	National Standard	
	1984–86	1986–88
(For adults)		
Placement rate	55 percent	63 percent
Cost per placement	$5,704	$4,374
Average wage at placement	$4.91/hour	$4.91/hour
Placement rate for trainees on welfare	39 percent	51 percent
(For youths)		
Placement rate	41 percent	43 percent
"Positive termination" rate	82 percent	75 percent
Cost per positive termination	$4,900	$4,900

SOURCE: Department of Labor, Division of Performance Management and Evaluation, *Summary of JTLS Data for JTPA Title IIA and III Enrollments and Terminations during Program Year 1985* (Washington: November 1986) (hereafter Department of Labor, November 1986), 15. Burt Barnow and Jill Constantine, *Using Performance Management to Encourage Services to Hard-to-Serve Individuals in JTPA* (Washington: National Center for Employment Policy Research Report, April 1988), 6.

While governors may adjust the targets when local circumstances warrant (within limits set by the Department of Labor), the standards do have teeth. If a program fails to meet the standards for one year, the governor is required to offer technical assistance to the troubled locality. If a program misses the mark for two years running, the governor must impose a reorganization plan, which means restructuring the Private Industry Council, blacklisting certain training contractors, or assigning authority for the program to a completely separate entity.[24]

Under CETA, evaluation had dealt far more with process, and less with product.[25] The Department of Labor assessment schedule allocated only 40 out of 150 points to performance measures, with much greater effort devoted to eligibility verification, equal-opportunity compliance, and administration. For example, of the twenty-one local CETA programs cited for serious deficiencies in 1980, only three citations had anything to do with actual training as opposed to administration. (Two of *these* three, moreover, concerned procedural defects in the way the training was conducted.)[26] Under JTPA performance standards rule. Explicit, output-based goals harmonize with and reinforce the rhetorical shift toward low-cost training oriented to private-sector jobs, as well as the organizational shift to business-dominated governing boards. Table 9.2 summarizes overall national achievement on JTPA's performance standards during the program's first two full years.

TABLE 9.2
JTPA Performance Standards and Results

Indicator	Standard	Average Results	
		1984–85	1985–86
(For adults)			
Placement	55%	69%	70%
Average wage at placement	$4.91	$4.87	$4.92
Welfare-recipient placement	39%	58%	62%
(For youths)			
Placement	41%	57%	51%
"Positive termination"	82%	68%	64%

SOURCE: Department of Labor, November 1986, 16.

The JTPA system, on average, exceeded by wide margins the placement targets set for adults, welfare recipients, and youths. Over 90 percent of the local programs sampled in a 1986 evaluation met or exceeded all placement and cost-per-placement standards, without requiring adjustments.[27] The Department of Labor does not report national cost data, but independent tallies indicate that training costs beat the target by an average of 40 percent.[28] The wage standard, on the other hand, at times has proven difficult to attain. In the first year, the nationwide average wage at placement fell just short of the standard; in the second year it just cleared it. Roughly one-fifth of the local programs studied missed the target.

The "positive termination" category requires some explanation. The JTPA legislation and regulations cast job placement as the only legitimate outcome for adult trainees. For young people of ages sixteen to twenty-one, however, Congress directed that performance standards should count as successes not only job placement, but also trainees who return to school, enroll in apprenticeship programs, enlist in the armed forces, or achieve "employment competencies recognized by the private industry council." Even with so broad a definition of success, fewer than one-half of the sampled local programs met the 82 percent target.[29] Accordingly, while most other standards have been stiffened in the late 1980s as their ease became apparent, this one was relaxed substantially.

Placement is the polestar of JTPA. Private Industry Council members, local officials, and contractors define their success in terms of getting eligible people placed in jobs. The most extensive study of JTPA implementation found that 86 percent of public and private officials involved in the program cited "placement and cost performance" as key achievements.[30] An official of the Illinois state training agency declared that meeting the placement standards was "the limit of our responsibility; other things are not in the law."[31]

This focus on placement has meant a sharp change in contractual arrangements between program officials and the organizations that actually do the training. Under CETA, "service providers" were generally paid on the bases of enrollment, days spent in class, certifications granted, or other input and process measures. But JTPA holds local officials accountable for results, which has had the intent and the effect of inspiring a shift toward performance-based contracting. The change came quickly. A study of local programs during the nine-month launch period for JTPA (October 1983 to June 1984) found that by the end of the period 46 percent of all contracts were performance based, with payment at least partially contingent on trainees' finishing their programs and finding jobs.[32] By the first full year of operation, roughly two-thirds of all contracts were performance based, heightening the importance of ensuring tight links between contractual mandates and real social value.

CREATING VALUE THROUGH SUBSIDIZED TRAINING

The Job Training Partnership Act is founded on the notion that output-based contracting is the best way to hold accountable the agents charged with preparing disadvantaged citizens for more rewarding roles in the economy. After the disappointing experience with CETA, this is an appealing proposition. The central question, however, is how well contractual provisions capture the value created as participants pass through the system. Examining this question requires a closer look at human capital investment, and at the logic of collective efforts to affect manpower development.

Looming behind any discussion of manpower policy is the fact that, entirely aside from the subsidized training discussed in this chapter, the American economy makes massive investments in human capital. A 1983 study by the Bureau of Labor Statistics found that more than one-half of all American workers reported taking some kind of occupational training to qualify for their current jobs, and that about one-third had upgraded their skills on the job.[33] In 1980, federal, state, and local government budgets for human capital development—counting elementary, secondary, and higher education plus vocational and military training and other, smaller categories—totaled around $160 billion.[34]

Private manpower investment includes individual tuition payments, as well as the sums business spends to run its own training programs and to cover employee tuition. It also includes the costs of on-the-job training, most of which—wasted materials, botched jobs, wear and tear on equipment, extra supervision and administration, missed sales, irritated customers—are difficult to distinguish from regular production costs, and so are seldom reported as human capital investments. Finally, private investments include all of the work that individuals do not perform and all of the income that they fail to collect *now* while in training to increase their production and income *later*. Estimates of direct private spending on skill development, not including these latter two categories, are in the range of $30 to $40 billion per year.[35] If on-the-job training costs, and the income people sacrifice while in training, are counted as well, private investment in education and training is probably at least as large as public investment. (If an average of 10 million people per year each sacrifice an average of $15,000 in current income while in school or training—which seems a rather low estimate of the real value of both figures—the cost in foregone income alone would come to $150 billion per year.) Total annual investment in human capital development in the United States, then, is probably $300 billion or more, a figure comparable to national spending on medical care or on defense.

Federal manpower programs account for only a minuscule fraction of this total. The Labor Department's budget for training America's disadvantaged is not much bigger than the IBM training budget. (IBM spends over $1 billion a year on employee training, while JTPA IIA spending for training is on the order of $1.5 billion.)[36] Of the 11 million people who upgraded their skills in the course of their careers, only 375,000 did so through government-sponsored programs. Nearly 5 million people, by comparison, got their training in employer-sponsored programs.[37] In a workforce of around 100 million people, the tally of subsidized trainees has never been much more than 1 million per year. But a Rand Corporation study suggests that, at a minimum, 10 million workers each year get *employer*-sponsored training.[38]

In short, JTPA—like its antecedents, and almost surely like its successors as well—deals with only a small, albeit possibly crucial, part of the whole training picture. This fact only highlights the importance of the basic question: What should subsidized training *do?* Arguments for collective financing of human capital development proceed from two quite different lines of reasoning. The first invokes the logic of market failure; the second invokes social solidarity.

Market Failure Arguments

The case for some public financing of basic education turns on external benefits. We are all better off, both economically and otherwise, when our fellow citizens are literate, schooled in the fundamentals of civics, and partake to some degree of our common culture. Basic education confers broad social benefits, and so society at large should pay part of the cost. But the case for public financing of *occupational* training is less obvious. If training boosts productivity, it yields extra income for the worker, or extra profit for her employer, or both. So why should not workers or employers pay for training themselves? To a great extent, as the figures cited above attest, they do. Individual and business spending on occupational training far exceeds public spending. But there is reason to believe that market arrangements, on their own, would result in too little investment in human capital.

The market failure argument for manpower policy turns on a distinction between *general* and *specific* human capital. Economist Gary Becker first established the distinction.[39] General human capital increases a worker's productivity across a wide range of economic activities. An extreme type of general human capital is basic literacy or numeracy; a somewhat less general type would be training in the fundamentals of microelectronics. *Specific* human capital investments increase productivity in some narrowly defined enterprise; for example, training in how to diagnose and repair chip failures in a Digital Equipment Corporation VAX–780. Most skills, of course, fall between these poles.

If markets worked perfectly, the right arrangement would be simple: Workers should pay for investments in general human capital, and employers should pay for investments in specific human capital. For an employer to train a worker in a strictly firm-specific skill is much the same as equipping her with a truck, drill press, or word processor to increase her productivity on the job. The employer pays for firm-specific training—just as he pays for capital equipment—and rightly lays claim to the resulting gain in production. General training, by contrast, belongs to the worker. She carries it with her from job to job, commanding a higher wage by virtue of her greater productive powers. Since the employee reaps the gains from general human capital, she should pay for it, either through schooling at her own expense or by accepting lower wages during apprenticeship.

In the world of the economic textbook, workers would invest in general human capital up to the point at which further increases in productivity were canceled out by the costs of further training. Employers would follow a similar calculus in training their workers, and there would be no role for government in manpower development. But the real world presents a number of complications.

Consider some impediments to investment in firm-specific training. Suppose an entrepreneur hires a worker with so little general training that her only other options are minimum-wage jobs. The employer pays to have the worker schooled in firm-specific skills. If the employer does his calculations correctly, the sums he spends on her training will be about equal to the extra profits he anticipates from her future work. But the worker knows that her labors are now worth, say, ten dollars per hour to her employer. She may demand an increase in pay to seven dollars per hour—despite the fact that her higher productivity is solely due to the employer's investment—and threaten to quit unless she gets it. If she quits, the employer loses his whole investment. If he meets her demand he loses much of his anticipated return and would have been better off not making the investment. Unless he can get the worker to commit herself not to expropriate the payoff, the employer is likely to shun many potential investments in human capital in favor of more appropriable investments in physical capital.[40] Having the worker pay for firm-specific training merely rearranges the vulnerability to exploitation. If the worker invests in skills with limited uses outside the firm, an opportunistic employer can profit at her expense by refusing to boost her wages in line with her investment.

The legal prohibition against indentured servitude bars workers from committing themselves to stay on the job after training. Resourceful companies and workers have found ways to circumvent this impediment—delaying the vesting of pension rights in order to retain workers, for example.[41] And a sense of loyalty and fair play in the workplace can often go far beyond contract law in allowing employers and employees to undertake such investments. But there is still reason to suspect that too little investment in specific human capital takes place.

Now consider *general* human capital. Training that increases productivity across a range of economic activities lets a worker command premium wages. So why would individuals fail to make the right level of investment in their own skills? One possible barrier is the imperfection of the financial markets. When a company buys a major new asset, it can usually borrow most of the money, using the asset for collateral and paying off the loan over time with the proceeds from the investment. Since people are legally barred from offering creditors a claim on their more-productive future selves as security for a loan, they may be unable to tap regular credit markets to finance human capital investments. If training must be financed out of savings, or out of cuts in consumption, individuals may spend too little on it.[42]

Even if people could easily finance human capital investments, they might have considerable difficulty in choosing the right kind of training to get, or the right sources from which to obtain it. Vocational training is a very long-lived asset. Making prudent human capital investments, in the face of a bewilderingly variable labor market, may require more economic sophistication than most people possess. The average American makes too few of such investments to develop great expertise in weighing the claims of alternative purveyors of training. Knowing of their inability to buy training wisely, or to accurately project the return on high-level skills, people may shun such investments. And even if they had extensive information about the cost and expected returns of various levels of human capital, people contemplating investments in training are exposed to the risk that the demand for skills will change, or that they have miscalculated the expected return. The same can be said, of course, about people contemplating investments in real estate or machinery. But investors in physical assets can *spread* that risk by selling shares in the undertaking. Human capital investments offer much less opportunity for diversification.[43]

While these barriers to investment in human capital have not demonstrably deterred substantial private spending on education and training, they almost surely *do* keep manpower development below its ideal level. *Public* investments can be seen as attempts to remedy these flaws in the market. But public spending to increase citizens' productivity is frequently promoted on quite different grounds.

Social Arguments

Occupational training most often appears on the public agenda as an instrument of antipoverty policy. The poor are disproportionately unskilled, and the perennial appeal of training programs for the disadvantaged reflects, in part, pragmatic judgments that making the poor employable will simply be cheaper than supporting them in idleness. But the proverb, "Give a man a fish and you feed him for a day; teach him to fish, and you feed him for life" (a proverb that seems to show up at some point in most writings on manpower policy), is not really about least-cost methods for dealing with the poor. The work ethic remains strong in America, and antipoverty training programs are popular *not* primarily because job training is seen as less expensive than welfare dependency, but because it is seen as morally preferable. A majority of Americans probably would favor subsidized training for the poor even if they were convinced that permanent income support would put less of a strain on the public purse.

Many current proposals for expanded job training programs also appeal, directly or indirectly, to economic nationalism. As the world economy becomes more integrated, international companies have broader options about where to locate various productive operations, ranging from research and administration to routine assembly and file-tending. While firms may be indifferent as to the choice between skilled labor, unskilled labor, automation, and overseas labor—selecting solely on the basis of costs and productivity—communities may *not* be indifferent. Citizens may prefer that their fellows be highly skilled and highly productive, and may care about the share of the world's more sophisticated work that takes place within their borders. A community might value a technologically proficient citizenry for reasons of security, independence, or simple pride, whatever the economic calculations.

Different rationales for manpower policy imply different (and not always consistent) goals and tactics. One response to the contractual problems that discourage human capital investments might be to adjust contract law to permit more binding long-term employment and wage agreements. Firms could be allowed to sue trained employees who quit before an agreed-upon interval, for example. (It is worth remembering, however, that there were reasons why we barred indentured servitude in the first place.) Or the government could produce (or certify) labor market projections, and regulate or standardize the claims of private training institutions in order to allow people to make human capital investments with better information and correspondingly greater confidence.

Beyond such attempts to mitigate market failures are more aggressive options for government action. We could decide that job training, like national defense, simply cannot be handled through private investment decisions but should be collectively financed. Perhaps workers or firms or both should be allowed to claim full tax credits for human capital investments. Or the government could establish public training programs open to all workers, or issue vouchers for training at nongovernmental institutions. "Just as government provides incentives for expanded business capital and technology investment," economist Pat Choate has argued, "it must offer incentives to stimulate investment in workers."[44]

But collective financing for *all* manpower development would mean something like a hundred-fold increase in the public training budget. Such a wholesale change, moreover, would squander much of the information that individuals and firms generate when they make their own decisions, with their own money, about human capital investments. Dispensing completely with the market would mean a different sort of inefficiency, but not necessarily less of it, than relying completely upon the market. The ideal seems to be a policy of *selective* intervention, using collective resources to fine-tune market forces.

Anything short of universal public financing, though, presents the problem of determining what training would take place *without* intervention. Choate's proposal, for example, includes the refinement that subsidies should apply "only to new efforts above and beyond present training and upgrading efforts." In much the same spirit, the JTPA legislation specifies that program funds "shall only be used for activities which are in addition to those which would otherwise be available."[45] This is undeniably a sensible proviso, but rather more difficult to put into effect than it seems at first blush.

In the case of on-the-job training, should we take "present efforts" to mean the training budget for each firm in the year the subsidy legislation passes? Or some average of the previous several years? What if the firm is growing, and would be expected to boost training anyway—or is shrinking, and would be expected to cut training? How much of the cost of on-the-job training (where learning is a by-product of marketable production) should be attributed to skill development? It is obviously in the firm's interest to depict as "incremental" as large as possible a portion of its training budget, and it is difficult to determine, from outside the organization, just what to take as the baseline.

The same problem appears if we shift attention from the corporation to the individual. Despite the impediments discussed above, most people make some investment in their own skill development. Some manage to invest just the right amount, and some doubtless invest too much. If the community prefers not to take on itself the whole burden of human capital development, how—without peering inside the mind of each potential trainee—can it know how much training people would pay for on their own without subsidies?

This is the same dilemma that arises when the federal government tries to increase corporate research and development spending through tax subsidies, or when a municipal government tries to lure office developers with various inducements, or, for that matter, when the U.S. tries to bolster European military defenses by supplementing the expenditures of its NATO allies. Unless it can distinguish *incremental* investments from investments that would take place in any event, the government may simply be shouldering more of the burden without increasing overall spending. The windfall problem bedevils any strategy of fine-tuning market mechanisms. Common sense insists that there must be some middle ground between a wholly public training system and a wholly private one. But the elusiveness of valid information about private willingness to pay for training makes that middle ground a mysterious bit of terrain.

The policy implications discussed so far have dealt mostly with market failure motives for intervention. Are the policy options linked to noneconomic motivations more tractable? They might be. Market failure strategies generally imply collective financing of *some* of the training costs for *most* people, while antipoverty motives imply collective financing of *most* of the training costs for *some* people. To the extent that subsidized training is restricted to the poor, the cost can be limited, and there seems to be less reason to worry about displacing private training investments. The poor do not invest much in their own training, presumably, since they have little money. If they are out of work, they are clearly not getting employer-sponsored training. If they *are* employed, it must be in marginal jobs where little is spent on skill development—otherwise, why would they be poor? When no human capital investment is going on, anything that results from public intervention counts as a net gain. Thus there are appealing practical reasons—beyond the obvious moral arguments—for focusing training programs on the disadvantaged.

Some problems remain, however. First, while the poor *do* get less training than other people, they still get some, so there is still a risk that government programs can substitute for private investments instead of supplementing them. (A 1980 survey of poor jobless Americans found that 11 percent of the men and 12 percent of the women got some training during the previous 17 to 21 months.)[46] Second, when public officials run targeted training programs with collective resources, there will generally be a degree of imprecision and inefficiency compared to the training decisions individuals and firms make on their own. Because of the extra organizational complexity, and the consequent muddying of accountability, it is somewhat more likely that the wrong people will be trained, or that the wrong skills will be emphasized, or that the training will be conducted inefficiently.

The third problem is that *the poor* is a generic term for a large and diverse group of people with different goals, different kinds of problems, and different capacities and inclinations to benefit from subsidized training. Should priority go to those in the direst circumstances, with the dimmest prospects for self-sufficiency in the absence of intervention? Or should it go to those who are best able to parlay job training into a permanent escape from poverty? If the former, at what level of disaffection, disability, or despair do we conclude that training is pointless and prescribe welfare instead? If the latter, how do we justify the exclusion of near-poor workers who may end up with worse labor market prospects than the recipients of subsidized training? The Job Training Partnership Act, as noted above, simply directs that resources will be concentrated on "those who can benefit from, and those most in need" of training, with no guidance as to the relative weights to put on these two potentially discordant criteria beyond calling for "equitable" treatment of different segments of the eligible population.[47]

The fourth problem is slightly complex, but crucial. Recall that roughly the poorest 20 percent of the American population is eligible for subsidized training under JTPA. Most people who are poor at some point in their lives escape poverty. It sometimes happens that the starving young artist becomes rich and famous. It frequently happens that the children of penniless immigrants become doctors and lawyers. And it routinely happens that people who slip for a time below the poverty line return, if not to affluence, at least to solvency.[48] Large numbers of the poor increase their incomes each year—more in a boom year, fewer in recessions—by virtue of talent, hard work, maturation, marriage, or simple good luck. This does not soften the hard truth that many other poor people stay poor. But it does vastly complicate efforts to assess the effect of manpower policies with an antipoverty rationale.

A training program for the disadvantaged creates value when, as a result of training, a participant's productivity and earnings exceed what they *would have been* absent any intervention.* In any random sample of poor Americans at any given time, a few are fated for prosperity, some for a modest but stable niche in the workforce, some for several years more of poverty and dependency, and some for deepening misery. We can easily observe a trainee's status *before* and *after* participation, but such comparisons conflate the whole gamut of forces determining a worker's prospects. The real effect of training programs is the difference created between each person's fate *with* and *without* the program. This we can never know for certain, and only by means of considerable care and effort can we know approximately. When a trainee earns dramatically more (or just the same, or less) after the program, it may be because the training was highly valuable (or ineffective, or harmful) or because she was, for entirely unrelated reasons, on an upward (or stagnant, or downward) earnings path. The *average* measured effect of a training program depends in part on the value the program creates. But it also depends on the mix of participants: With a larger proportion of high-potential trainees, the program looks better; with a larger proportion of low-potential trainees, it looks worse, *no matter what* real but unobserved changes take place in the prospects of participants. The true impact of manpower policies, in other words, can be either more or less than meets the eye.

---

*This is strictly true only under full employment; if any nonparticipant loses a job to a participant, the waste due to his unemployment must be netted out.

In a world far richer than our own in information, performance-based training contracts would be easier to arrange and enforce. Imagine that the Private Industry Council, its governmental partners, and a collection of rival contractors all shared complete information about each potential trainee. An eligible citizen walks through the door, and by some means—it does not matter for purposes of this fantasy whether through an exhaustive analysis of his educational and sociological characteristics or by reading his palm—everybody knows what kinds of jobs he can hope to obtain, how productive he will be, and what wages he can expect to command for the rest of his life, given his current stock of human capital. When he is assigned to some attitude-improvement seminar, or to a course in engine repair, or to a regime of on-the-job training, it is obvious at each point (and especially at the end of the training) what his *new* prospects are. Everyone knows when training creates value. Alternative types of training, and alternative training organizations, can be readily compared. In such a fantasy world, it would make eminent sense to let organizations simply bid on the basis of price, and to compete to add productive value to the people they train.

In the real world, though, human capital is hard to measure. The greater the uncertainty over a participant's prospects (both before and after training), the less precisely can the value created in the course of the training be assessed. The less measurable is value, the less efficient is contracting for manpower development. Superior training organizations will be less able to capitalize on their expertise and, if motivated chiefly by profits, will be correspondingly less driven to develop expertise. Training organizations with wasteful approaches or sloppy management will be less likely to face penalties, and correspondingly less anxious to improve.

Data Constraints on Performance Contracting

The more information is available, the more realistic and efficient performance contracting will be. But knowledge is expensive, and the federal government has opted to limit spending on information about JTPA. In the year between its passage and its implementation, the Labor Department designed a JTPA information system requiring local programs to report in some detail on the characteristics and employment experience of each trainee before participation, at the end of training, and at a thirteen-week follow-up interview. Smaller samples of participants would be analyzed at greater length both before and after participation, and would be compared with a large control group for a finer estimate of the value added by training. But the Office of Management and Budget protested that so elaborate a measurement system would be unduly expensive and intrusive.[49]

The information system the Office of Management and Budget finally allowed includes only gross indicators of pretraining characteristics: sex; race; age; employment experience in the past one-half year; welfare status (food stamps, AFDC, or other); handicapped status; veteran status; educational level.[50] The plans for large-scale studies comparing participants with otherwise-similar nonparticipants— before training, and at six-month, twelve-month, and two-year intervals after training—were also scrapped.[51] Between 1980 and 1984, as the process-oriented CETA gave way to the declaredly performance-oriented JTPA, the performance evaluation budget of the Employment and Training Administration fell by around 66 percent, while the evaluation staff shrank from thirty-eight to five.[52]

The *before* information about JTPA participants, in short, is highly limited. The *after* information is restricted to whether participants found a job at some point soon after training and how much that job paid (as reported by contractors and local programs according to rather broad-minded definitions of "placement"). The following sections use what information exists to explore the link between the contractual provisions of JTPA, the patterns of participation and of training that result, and the logical requirements for creating value through subsidized training.[53]

Patterns of Participation

To be eligible for subsidized training, a citizen must have a family income below either of two alternative definitions of relative poverty, or be on some form of public assistance. He need not be unemployed, and there are no restrictions on either the degree or the duration of economic disadvantage. Baseline data from the 1980 Census identify 43 million Americans as disadvantaged by these criteria, including 29 million who are old enough for JTPA training.[54] Moreover, up to 10 percent of participants with special "barriers to employment"—including the handicapped, older workers, veterans, alcoholics and drug addicts, ex-offenders, and "displaced homemakers"—may be exempted from any means test.[55] Out of this universe of potential participants, the number of actual participants is roughly 1 million per year. In other words, something like one out of thirty eligibles gets training.

By what criteria are the few participants to be chosen from among the many eligibles? Aside from the stipulation that 40 percent of the funds must go for training young people, and repeated exhortations to serve welfare recipients, and other subgroups "equitably," the selection of participants is left up to local programs officials and contractors.

Table 9.3 summarizes the overall pattern of participation in the JTPA. The first column gives a breakdown of participants by sex, race, welfare status, and education. The second column shows each group's representation in JTPA enrollment relative to its proportion of the eligible population. For example, Hispanics constitute 10 percent of actual enrollees, but are closer to 11 percent of the eligible population; thus they are underrepresented by about 9 percent relative to strictly proportional participation.

TABLE 9.3
Participation Patterns in JTPA Programs

Category	Percentage share of trainees	Relative representation (by percent)
Male	46	Overrepresented by 9 percent
Female	52	Underrepresented by 7 percent
White	55	Underrepresented by 13 percent
Black	32	Overrepresented by 39 percent
Hispanic	10	Underrepresented by 9 percent
Welfare recipients	40	Underrepresented by 15 percent
No high school diploma	40	Underrepresented by 22 percent
At least high school	60	Overrepresented by 23 percent

The U.S. General Accounting Office examined *changes* in participation between 1980 (under CETA) and 1984 (under JTPA), and found that the same groups that are underrepresented in JTPA generally suffered a drop in participation in the shift. (The exception is blacks, who are overrepresented in JTPA programs, but were still more overrepresented in CETA programs.) The proportion of high school dropouts fell 23 percent, while graduates rose 17 percent. The unemployed, women, and minorities all fell slightly as a fraction of total trainees, while the fractions of whites, of the employed or recently employed, and of males increased.[56] In other words, the pattern of participation hints at a shift toward the less disadvantaged, more employable fraction of the large and diverse pool of citizens eligible for JTPA training.

Anecdotes and commentary from manpower policy specialists have emphasized a pattern of "screening" or "cream-skimming" in which local JTPA programs and contractors systematically select the more promising candidates for training while weeding out the troubled and troublesome, the untalented, and the disaffected. The head of one agency reported that under JTPA, his organization had changed its mission from "taking the tough cases, to becoming an efficient personnel office for local businesses."[57] The director of a Boston training organization operating under JTPA contracts has explained: "Of course we're going to pick candidates from the pool available who we think are most likely to succeed. The problem is if you get fifteen people eligible, and you take ten, the five you don't take are the ones who need extra help." But accepting the harder cases means that "it might be difficult to meet the performance standards."[58]

A study of twenty-five local programs found that they "have largely spurned the 'most in need' issue as a vague exhortation amidst seven clearly stated performance standards by which they are judged."[59] The prevalence of performance-based contracts in JTPA programs has meant that "service providers choose program participants very carefully."[60] There is some evidence of especially intense screening by proprietary vocational schools, where performance-based contracting, coupled with the concentrated financial incentives of private ownership, makes low-potential trainees particularly unattractive. A for-profit organization training bank tellers screened 118 applicants to fill 19 training slots, for example, and another proprietary school accepted only 1 out of 25 applicants.[61]

Most local programs expect applicants to take the initiative in seeking training, which tends to weed out the less motivated even prior to any formal screening. About one out of every six local programs has formal arrangements whereby schools, community groups, or social workers recruit people who need training; few report that they explicitly instruct contractors to recruit and train people from especially disadvantaged groups. But most make little or no provision for countering the powerful incentives to select the most "job-ready" applicants.[62]

Table 9.4 displays the rate of participation of various demographic groups, each group's rate of post-training job placement relative to the rate for all groups, and its relative wage at placement. The table also records (in the second column) whether the participation of each group in manpower programs rose, fell, or stayed the same during the transition from CETA to JTPA.

Blacks remain overrepresented and whites underrepresented, despite a higher relative placement rate for whites. But for every other group, the level of representation under JTPA parallels the group's relative ease of placement. The same relationship usually holds between the representation of each group and the average wage earned at placement. Without exception, every group that showed an *increase* in its proportion of total trainees in the transition to JTPA tends to score better than average on placement and wages. With one exception—Hispanics—every group that decreased in its proportion of total trainees tends to score worse than average. In short, the evidence on nationwide patterns of participation suggests that local programs and contractors tend to select trainees with an anxious eye to wage and placement standards.

TABLE 9.4

JTPA Participation and Placement (by group)

Group	Representation relative to overall average (by percent)	Change 1980–84	Placement relative to overall average (by percent)	Wage at placement relative to overall average (by percent)
Blacks	139	fell	89	95
Graduates	123	rose	115	107
Males	109	rose	102	106
Females	93	fell	98	94
Hispanics	91	fell	98	100
Whites	87	rose	106	102
Welfare recipients	85	same	92	96
Dropouts and students	78	fell	72	87

SOURCE: Derived from Department of Labor, division of performance management and evaluation, compilations from the *Summary of JTLS Data for JTPA Title IIA and III Enrollments and Terminations* (Washington: November 1984, November 1986); and General Accounting Office, *The Job Training Partnership Act: An Analysis of Support Cost Limits and Participant Characteristics* (Washington: November 1985).

The data displayed here, moreover, reflect only those few trainee characteristics for which national breakdowns are published. Within the broad categories of *men, women, Hispanics, dropouts, welfare recipients,* and so on, there is room for enormous variation in experience, ability, motivation, and other factors affecting need for training, ability to benefit from it, and prospects for placement with *or without* any increment in human capital. Training specialist Michael E. Borus has identified some forty "personal variables" affecting labor market success. Certain of these variables ("skills and abilities" and "access to transportation") can be readily altered by government programs. Others (such as "perceived limitations on ability" and "attitude toward working") can be changed only with difficulty. Still others ("age," "intelligence level," and "attitudes of other family members toward work") are largely or entirely resistant to intervention.[63]

Local training officials and contractors will often be able to *observe* such characteristics—through means such as interviews, application forms, data-sharing with welfare and social agencies—even when they cannot *affect* them. Recall that roughly one-half of the poverty population at any given time consists of those who (for a myriad of reasons) are destined for many years of dependency. The other one-half are the transitory poor, who will escape from poverty fairly quickly. We know that the JTPA system tends to enroll high school graduates, males, and other groups with good average placement prospects at a higher rate than it does dropouts, females, and other groups with poor average placement prospects. Given this pattern, it would be surprising if the one welfare recipient out of twenty-five who participates in JTPA, for example, comes from the least promising fraction of that diverse group. Similarly, it seems likely that JTPA tends to take in the less troubled dropouts, the less encumbered women, the Hispanics who speak better English, and so on.

Local JTPA programs, in sum, have more detailed information about participants than has the Department of Labor. Training contractors usually have better information than have local officials. Performance standards provide officials and contractors with powerful incentives to select, from the universe of eligibles, those trainees most likely to succeed—with or without intervention. Anecdotes, incentives, and the statistical data all strongly suggest that, with one systematic exception (blacks are overrepresented), the norm in JTPA is to recruit participants who are likely to fare relatively well in any event.

The significance for the broader issue addressed in this chapter—does JTPA's contractual system constrain agents to create value?—is that the pool of eligibles is large enough and diverse enough that painstaking screening *alone* goes far enough to explain much of the impressive placement and wage scores, whether or not there is any real value added. Ivy League graduates indisputably tend to earn more, over the course of their careers, than the national average. If Ivy League schools selected their students randomly, this would be clear evidence that sitting through four years of lectures boosted their earning power. But students are not selected randomly. The screening process is sufficiently rigorous that the people selected for admission would *still* tend to earn more than average even if they spent their four years in the Peace Corps, or learning to play the harp, instead of attending classes in prestigious settings. It is impossible to distinguish conclusively between the value *added* by the professors and the value *identified* by the admissions office. A similar uncertainty complicates JTPA's contractual system of accountability.

Patterns of Training

Manpower policy features four broad categories of assistance: classroom instruction, on-the-job training, placement assistance, and work experience programs. Table 9.5 shows how the allocation of people and money has changed with the transition from CETA to JTPA.[64]

Table 9.5 illustrates a pronounced tilt toward the kinds of training that most expeditiously pump up placement rates. Next, consider changes in the allocation of trainees *within* a single category, on-the-job training. Table 9.6 displays the breakdown of on-the-job trainees in 1980 and 1985; the change in each group's

TABLE 9.5

Changing Training Patterns 1980–85

	Percentage change in enrollment 1980–85	Percentage placement rate 1985	Average days of participation per placement*
Work experience	−84	42	323
Classroom training	−19	54	233
On-the-job training	+80	76	131
Job-search assistance	+535	75	34

*Average days of participation per placement is derived from the average days of training per participant, the termination rate, and the placement rate.
SOURCE: Derived from Robert Taggart, *A Fisherman's Guide: An Assessement of Training and Remediation Strategies* (Kalamazoo, Mich.: W.E. Upjohn Institute, 1981), 22 (hereafter referred to as Taggart, *A Fisherman's Guide*); and Department of Labor, Statistical Appendix B, November 1986.

share of on-the-job training slots; and each group's placement rate, relative to the average for all on-the-job trainees.

TABLE 9.6

On-the-job Trainees

	CETA 1980	JTPA 1985	Percentage change	Relative placement rate, 1985
Male	63	56	−11	97%
Female	37	44	+19	103%
White	60	65	+ 8	104%
Black	26	22	−15	92%
Hispanic	11	10	− 9	99%
Under 22	33	30	− 9	90%
22 or over	67	70	+ 5	106%
Dropouts	33	25	−24	100%
Graduates	65	72	+11	101%

SOURCE: CETA figures are based on Department of Labor data reprinted in Taggart, *A Fisherman's Guide*, 36; JTPA figures are from Department of Labor, Statistical Appendix B, November 1986.

With the transition to a performance-based evaluation system, more on-the-job training slots have been reserved for participants who are relatively easy to place. In four of the five cases where group representation declined, that group had a lower than average placement rate. In all four cases where group representation increased, that group had a placement rate higher than average.

A 1988 General Accounting Office study, covering 5,500 participants in sixty-three local programs, confirmed that applicants who were less "job-ready" received less intensive training than did people who could be more easily placed in jobs. What training they *did* receive, moreover, tended to be in low-skill occupations like custodial work, housekeeping, or laundering.[65]

The pattern is straightforward and quite consistent. The more quickly and reliably a type of training leads to placement, the greater the emphasis on that type of training. The assignment of trainees across programs also accords with the imperative to maximize placement rates. In sum, the evidence supports the proposition that the pattern of training in the JTPA is strongly placement-driven. Of course, this is precisely what one would expect from the contractual arrangements of the JTPA system. This is what players in the system *say* they are doing. Local officials, contractors, and the legislators and federal officials who crafted the system all would argue that this is the whole idea of moving from a bureaucratic, process-oriented manpower policy to a businesslike, output-oriented policy. JTPA works, in the sense that its structure of incentives animates and enforces the mandate to get people placed in jobs. The question, though, is how closely this mandate reflects real social value.

PLACEMENT AS A MEASURE OF VALUE

One basic problem is that neither the JTPA nor Department of Labor regulations define job placement with much precision. (In a much-ballyhooed 1988 reform, a trainee was required to keep his job for thirty days for a placement to count. Prior to that, one day on the job was usually enough.) Those states that have developed criteria more restrictive than "working for some time, in some job, at some point after training," have such varied standards that national compilations are very close to meaningless. Graduates may be given two to six months to find a job before they are recorded as *not* placed. Participants who drop out at any point are generally not counted at all, which allows considerable scope for fudging the statistics. For example, a research team found that many Illinois training organizations routinely delay submitting paperwork on trainees until they have ascertained which of them have good job prospects lined up. By officially enrolling only the best bets, they prop up their reported placement rates.[66] Since the JTPA information system has no long-term follow-ups and no provisions for comparing trainees with nonparticipants, it is impossible to say with certainty how well the placement figures measure real value creation. There *is*, however, some suggestive evidence from earlier training programs.

Late in the CETA era, as doubts about the program mounted, there were efforts to develop performance indicators. Michael Borus studied 323 people who had graduated from government training programs several years previously. He used multiple regression analysis to explain postprogram differences in earnings, employment, and welfare dependency as between participants and nonparticipants, controlling for twenty-four separate variables including education, race, sex, age, and preprogram employment and earnings.[67] Participants, on average, did turn out to work and earn more, and to collect less welfare, than did nonparticipants.[68] But Borus discovered that no short-term indicator worked very well as a proxy for long-run benefits.

Having a job one month after training—corresponding to the newly stiffened placement standard in JTPA—was a valid but weak proxy. It explained only about 7 percent of long-run earnings gains, and had no significant link to long-run weeks worked per year, reduced welfare dependency, or any other benefits. Whether or not a participant finished his training curriculum proved to be a slightly better proxy than short-run job placement.[69] The only truly powerful proxy, Borus found, was staying off welfare for at least thirty days after training, a measure that has no counterpart in the JTPA.

Short-term results may also be weak measures of the *relative* effectiveness of different types of training. One large-scale study compared CETA participants with a matched sample of nonparticipants drawn from the Census Bureau's Current Population Survey. The first year after training, on-the-job trainees reported earnings increases two and one-half times as large as those of classroom trainees. But one year later, annual benefits had risen for classroom trainees and fallen for on-the-job trainees, and the apparent advantage of on-the-job training had narrowed sharply.[70]

The average length of classroom training decreased by 40 percent in the transition from CETA to JTPA.[71] If the real value of an additional week in the classroom drops off fairly rapidly, this can be credited to JTPA's results-oriented ethic as a sound economic move. One training expert, however, has found evidence of a positive link between the length of classroom training and postprogram earnings and employment gains.[72] But this link only shows up over time, as table 9.7 displays. In the short-term, studies from the CETA era show little benefit from additional time in the classroom. The extra gain develops well beyond the time horizon covered by JTPA's contractual system.

Research from the CETA era suggests that the long-term benefit of on-the-job training comes largely from workplace socialization, not actual skill development, and that such socialization is most useful to people who are weakly attached to the labor force. In other words, the "general" skills imparted are cultural and psychological rather than technical. Large-scale comparison group studies suggest

TABLE 9.7

Employment Rates of CETA Classroom Trainees

Length of training	Percent employed three months after training	Percent employed two years after training
Two months or less	44	55
More than two months	43	60
More than six months	46	65

SOURCE: Department of Labor data reprinted in Taggart, *A Fisherman's Guide*, 221–22.

that young people and minorities reap somewhat greater benefits from on-the-job training—presumably because fewer of them have ever held good jobs before—than do adults and whites.[73] But whites and adults are better placement prospects. The imperative of postprogram placement dominates the logic of long-term benefits in JTPA: White participants are more than twice as likely as blacks to fill on-the-job training slots, and participants over twenty-one are more than twice as likely as younger applicants to be assigned to on-the-job training.

All of this is *not* to charge that those making allocation decisions in JTPA are perverse, or bigoted, or careless. It is not that PICs, local officials, and training contractors *disregard* long-run effects; they cannot *observe* long-run effects. The point is that short-run placement has been assigned a far more central role to play in JTPA's contractual system than so feeble a proxy can carry off.

CONTRACTING FOR ON-THE-JOB TRAINING

The JTPA legislation expressly forbids subsidized employment (with the exception of limited work-experience programs for young people).[74] But it allows, and even encourages, local programs to pay up to one-half of the wages of eligible workers undergoing training while working for profit-seeking firms. Probably the most important difference between CETA and JTPA is the expanded role of on-the-job training. The contracts governing the relationships between the trainee, his employer, and JTPA officials are correspondingly central.

The intuitive appeal of assigning to profit-making firms the responsibility for delivering training is considerable. Who knows the value of skills better than do the people on the buyer side of the labor market? Many firms already do a good deal of formal and informal training, and are already equipped with machines, material, and staff expertise. Most generally, organizations that are accustomed to facing competition and to meeting a payroll, the logic goes, should be leaner, more tightly run, and better able to deliver value for money than the public agencies and community nonprofits that dominated the delivery of training services under CETA.

There are several ways in which subsidized on-the-job training, in principle, can create public value. An employer can endow trainees with *general* skills. This is the idea behind apprenticeship programs in trades like construction or plumbing. Training in general skills creates value the employer cannot appropriate, which is why someone else (the trainee, his parents, or the government) must pay for apprenticeship training, either directly or by providing an appropriate amount of low-wage labor. (When the young Benjamin Franklin left Boston midway through his apprenticeship to a printer—after he had learned the trade, but before he had worked his appointed term—he was, in effect, skipping out on a debt.)

On-the-job training can amount to subsidized work in disguise and still be valuable, under certain conditions. Suppose the community has a legitimate political commitment to improving the job prospects of a particular group of people. If on-the-job training contracts lead companies to increase their hiring of people who would otherwise be jobless or underemployed, then (though it is somewhat disingenuous to declare them *training* subsidies instead of temporary wage subsidies) payments to employers could buy something of value to the community.

Another way in which such subsidies can create value, even without developing general human capital, is somewhat more subtle. Assume that, first, productive potential cannot be fully observed. An employer cannot be certain how intelligent, honest, diligent, and adaptable a job applicant will turn out to be. Suppose, next, that members of certain groups—high school dropouts, for example—tend *on average* to be bad bets. *Some* dropouts would make spendid employees, but the employer cannot know which ones they are. He may thus choose to avoid the whole group. This is bad for the employer, bad for the high-potential dropouts, and bad for society as a whole. Temporary subsidies for on-the-job training could alleviate this problem if they compensate the employer for the costs and risks of experimenting with classes of workers he would otherwise shun.

So subsidies for on-the-job training may create value if they lead to the development of general human capital, or if they increase the quantity or quality of jobs (by subsidizing wages, or screening costs, or both) held by members of groups the community has resolved to help. The important point for JTPA's output-based system of accountability is that, in each instance, the interests of employers are in partial conflict with JTPA's goals. The employer is better off training workers in strictly firm-specific skills. The employer is also better off accepting wage or screening subsidies (packaged as on-the-job training subsidies) without departing from normal hiring patterns.

If we want employers to *alter* their decisions in response to subsidies, we have two broad options. The first is to assume that integrity and public spirit will lead employers to select and train subsidized workers in a manner that creates public value, forswearing the opportunity to collect extra profits. Most employers involved in subsidized training programs surely *are* honorable and public-spirited. But some are not. Creating value through on-the-job training, moreover, is a sufficiently subtle undertaking that, if left to their own devices, even employers acting in the best of faith might lack the information needed to carry it off. Furthermore, the emphasis on tough performance standards, the competitive bidding for on-the-job training contracts, and the market rhetoric that characterize JTPA all suggest that this is not the mechanism of accountability that JTPA's architects had in mind.

The second approach is a contractual framework that is complete enough, specific enough, and enforceable enough to ensure that on-the-job training subsidies buy real public benefits at an acceptable cost. The JTPA legislation stipulates that the temporary subsidies paid to firms hiring and training eligible workers "shall be deemed to be in compensation for the extraordinary costs associated with training participants . . . and in compensation for the costs associated with the lower productivity of such participants."[75] Yet it is exceedingly difficult to ensure that subsidized trainees differ to any meaningful degree—in their initial characteristics or in the training they receive—from unsubsidized employees.

It is impossible to say what proportion of on-the-job training subsidies under JTPA create value, by any of the measures outlined above, and what proportion simply reward employers for hiring essentially the same kinds of workers, and training them in essentially the same way, as they would in any event. Even if JTPA's information system were far more elaborate than it is, it would be difficult to imagine any feasible method for ascertaining, for each on-the-job training contract, what employers would have done without subsidies. Private Industry Council members and others involved in JTPA fervently believe that they are doing something useful when they line up on-the-job training slots, and it is obvious why they think this: What they see is disadvantaged people signing up for training, learning to do demonstrably useful things, and in three cases out of four, ending up with an unsubsidized job. They are less aware of similar outcomes, at other firms, at other times, that occur *without* public financing. (And the people who otherwise would have landed the job that went instead to a subsidized trainee remain unidentified.)

Consider the types of jobs and the types of companies that typify JTPA's on-the-job training programs. Fully 40 percent of training slots are in low-skill occupations such as food service and dishwashing. The average contract allows a firm about fifteen weeks to train a worker in the janitor's craft, for example, with the government paying one-half of the wage bill.[76] Among the most important on-the-job training contractors in many local programs are fast-food restaurants and convenience stores. Both types of enterprises hire large numbers of people—generally young, frequently at the lower end of the income distribution—and train them in a limited range of fairly firm-specific skills applicable to low-wage, high-turnover jobs. It seems prudent to wonder how much the firms change their hiring or training—indeed, how much *room* there is for them to change their hiring or training—in response to subsidies.[77]

Consider, too, the demonstrated lack of awareness among many JTPA decision-makers of the contractual complexity of subsidized on-the-job training. With few exceptions, the perception seems to be that to reward firms for training eligible workers in any skills whatever is, in itself, a valuable intervention in the labor market. In the words of one Pittsburgh entrepreneur involved in JTPA: "Just because a businessman has an on-the-job training contract and his two sons are his only employees, where's the conflict of interest? Is it wrong to upgrade the skills of your children?"[78] Few officials or contractors, to be sure, are quite so unclear on the concept. But the basic problem is neither nepotism nor conflict of interest in this blatant sense. Rather, the problem is the general lack of attention to the delicate task of singling out for subsidies only *incremental* human capital investment. It is quite probable that the gentleman in Pittsburgh would have trained his sons without subsidies. It is less obvious, but equally true, that most businessmen in the United States find it in their interest to train people, including large numbers of JTPA-eligible people, without subsidies. The annual report published by the Houston Public Industry Council declared that its on-the-job training program was designed "for businesses that want to reduce labor cost and increase profits."[79] Even if one makes allowances for the public relations function of such reports, this statement is rather starkly at odds with the logic of creating public value through targeted subsidies for incremental training.

INCOMPLETE CONTRACTS AND COVERT WASTE

The National Alliance of Business entitled its 1986 study of JTPA *Is the Job Training Partnership Working?* The study concluded: "Several key facts indicate that the answer is a resounding 'Yes!' " The key facts, which the Alliance assembled from official statistics and an extensive survey of Private Industry Council members and of local training officials: Two-thirds of the adult trainees found jobs, over 60 percent of the youths participating had some kind of positive outcome, and, on average, local programs met most of the performance standards.[80] One staff director offered a fairly typical perspective: "Our placement rates and costs beat the federal standards. That proves we're efficient."[81]

It proves nothing of the sort. There can be no doubt that JTPA does some good; it would be astonishing if the public and private partners, equipped with noble intentions and $2 billion a year, did *not* do some good. But there can also be little doubt that JTPA does much less good than the raw statistics suggest and its proponents assert.

The problem, at base, is a preposterously underspecified contractual relationship. Most disadvantaged people work, most of the time. The local officials and contractors who implement JTPA are required only to select a small minority of the disadvantaged and to get them placed in jobs. The program deals with around 2 or 3 percent of the poor each year. But over 10 percent of the poor escape from poverty each year, most for reasons that have absolutely nothing to do with government manpower policy.[82] The typical JTPA trainee ends up in a job paying little more than one-half the average wage. Most of the working poor move in and out of such jobs with dismal regularity, with or without government help. There is little within the contractual structure of JTPA to constrain local programs or training organizations to concentrate on people who would otherwise remain unemployed and impoverished. There are powerful incentives to select trainees from among the minority of the eligible population who—for wholly separate reasons—have the best prospects.

This is not to imply that the contractual approach to subsidized human capital development cannot work, but only that the contractual architecture of JTPA's Title IIA program falls far short of enforcing, or even acknowledging, the complex requirements for creating value through subsidized training. Interestingly, a separate piece of American manpower policy, the Job Corps, exemplifies a more realistic model of contracting with profit-seeking agents.

The Job Corps was launched in 1964 as part of the Equal Opportunity Act, was brought under the aegis of the Department of Labor in 1969, became incorporated as a title of the CETA in 1973, and continues to be authorized as a title of the JTPA, although it is administered separately.[83] The basic idea behind the Job Corps is to send seriously disadvantaged young people away to residential centers for long-term, intensive remedial education and vocational training. Most of the Job Corps centers—about 70 percent—are managed under contract, and most of these—about 80 percent—are run by for-profit companies.[84] Companies bid competitively for two-year management contracts, and there is some evidence the competition is serious. Incumbent firms lost out to challengers ten times between 1971 and 1980, and one study found "frequent changes in the staffs of particular centers, in response to poor performance and under threat of losing out in the next competition."[85] The key feature distinguishing the Job Corps from JTPA is that the organizations responsible for Job Corps *training* have no control over the *recruitment* of participants or over subsequent *placement* efforts. These tasks are handled by volunteer groups, social agencies, unions, schools, and local employment offices.[86]

Unlike JTPA's local officials and training contractors, the companies running Job Corps centers cannot affect their measured performance by screening applicants or by securing job slots for graduates. Far more than JTPA contractors, Job Corps contractors are constrained to compete on the basis of the changes they produce in the trainees consigned to their charge. Most studies indicate that this arrangement has been effective in concentrating the energies of private contractors on valuable human capital development. The Job Corps serves a deeply troubled population. Its graduates work and earn more, collect less welfare, and commit less crime than nonparticipants.[87] But these benefits show up only in long-term assessments of participants and of matched comparison groups. In the short term, trainees returning from Job Corps centers work and earn *less* than nonparticipants, as they adapt to life back at home; the benefits are not measurable for six months or so, but they last for several years.[88] Under JTPA's placement-based system of accountability, Job Corps training would be counted as a failure, inferior to the most perfunctory job-search assistance for the most mildly disadvantaged clientele.

Public versus *private* thus does not exhaust the alternatives. What *kind* of private arrangement matters too. The problem with JTPA is not the involvement of private individuals and organizations, but rather the rickety arrangements for holding these agents to account. It is as if Medicaid physicians were presented with a population of patients suffering from complaints ranging from tendonitis to brain tumors, were asked to choose 2 or 3 percent for treatment, and then were paid on the basis of how many were still breathing when they left the hospital. Many officials in the JTPA system, public and private, are fully aware of the inherent tension between short-term performance measures and the unenforced imperative to create value. Both critics and troubled proponents recognize that JTPA generally concentrates on the most job-ready portion of the eligible population. But charges of "cream-skimming" miss an important part of the problem. The tendency to avoid the hard cases is seen as lamentable on ethical grounds, and it is. But it also means that the real impact of JTPA is far less than advertised. There is no compelling evidence that the Job Training Partnership Act system, on balance, makes much difference for the employment, earnings, and productive capacity of American workers.

PART FOUR

CONCLUSIONS

CHAPTER 10

THE (LIMITED) PROMISE

OF PRIVATIZATION

TWO CONCEPTS share the same word—*privatization*. The first concept (which might, even less euphoniously, be called "desocialization") involves removing certain responsibilities, activities, or assets from the collective realm. This is the chief meaning of privatization in countries retreating from postwar, postcolonial experiments with socialism, as they separate factories, mines, airlines and railroads from public control. The United States, for most of its history, has so tenaciously resisted collectivism that there is not much of a socialized sector to dismantle, however favorable the political winds may be. This book deals mostly with the second meaning of privatization: retaining collective financing but delegating delivery to the private sector. Here there has been a great deal of discussion and experimentation at all levels of American government, and the trend bids fair to continue. Is this good news?

There is a large element of nonsense in the privatization debate. Proponents are fond of invoking the efficiency that characterizes well-run companies in competitive markets and then, not troubling with any intervening logical steps, trumpeting the conclusion that private firms will excel in *public* undertakings as well. To go from the observation that private companies tend to do what they do better than public agencies, to the assertion that companies should take over the agencies' duties, is rather like observing that the clients of exercise spas are healthier, on average, than the clients of hospitals, and concluding from this that workout coaches should take over for doctors. Public tasks are different, and mostly harder.

At the same time, it is perverse to reject privatization simply because some enthusiasts favor it for the wrong reasons. Even for those who believe in govern-ment—perhaps *especially* for those who believe in government—any opportunity to serve the public interest more efficiently warrants respectful appraisal. Govern-ments in the United States spend roughly half a trillion dollars per year paying public workers to deliver goods and services directly. If only one-quarter of this total turned out to be suitable for privatization, at an average savings of, say, 25 percent—and neither figure is recklessly optimistic—the public would save over $30 billion. The prospects of government spending that much less, or of being able to *do* that much more, should appeal to Americans of whatever political leanings.

An openness to privatization by no means implies contempt for government bureaucracy. Productive efficiency is simply not the cardinal virtue of civil service organization. Public agencies characteristically are structured to guarantee due process and administrative fairness, to ensure that all considerations get proper weight and that no citizen's rights are violated. Governmental institutions hew to these values for excellent reasons. But such an orientation is at odds with the unencumbered administrative flexibility and concentrated decision-making au-thority that allows for the fastest technical adaptation and the greatest devotion to cost control. Different organizational designs have different virtues and defects. The trick is to match the design to the task, choosing civil servants where pro-cedural fairness matters most, choosing profit-seekers where productive efficiency matters most.

A related issue concerns our culture's capacity for public management. While different citizens would put different items on the list, most would agree that certain functions—defending the commonwealth, managing criminal courts, ad-ministering the tax system—can only be performed by public organizations and must be performed well. Are such duties likely to be discharged better, or worse, if we seize every opportunity to delegate *other* tasks to outside suppliers? In other words, are the essential resources of good public management—dedicated officials, alert investigative reporters, the citizenry's attention and patience, legislative oversight time, and so on—constrained and exhaustible? Or does our public man-agement expertise grow through practice? Should we worry more about wasting our capacity to run good bureaucracies, or about letting it atrophy? There are defensible arguments either way. Of course, if government reserved for itself *only* the messiest, most failure-prone undertakings, privatizing everything else, the con-sequences for civil servants' morale and reputation could be crippling. But on balance, the cause of good government would be better served by delegating when it is possible to delegate, and by concentrating the attention of public managers on tasks that are central to the mission of governance.

When it works well, privatization can boost efficiency through accelerated innovation, more appropriate technologies or management styles, or a more sensible scale of operation. It can clarify the public purpose by passing mandates through the focusing filter of explicit contracts. It can allow for more flexibility and variety in public services, spare public managers from occupying themselves directly with peripheral functions, and improve spending decisions by highlighting costs. When it works badly, of course, privatization can muddy public finance, make public management more complex and awkward, strip away vital dimensions of the public purpose that are hard to pin down contractually, transfer money from public workers to contractors without any savings to the collective fisc, allow quality to decay, and *increase* costs. Previous chapters have presented ample evidence of both the bright side and the dark side of privatization, and have, in the process, offered some lessons.

SPECIFICATIONS, PROCESS, AND COMPETITION

The first lesson seems simple enough, yet it often goes unheeded. If government does not specify what it wants from suppliers, or does not evaluate what it has received, it should not expect to get what it needs. Many municipal services *are* readily definable and easy to measure and evaluate, which explains the encouraging findings of chapter 7. But prison management, by and large, is not. The lesson is most poignantly illustrated by the Job Training Partnership Act, where the goal is to enhance the productive capacity of disadvantaged citizens. Numerical standards define expectations for graduates' employment and earnings. But private trainers are free to select a very few participants from a very large and diverse eligible population. Contractors, in effect, are allowed to choose between *making* skill-deficient citizens employable, or *selecting* citizens who are employable in the first place. So loosely drawn a contract leaves ample room for waste, inefficiency, and arrangements that in many other contexts would invite the label of fraud.

The second lesson concerns the burden of process. The privatization movement is propelled in part by the longing of public officials to escape bureaucratic complexities, substituting the supposed simplicity of arm's-length contracts. Chapter 6, on military procurement, demonstrates at (perhaps discouraging) length how very complicated contracting can be. Perhaps the most common error in thinking about privatization is to concentrate on *potential* efficiency gains without considering, in the laborious detail required, how to realize this potential. Vague calls for careful legal draftsmanship and monitoring beg the question. Even when the private sector enjoys an overwhelming technical edge, in short, harnessing private energies to public purposes can be a difficult exercise in contractual architecture. (While the evidence is not yet in, it seems a safe bet that some jurisdictions opting for private prisons will discover contracting to be more onerous than they had anticipated, while others will discover, to their dismay, the consequences of inadequate structures of accountability.)

The third lesson concerns the cardinal importance of competition. Organizations (including public ones) that must match the pace set by ambitious rivals are virtually always more efficient than organizations (including private ones) that are secure against challenge. Most of the kick in privatization comes from the greater scope for rivalry when functions are contracted out, not from private provision *per se*. The evidence is overwhelming that where corruption, negligence, or the nature of the service itself undercuts competition, the benefits of privatization shrink or vanish. Efforts to compensate by other means for the missing discipline of competition will seldom be fully successful. Those public services for which it is technically or politically impossible to keep contractors in a state of healthy insecurity offer, at best, limited potential for privatization.

The preceding chapters present a selective, by no means systematic overview of the private sector's role in the public realm. There are countless other examples. Some have been extensively analyzed already, some are too recent to have attracted much comment, and some are rarely recognized to be *contracting* issues. City governments have taken to requiring real estate developers to deliver social services and to provide civic amenities as a quid pro quo for zoning variances and other benefits, a complex and indirect form of contract that replaces public with private services.[1] Philadelphia has no municipal homeless shelters, relying on contractors (including many for-profit operations) to provide beds (at a per-person fee) for people who would otherwise sleep on the streets.[2] Several smaller airports have privately run control towers, and corporate bids to expand the private role in the air-traffic control system have been well received by federal officials.[3] Washington has sharply expanded its use of temporary-worker agencies.[4] And the Department of the Interior plans to contract out for maintenance and tourist services in some national parks, as well as for the map-making functions of the Geological Survey.[5]

These and other policy issues invite the basic questions that run through this book. Does the "contract" between the government and the profit-seeker accurately specify the community's goals and reflect the community's values? Is it precise enough to permit meaningful bidding? Is competition possible throughout the project? Will the contract be enforceable—and enforced? Are profit-seekers dangerously well placed, or especially well motivated, to influence spending decisions?

Calls to improve public education through private sector involvement arise periodically, and it is hard to contemplate the current state of American schools without sharing the general sentiment for reform. Yet experiments with educational contracting have been mostly discouraging. In some cases, for-profit organizations showed no efficiency edge; in others, profit-seekers proved all too adept at concentrating their efforts on the narrow performance indicators covered in the contracts while ignoring other dimensions of educational quality.[6] The problem is that higher math test scores, fewer dropouts, more frequent recitations of the Pledge of Allegiance, and other such measurable results are not all that we expect of our schools. "Education" also includes subtler factors that are hard to specify, harder still to monitor, and this limits the ability of a school district to easily choose the most attractive bidder among education contractors.

When a government-insured financial institution becomes insolvent, the regulating agency—the Federal Savings and Loan Insurance Corporation or the Federal Deposit Insurance Corporation—has two alternatives. It can either assume control of the failed bank or thrift itself, pay off insured depositors, and manage or (more frequently) liquidate the assets. Or it can delegate the task, adding to the assets of the defunct institution in order to entice a private firm to take it over. As financial institutions failed at a dizzying pace in the late 1980s, concerns arose as to the terms of the deals between the government and the firms agreeing to subsidized mergers. Were there enough potential buyers to ensure the public a decent deal? Did agreements apportion risk and reward fairly between the government and the private rescuer? When should the government handle failing financial institutions itself, instead of paying the private sector to take the chore off its hands?

States and localities seek to spur economic development by offering incentives to businesses, including tax breaks, special water, sewer, and road construction, subsidized loans, and even outright grants. Such relationships can be analyzed as transactions between governments and profit-seekers—subsidies in exchange for providing things the community values—and the propositions developed here apply. Do the subsidy programs reflect real community priorities? Are the anticipated public benefits—jobs, tax revenues, and so on—well understood and clearly spelled out? What provisions are there for monitoring adherence to the terms of the deals, and what recourse does each side have if the other reneges?[7]

Among the most important applications of private means to public ends (and very likely the most complex) is health care, where public financing and private delivery has become the norm. Recent trends in American health care policy can be seen as efforts to refine the terms of the contract between the government and the physicians and hospitals (most of which are private, and many of which are profit-seeking) that actually deliver the care. Paying private providers on the basis of *inputs*, the contractual form that prevailed until the 1980s, gave no incentives to economize and, indeed, tempted physicians and hospitals to insist on excessive tests and procedures. Like civil servants, health care providers were managed by reference to procedures, rather than to results. But unlike most civil servants, the incomes of these providers varied directly with the amount of work they did. Anxious to blunt the incentive to excessive care, governments have attempted to link providers' pay more clearly to *outputs*. Hospitals (and increasingly physicians) are paid a fixed fee for tending to each malady. This looks more like standard models of contracting with profit-seekers and is meant to inspire efficiency. But the link between specified outputs and patients' health remains complex and controversial. The payment system is vulnerable to misuse. And health care providers retain a good deal of influence over the effective public demand for medical care.[8]*

PRIVATIZATION AND THE SIZE OF GOVERNMENT

Debates over the competence of governmental organizations frequently become confused with debates over the proper boundaries of collective activity. The issues, while undeniably related—if the government does very little, there are correspondingly few decisions to make about public versus private delivery—are separable. It is no offense against logic to believe that bureaucracy is inherently inefficient,

---

*As this book goes to press, it is becoming increasingly clear that the dark side of the profit motive prevailed during the 1980s at the Department of Housing and Urban Development, the federal government's privatization pacesetter in the Reagan years. Favoritism and insouciant supervision led to a gross erosion of accountability in several housing programs. Influence-peddling made a mockery of competition among suppliers. The size of contractors' rewards lost all connection to the public value they produced. And the allocation of scarce collective resources—among different programs, and across communities—was governed not by any calculus of social needs but by the prospect of profit for well-connected developers and consultants.

and at the same time to believe that expediency or justice call for an expansive common realm. Someone who feels that the government does vital things, but tends to do them badly, would eagerly seek out ways to privatize the performance of collective undertakings. Similarly, there is nothing irrational about the belief that government bureaucracies do what they do quite well, but ought to do much less of it.

In practice, though, citizens' views on the *efficiency* and on the *legitimacy* of governmental undertakings tend to run in tandem. Conservatives typically welcome private delivery of public goods and services as the next best thing to cutting them out of the government budget altogether. Most liberals lament private delivery as a retreat from the principle of collective action. But the questions raised here ought to spark far less ideological passion than do more fundamental debates about the proper size of government.

Yet means might matter. This book has been concerned almost entirely with the pragmatic dimension of privatization. If a private organization can do the job better, or cheaper, with no fewer positive side effects and no more negative ones than the public alternative, then private delivery is superior; otherwise, not. In the discussion in chapter 8 on private corrections I explicitly assign the symbolic dimension a subordinate status, and in most other cases I simply do not deal with it. The pragmatic issues are rich enough in themselves to fill many pages, and this book is long enough already. And even if we care greatly, for reasons other than instrumental ones, about how public agents are organized, these concerns still must be balanced against more mundane considerations. The point was raised briefly in chapter 8: We might object intrinsically to the idea of prisons for profit, but if private prisons turned out to be sufficiently cheaper, more accountable, or more humane than public prisons, most of us would probably set aside our misgivings. Finally, people might simply disagree about which way the symbolism issue cuts. One citizen might feel that providing public goods through civil service organizations reinforces the communal character of those goods, while the profit motive would pollute it. Another might feel that to accomplish our common goals through private institutions affirms our individualistic culture and that— precisely *because* symbolism matters—Americans should shun bureaucracy, even when it would be cheaper or more accountable than private contractors. Let that debate continue.

*   *   *

In most of the world, "privatization" means getting the government entirely out of the airline business, or the car business, or the hospital business, while in the United States the term more often refers to the private delivery of goods and services that are still paid for collectively. One can debate at length, for each particular enterprise, the merits of the first form of privatization. But few would dispute that selling public assets and repudiating public duties *does* tend to shrink the size of government. There is no cause for confidence that this will usually be the case with American-style privatization, and considerable reason to suspect that it will not.

The expansionary appetites and resistance to cutbacks of bureaucratic organizations are classic conservative laments. But profit-seeking organizations are usually at least as eager and at least as able to affect the public spending agenda. The same features of private institutions that concentrate incentives for efficiency provide for a similarly concentrated interest in exercising political influence. Those who fear the political might of civil servants and prescribe wholesale privatization as a corrective have not thought things through.

I have argued that getting the government to do the right things may ultimately be more important than getting government to do things right. In an era plagued by both straitened public finances and urgent, unmet needs, privatization summons concerns about the *composition* of government action, and not just its scope. An unwelcome but all too likely prospect is that aspiring private contractors will push hardest for privatizing precisely the wrong functions—those where it is most difficult to write and to enforce contracts, to ensure competition, and to bridle suppliers' pressures for increased spending. Civil servants, meanwhile, will most vigorously resist privatization just where it offers the greatest cost savings for the public.

The pursuit of the common interest requires a carefully designed structure of accountability that ensures for citizens the best efforts of those who act on their behalf. This is hard to arrange, and there is no reason to believe that a private form of organization will always, or even usually, improve accountability. Private firms in competitive markets *are* frequently more efficient than government bureaucracies, but it is romantic to infer from this that the mere fact of private organization, *without* competition and *without* market tests, leads to efficiency. The troublesome aspects of government spending, as the early chapters argued, are rooted in the conflicts and ambiguities of collective *decision*, not merely in collective action. This observation summons no conclusions on the proper level of government activity: Some things are important enough to be worth doing awkwardly. Delegating tasks to profit-seekers can make public action *less* awkward—more efficient, more accountable, more firmly under the citizenry's control—when contracts can be clearly written and fairly enforced, and when suppliers' efforts to affect decisions can be contained. It would be wrong, and wasteful, to deny the considerable potential of privatization in these cases. But it would be reckless to claim that private delivery is any sweeping remedy for the fundamental complexity of the public realm.

NOTES

Chapter 1

1. Butler is quoted in Peter Kilborn, "Reagan Plan to Privatize Government Is Gaining Support from Democrats," *New York Times* 15 Feb. 1988

2. Peter Drucker, *The Age of Discontinuity* (New York: Harper & Row, 1978), 234–35, and Anthony H. Pascal, "Clients, Consumers, and Citizens: Market Mechanisms for the Delivery of Public Services" (paper presented at the Conference on Centrally Planned Social Change, Quail's Roost, North Carolina, April 1972).

3. Bureau of the Budget, *Bulletin 55-4*, 1955.

4. Office of Management and Budget, *Circular A-76*, rev. August 1983.

5. Madsen Pirie, *Dismantling the State* (Dallas: National Center for Policy Analysis, 1985), offers a representative summary of the British approach to privatization.

6. E. S. Savas, *Privatizing the Public Sector* (Chatham, N.J.: Chatham Publishing, 1982).

7. James T. Bennett and Manuel H. Johnson, *Better Government at Half the Price* (Ottawa, Ill.: Caroline House Publishing, 1981).

8. Stuart M. Butler, *Privatizing Federal Spending: A Strategy to Eliminate the Deficit* (New York: Universe Books, 1985).

9. Alan Murray, "Miller Expects Congress to Accept Increase in Sales of Federal Assets," *Wall Street Journal*, 6 Jan. 1987. See also President Ronald Reagan, "Performance of Commercial Activities," Executive Order 12615, Fed. Reg., 19 Nov. 1987, 52: 225.

10. See, for example, Robert W. Poole, *Cutting Back City Hall* (New York: Universe Books, 1980).

11. See Heritage Foundation, *Backgrounder* no. 494 (Washington: 31 March 1986).

12. President's Commission on Privatization, David F. Linowes, chairman, *Privatization: Toward More Efficient Government* (Washington: March 1988).

13. U.S. Office of Technology Assessment, "Assessing Contractor Use in Superfund," U.S. Government Printing Office, January 1989; Martin Tolchin, "U.S. Hires Private Concerns to Check Job Seekers," *New York Times*, 1 Feb. 1986; Robert Pear, "U.S. Expanding Use of Private Groups to Collect Debts," *New York Times*, 26 March 1987; and David Rampe, "U.S. Services Agency to Hire an Outside Firm on Auditing," *New York Times*, 12 Jan. 1989.

14. See Arlen J. Large, "High Hopes Riding on Privatized Landsat," *Wall Street Journal*, 18 March 1986; Reginald Stuart, "Transit Agencies Get New U.S. Rule," *New York Times*, 27 Nov. 1985; and Martin Tolchin, "Private Concerns Gaining Foothold in Public Transit," *New York Times*, 29 April 1985.

15. See Peter Young, *Privatization around the Globe: Lessons for the Reagan Administration* (Houston: National Center for Policy Analysis, January 1986); Peter Young and Stuart Butler, *Privatization: Lessons from British Success Stories* (Washington: Heritage Foundation, 1987); Christopher Barclay and Neil Marsland, *Privatisation*, House of Commons Library Research Division Background Paper, 12

April 1985; George Yarrow, "Privatisation in Theory and Practice," *Economic Policy,* 1 April 1986; and "Privatisation: Everybody's Doing It Differently," *Economist,* 21 December 1985.

16. See Shawn Tully, "Europe Goes Wild over Privatization," *Fortune,* 2 March 1987; Richard Alm, "When the Government Sells Out," *U.S. News and World Report,* 10 Nov. 1986; and Jeanne Villeneuve, "Privatisation: le reflexe nationalistise," *L'Express,* 21 March 1986.

17. See Katsuro Sakoh, *Privatizing State-Owned Enterprises: A Japanese Case Study* (Washington: Heritage Foundation Asian Studies Center, 1986).

18. For Turkey's sale of Bosphorus bridge, see "Wooing the Investor," *Euromoney,* Jan. 1985. Chile launched the developing world's earliest, most radical, and most ideological privatization campaign in the 1970s. See Jonathan Aylen, "Privatization in Developing Countries," *Lloyds Bank Review* (January 1987). See also Gabriel Roth, *The Private Provision of Public Services in Developing Countries* (New York: Oxford University Press, 1987).

19. For examples, see Young, *Privatization around the Globe,* and Stuart Butler, *How Reagan Can Put Privatization Back on Track* (Washington: Heritage Foundation, 1986).

20. From Dennis Encarnation, "Note on Comparative Political Economy" (case study, Harvard Business School), 9, ex. 1.

21. See Thomas K. McCraw, "The Public and Private Spheres in Historical Perspective," in Harvey Brooks et al., *Public-Private Partnerships* (Cambridge, Mass.: Ballinger, 1984), 34–35, fig. 2.1.

22. In 1986, the National Aeronautics and Space Administration was instructed to concentrate on military and scientific payloads, and to leave commercial business to the private sector. See David E. Sanger, "Price NASA Will Pay for 4th Orbiter," *New York Times,* 16 Aug. 1986, and Philip M. Boffey, "Commercial Launching by NASA Ordered Shifted to Private Sector," ibid.

23. Bob Davis, "A Supersecret Agency Finds Selling Secrecy to Others Isn't Easy," *Wall Street Journal,* 28 March 1988.

24. Eduarco Lachica, "Federal Labs Give Out Fruit of More Research for Commercial Uses," *Wall Street Journal,* 1 Feb. 1988.

25. Figures derived from U.S. Department of Commerce, *Survey of Current Business* (Washington: June 1989), table 3.7B.

Chapter 2

1. Adam Smith, *The Wealth of Nations* (Bungay, Suffolk: The Chaucer Press, 1979), 117. Consider, for example, how rapidly capitalists met such new needs as those for environmentally benign chemical solvents, or for shoes designed for marching backward. Philip H. Dougherty, "Marketing Shoes for Marching," *New York Times,* 2 Dec. 1986; Philip Shabecoff, "New Compound Is Hailed as Boon to Ozone Shield," *New York Times,* 14 Jan. 1988.

2. Abraham Lincoln, "Fragment on Government, July 1854," in *The Collected Works of Abraham Lincoln,* ed. Roy P. Basler (Westport Conn.: Greenwood Press, 1974), 2:220–21. I am grateful to Jeremy Rosner for bringing this quotation to my attention.

3. Classic examples include Paul Samuelson, "The Pure Theory of Public Expenditure," *Review of Economics and Statistics* 36 (1954); Francis Bator, "The Anatomy of Market Failure," *Quarterly Journal of Economics* 72 (1958); and Kenneth Arrow, "The Organization of Economic Activity: Issues Pertinent to the Choice of Market versus Nonmarket Allocation," in Edwin Mansfield, ed., *Microeconomics: Selected Readings,* 3d ed. (New York: W. W. Norton & Co., 1979).

4. Edith Stokey and Richard Zeckhauser, *A Primer for Policy Analysis* (New York: W. W. Norton & Co., 1978), 298–308.

5. These categories are neither exclusive nor exhaustive. Charles Lindblom, *Politics and Markets* (New York: Basic Books, 1977), 81–85, goes somewhat beyond the utilitarian framework to list six other potential problems. Of course, Socialists, philosophers, and some religious thinkers have still more fundamental complaints.

6. Smith, *The Wealth of Nations,* 379.

7. Robert Dorfman, "General Equilibrium with Public Goods" (paper delivered to International Economics Association Conference on Public Economics, Sept. 1966), 4; Edward Birdsall, "A Study of the Demand for Public Goods," in Richard Musgrave, ed., *Essays in Fiscal Federalism* (Washington: The Brookings Institution, 1965), 235.

8. A good treatment of the rivalry and exclusion concepts can be found in Richard A. Musgrave and Peggy B. Musgrave, *Public Finance in Theory and Practice,* 3d ed. (New York: McGraw-Hill, 1980), 55–58.

9. Julius Margolis, "A Comment on the Pure Theory of Public Expenditures," *Review of Economics and Statistics* 37 (November 1955); Francis Bator, *The Question of Government Spending* (New York: Harper & Brothers, 1960), 95–98; Robert M. Spann, "Collective Consumption of Private Goods," *Public Choice* 20 (Winter 1974); and Richard Zeckhauser, "The Muddled Responsibilities of Public and Private America," in Winthrop Knowlton and Richard Zeckhauser, eds., *American Society: Public and Private Responsibilities* (Cambridge, Mass.: Ballinger, 1986).

10. The question is whether he is motivated by the goal itself or by his satisfaction in his own generosity. For a related discussion, see Harold M. Hochman and James D. Rodgers, "Pareto-Optimal Redistribution," *American Economic Review* 59 (September 1969).

11. Hans Ritschl contended that "objective communal needs are subjectively felt by the competent public authorities and by individuals, in so far as they think, feel, and act as members of the community." Hans Ritschl, *Communal Economy*, 1931, excerpted in Richard A. Musgrave and Alan T. Peacock, eds., *Classics in the Theory of Public Finance* (New York: St. Martin's Press, 1967), 235.

12. In his distopian "Constitution of the Second Republic," Theodore Lowi's Article VI states: "The public interest shall be defined by the satisfaction of the voters in their constituencies. The test of the public interest is reelection." Theodore Lowi, *The End of Liberalism*, 2d ed. (New York: W. W. Norton & Co., 1979), xiii. Lowi intends his "Constitution" as a polemical parody of the degeneracy of American politics. But—again, within the constraints on public action set by the Constitution of 1787—the criterion is essentially sound, however uncongenial it may be to Aristotelian sensibilities.

13. Those interested in the intellectual history of the social welfare function debate should consult Abram Bergson, "A Reformation of Certain Aspects of Welfare Economics," *Quarterly Journal of Economics* (February 1938); Paul Samuelson, *Foundations of Economic Analysis* (Cambridge, Mass.: Harvard University Press, 1947), especially chapter 8; Kenneth Arrow, "A Difficulty in the Concept of Social Welfare," in Mansfield, ed., *Microeconomics*; Murray C. Kemp and Yew Kwang Ng, "On the Existence of Social Welfare Functions, Social Orderings, and Social Decision Functions," *Economica* 43 (February 1976); and Paul Samuelson, "Reaffirming the Existence of 'Reasonable' Bergson-Samuelson Social Welfare Functions," *Economica* 44 (February 1977). An invaluable secondary source is Alfred F. MacKay, *Arrow's Theorem: The Paradox of Social Choice* (New Haven: Yale University Press, 1980).

14. Max Weber, "Politics as a Vocation," in H. H. Gerth and C. Wright Mills, eds., *From Max Weber* (New York: Oxford University Press, 1946), 78.

15. For thoughts on the philosophical virtues and the practical defects of consensual systems of public finance, see the 1896 study by Knut Wicksell, "A New Principle of Just Taxation," in Musgrave and Peacock, eds., *Classics in Theory* (New York: St. Martin's Press, 1967), and T. Nicolaus Tideman and Gordon Tullock, "A New and Superior Process for Making Social Choices," *Journal of Political Economy* 84 (December 1976).

16. Alexis de Tocqueville, *Democracy in America* (New York: New American Library, 1956), 114.

17. Madison argued that one central advantage of an extensive republic is that, with a variety of diverse interests, it will be less likely that a single group will find a "common motive to invade the rights of other citizens," and that even if there is some latent capacity to form a dominant group, "it will be more difficult for all who feel it to discover their own strength and to act in unison with each other." Alexander Hamilton, James Madison, and John Jay, "The Federalist No. 10," *The Federalist Papers* (1788; reprint, New York: New American Library, 1961), 83.

18. In 1986 Governor Michael Dukakis declared the corn muffin to be the official muffin of Massachusetts. Had his decision been an authoritative decision on baking policy in the state rather than a nonbinding endorsement, the cost of majority rule would have been the discontent of blueberry- and bran-muffin partisans.

19. Some years before he became the Reagan administration's budget director, James Miller suggested scrapping representative democracy and replacing the House and Senate with in-home electronic devices on which citizens would register their preferences on each issue. James Miller, "A Program for Direct and Proxy Voting in the Legislative Process," *Public Choice* 7 (Fall 1969).

20. "A Sad Basel Offers Dirge for 'Fluvius Rhinus,'" *New York Times*, 16 Nov. 1986.

21. Hamilton, Madison, and Jay, "The Federalist No. 10," *The Federalist Papers*, 82.

22. For a related discussion, see Hanna F. Pitkin, *The Concept of Representation* (Berkeley: University of California Press, 1967), especially 216–18, 222.

23. For a survey of the virtues and defects of group politics, see William Kelso, *American Democratic Theory* (Westport, Conn.: Greenwood Press, 1978); David Truman, *The Governmental Process* (New York: Alfred A. Knopf, 1951), especially chapter 10, Mancur Olson, *The Logic of Collective Action*

(Cambridge, Mass.: Harvard University Press, 1965), and *The Rise and Decline of Nations* (New Haven: Yale University Press, 1982); Theodore Lowi, *The End of Liberalism* (New York: W. W. Norton & Co., 1979); and Robert A. Dahl, *Dilemmas of Pluralist Democracy* (New Haven: Yale University Press, 1982). Interestingly, Jean-Jacques Rousseau, certainly no partisan of the economist's gospel of individualism, also seemed suspicious of interest-group politics: "In order for the general will to be well-expressed, it is imperative that there should be no sectional associations in the state, and that every citizen should make up his own mind for himself." Jean-Jacques Rousseau, *The Social Contract* (Harmondsworth, Middlesex: Penguin Books, 1968), 73.

24. Sigmund Freud, *Civilization and Its Discontents*, trans. James Strachey (New York: W. W. Norton & Co., 1961), 23–24, 32.

25. A seminal article is George Stigler, "The Economics of Information," *Journal of Political Economy* (June 1961).

26. Alston Chase, *Playing God in Yellowstone* (Boston: Atlantic Monthly Press, 1986).

27. See Eva Mueller, "Public Attitudes toward Fiscal Programs," *Quarterly Journal of Economics* (May 1963); Paul N. Courant, Edward M. Gramlich, and Daniel L. Rubinfeld, "Why Voters Support Tax Limitation Amendments: The Michigan Case," *National Tax Journal* 33 (March 1980); Susan Welch, "The More for Less Paradox: Public Attitudes on Taxing and Spending," *Public Opinion Quarterly* 49 (1985). For a federal perspective, see Andre Modigliani and Franco Modigliani, "The Growth of the Federal Deficit and the Role of Public Attitudes," *Public Opinion Quarterly* 51 (1987).

28. Puviani's work is discussed in James M. Buchanan, *Fiscal Theory and Political Economy* (Chapel Hill: University of North Carolina Press, 1980), 60.

29. Herman B. Leonard, *Checks Unbalanced: The Quiet Side of Public Spending* (New York: Basic Books, 1986), 6.

30. Max Weber, "Bureaucracy," in Gerth and Mills, eds., *From Max Weber*, 233.

31. For an example of one exceptionally baffling and wasteful program, see John D. Donahue, "The Political Economy of Milk," *Atlantic Monthly*, Oct. 1983.

32. Representative Clarence Brown, an Ohio Republican, in U.S. Congress, Joint Economic Committee Staff Study, *The Economics of Federal Subsidy Programs* (Washington, 1972), 22–23.

33. Gregg Easterbrook, "Sack Weinberger, Bankrupt General Dynamics, and Other Procurement Reforms," *Washington Monthly*, Jan. 1987, 42.

34. For a related discussion, see George A. Akelof, "The Market for 'Lemons': Quality Uncertainty and the Market Mechanism," *Quarterly Journal of Economics* 84 (August 1970). See also Harry Frankfurt, "On Bullshit," *Harper's*, Feb. 1987.

35. See Max Weber, "Bureaucracy," in Gerth and Mills, eds., *From Max Weber*, 205–7.

36. William Orzechowski, "Economic Models of Bureaucracy: Survey, Extensions, and Evidence," in Thomas E. Borcherding, ed., *Budgets and Bureaucrats: The Sources of Government Growth* (Durham, N.C.: Duke University Press, 1977), 251–53.

Chapter 3

1. Office of Management and Budget, *Circular A–76* rev., August 1983, para. 4(a).

2. For a good overview of agency theory, see the introductory chapter by editors John W. Pratt and Richard J. Zeckhauser, *Principals and Agents: The Structure of Business* (Boston: Harvard Business School Press, 1985). See also Daniel Levinthal, "A Survey of Agency Models of Organizations," *Journal of Economic Behavior and Organization* (March 1988).

3. John Stuart Mill, *Principles of Political Economy* (London: Longmans, Green, and Co., 1929), 139.

4. Adam Smith, *Wealth of Nations* (Bungay, Suffolk: The Chaucer Press, 1979), 271.

5. A good discussion of this issue can be found in Oliver E. Williamson, *Markets and Hierarchies* (New York: The Free Press, 1975), chapter 4.

6. The problem of setting compensation to equal marginal product in a joint production effort is discussed in Armen A. Alchian and Harold Demsetz, "Production, Information Costs, and Economic Organization," *American Economic Review* 62 (Dec. 1972).

7. Among other reasons, this will be the case if the principal is less averse to risk than the agent, or has greater control over the sources of risk, or knows more about the environment than he can convincingly convey to the agent. For one example of the effect of risk on contractual arrangements, see the account of currency and commodity price turbulences in the 1970s and their impact on the

aluminum industry in Jean-Francois Hennart, "Upstream Vertical Integration in the Aluminum and Tin Industries," *Journal of Economic Behavior and Organization* 9 (April 1988); especially 287.

8. Mill, *Principles of Political Economy*, 977.

9. This section draws on Williamson, *Markets and Hierarchies*, 64–72.

10. Discussed in Tony Tanner, review of *Playboys and Killjoys*, by Harry Levin, *New York Times*, 8 March 1987.

11. For the classic treatment of this issue, see R. H. Coase, "The Nature of the Firm," *Economica* (November 1937): 391, 403–4.

12. For some observations on a related theme, see Sanford J. Grossman and Oliver D. Hart, "The Costs and Benefits of Ownership," *Journal of Political Economy* 94 (Dec. 1986).

13. Ludwig von Mises, *Bureaucracy* (New Haven: Yale University Press, 1944), 1.

14. Max Weber, "Bureaucracy," in Gerth and Mills, eds., *From Max Weber*, 214.

15. Ibid., 196–99.

16. Max Weber, "Politics as a Vocation," in Gerth and Mills, eds., *From Max Weber*, 95. Herbert Simon similarly stressed that the bureaucrat's duty involves not the accomplishment of a specified result by whatever means he chooses, but rather allegiance to authority; the bureaucrat accepts "a general rule which permits the communicated decision of another to guide his own choices." Herbert Simon, *Administrative Behavior* (New York: Macmillan, 1947), 125.

17. Weber "Bureaucracy," 197. Weber discerned that the same essential organizational structure was being replicated in both state agencies and in the big industrial organizations taking shape in the Europe of his day. He argued that "the very large, modern capitalist enterprises are themselves unequaled models of strict bureaucratic organization," having become assemblages of professional functionaries operating "according to calculable rules." Ibid., 215.

18. Anthony Downs, *Inside Bureaucracy* (Boston: Little, Brown and Company, 1967), 24–25. See also William Niskanen, *Bureaucracy and Representative Government* (Chicago: Aldine-Atherton, 1971), 15, and Hal G. Rainey, Robert W. Backoff, and Charles H. Levine, "Comparing Public and Private Organizations," *Public Adminstration Review* (March/April 1976).

19. On this matter see Simon, *Administrative Behavior*, 173.

20. Harvey Leibenstein, "Allocative Efficiency versus X-Efficiency," *American Economic Review* (June 1966).

21. Albert O. Hirschman, *Exit, Voice, and Loyalty: Responses to Decline in Firms, Organizations, and States* (Cambridge, Mass.: Harvard University Press, 1970), 15.

22. There is a vast literature on the consequences of the separation of ownership from control, including the seminal work by Adolph Berle and Gardiner Means, *The Modern Corporation and Private Property* (New York: Harcourt, 1932). For a far earlier (and essentially complete) statement of the problem, see Mill, *Principles of Political Economy*, 960–61.

23. On this last-cited extreme, see the discussion of the United Nations Food and Agriculture Organization in Charles Wolf, Jr., "A Theory of Nonmarket Failure: Framework for Implementation Analysis," *Journal of Law and Economics* 22 (April 1979): 126.

24. The importance of this point was stressed by Armen Alchian, "Some Economics of Property Rights," *Il Politico* 30 (December 1965).

25. The usage is rooted in the economics of farmland and was first analyzed by David Ricardo. Since a parcel of land cannot be moved, its alternative uses are limited to what can be grown or built on it. The parcel has no perfect competitors sharing its attributes *and* location. Thus the owner of a particularly fertile or well-located parcel can charge a premium price for its use that corresponds roughly to what modern economists mean by rent.

26. See, for example, Anne O. Krueger, "The Political Economy of the Rent-Seeking Society," *American Economic Review* (May 1974); Jagdish Bhagwati, "Directly Unproductive, Profit-Seeking Activities," *Journal of Political Economy* (October 1982); and James M. Buchanan, Robert D. Tollison, and Gordon Tullock, eds., *Toward a Theory of the Rent-Seeking Society* (College Station, Tex.: Texas A&M Press, 1980).

27. Buchanan, "Why Does Government Grow?" 11.

28. Richard Craswell, "Self-Generating Growth in Public Programs," *Public Choice* 21 (Spring 1975): 92. Worries about the political effectiveness of self-seeking suppliers are not limited to conservative scholars. John Kenneth Galbraith, for example, has argued: "For important classes of products or services . . . decisions are taken not by the individual citizen and voter and transmitted to the state. They are taken by the producers of public services. . . . The Congress and the public are then persuaded or commanded to acceptance of these decisions." See "Economics as a System of Belief," in John Kenneth Galbraith, *Economics, Peace, and Laughter* (Boston: Houghton Mifflin, 1971), 70.

29. This section owes much to Mancur Olson, *Logic of Collective Action* (Cambridge, Mass.: Harvard University Press, 1965).

30. Two scholars have attempted to document the political activism of government employees, concluding somewhat boldly from their study of voting data in one city in 1933 that it is "clear now why at one time bureaucrats were not permitted to vote in the political unit where they worked." Winston E. Bush and Arthur T. Denzau, "The Voting Behavior of Bureaucrats and Public Sector Growth," in Thomas E. Borcherding, ed., *Budgets and Bureaucrats: The Sources of Government Growth* (Durham, N.C.: Duke University Press, 1977), 97.

Chapter 4

1. Department of Commerce, *Statistical Abstract of the United States 1987* (Washington: 1987), 191, table 335.

2. E. A. Pearson and H. B. Gotaas, "Refuse Collection and Disposal in California," *Western City* (Dec. 1952): 8.

3. Faye Rive, "Where Will We Put All That Garbage?" *Fortune*, 11 April 1988; William K. Stevens, "Trash Disposal Problem Besieging Philadelphia," *New York Times*, 20 Jan. 1988; and Bill Paul, "Heard on the Street," *Wall Street Journal*, 3 June 1987.

4. These figures are from a 1975 Columbia study of 1,378 communities reported in E. S. Savas, "Policy Analysis for Local Government: Public vs. Private Refuse Collection," *Policy Analysis* 3 (Winter 1977): 54–55.

5. These figures are from Dennis Young, *How Shall We Collect the Garbage?* (Washington: The Urban Institute, 1972), 12, and Carl Valente and Lydia Manchester, *Rethinking Local Services: Examining Alternative Delivery* (Washington: International City Management Association, 1984), xv, table B, reprinted in National Center for Policy Analysis, "Privatization in the U.S.: Cities and Counties" (Dallas: NCPA, 1985), 4, table 1. A 1972 study termed private garbage collection a "youthful" industry; by 1986, total annual revenues had reached $15 billion. See Young, *How Shall We?* 14; and Bill Richardson, "U.S. Targets Waste Haulers in Big Inquiry," *Wall Street Journal*, 4 June 1987.

6. J. T. Bennett and M. H. Johnson, "Public versus Private Provision of Collective Goods and Services: Garbage Collection Revisited," *Public Choice* 34 (1979): 61–62.

7. Ibid., 61.

8. Warner Z. Hirsch, "Cost Functions of an Urban Government Service: Refuse Collection," *Review of Economics and Statistics* 47 (February 1965).

9. Young, *How Shall We?* 5–7.

10. E. S. Savas, "Policy Analysis." Savas and Barbara J. Stevens (see note 13) drew from the same large data collection effort, which they conducted jointly.

11. See ibid., 68, table 7, for a fuller display of results. Young reached the same conclusion and attributed it to the average regulatory commission's chronic "preference for amicable rather than efficient solutions," with the frequent result that, in a regulated monopoly franchise, "management may become fairly relaxed about efficiency considerations." Young, *How Shall We?* 30.

12. Peter Kemper and John M. Quigley, *The Economics of Refuse Collection* (Cambridge, Mass.: Ballinger Publishing, 1976), 110.

13. Barbara J. Stevens, "Scale, Market Structure, and the Cost of Refuse Collection," *Review of Economics and Statistics* 60 (March 1977). Stevens did not, however, net out the taxes and profits of private firms, so her analysis tends to underestimate their real economic advantage. Ibid., 442.

14. Ibid., 444, tables 1, 1B, 1C. Stevens has no category for large cities—of population two hundred thousand or greater—so there is no test for possible diseconomies of scale.

15. This result holds up at the 95 percent confidence level. Ibid., 445, 446, table 2.

16. James C. McDavid, "The Canadian Experience with Privatizing Residential Solid Waste Collection Services," *Public Administration Review* 45 (1985): 603, 604, table 2, 606, n. 19.

17. John Cubbin, Simon Domberger, and Shirley Meadowcroft, "Competitive Tendering and Refuse Collection: Identifying the Sources of Efficiency Gains," *Fiscal Studies* (August 1987): 52, 54, table 1.

18. See Barbara J. Stevens, "Scale, Market Structure," 45, n. 17.

19. Jeffrey Klein of Kidder, Peabody and Company, quoted in "Taking Out the Garbage," *New York Times*, 2 May 1987.

20. Young, *How Shall We?* 34.

21. See Arnold H. Lubasch, "Witness Tells of Bid-Rigging by Garbage Carters," *New York Times*, 20 April 1986. See also Bill Richards, "U.S. Targets Waste Haulers in Big Inquiry," *Wall Street Journal*, 4 June 1987; Richard W. Stevenson, "Three Trash Haulers Charged on Los Angeles Pricing," *New York Times*, 10 June 1987; Bill Richards, "Waste Management Faces More Inquiries," *Wall Street Journal*, 28 Sept. 1987; and Ralph Blumenthal, "Mob Ruling and Empire of Garbage," *New York Times*, 24 Jan. 1988.

22. See Stanley Penn, "NYC Will Confront Mafia in Chinatown by Bidding to Haul Garbage of Some Businesses," *Wall Street Journal*, 25 April 1988.

23. National Serv-All is described in Eugene Linden, "Entrepreneurs Can Do Everything Government Can Do, Only Better—Or Can They?" *Inc.*, Dec. 1984, 173. It is worth noting that not all cities have been fully satisfied with this firm's services.

24. See Lindsey Gruson, "Philadelphia Services Strike a Challenge for the Mayor," *New York Times*, 2 July 1986, and William Stevens, "Philadelphia Trash Haulers Ordered Back to Work," *New York Times*, 17 July 1986.

25. In smaller cities, the public sector absentee rate is 60 percent higher than is that of the private sector; in larger cities, the public sector rate is twice as high. See Stevens, "Scale, Market Structure," 447. Savas, who shared Stevens's data, reported that public garbage agencies averaged 12 percent absenteeism versus 6.5 percent for contractors; that municipal crews averaged 3.26 persons versus 2.15 persons for contractors; and that municipal agencies spent 4.35 hours per household per year versus 2.37 hours per year for contractors. Savas, "Policy Analysis," 70.

26. See E. S. Savas, "Intracity Competition between Public and Private Service Delivery," *Public Administration Review* 41 (January–February 1981).

27. Chuck Walbridge, manager of National Serv-All, quoted in Linden, "Entrepreneurs Can Do," 172.

28. E. S. Savas, "An Empirical Study of Competition in Municipal Service Delivery," *Public Administration Review* 37 (November–December 1977): 721, table 1.

29. Young, *How Shall We?* 73.

30. Department of Defense, *Report to Congress on the Commercial Activities Program* (Washington: March 1984).

31. Department of Defense, *Report to Congress, Department of Defense Commercial Activities Program* (Washington, April 1986), table 4.

32. General Accounting Office, *DOD Functions Contracted Out Under OMB Circular A–76: Contract Cost Increases and the Effects on Federal Employees* (Washington: April 1985).

33. Ibid., 4, appendix II, 38.

34. See the March 1984 Department of Defense "Commercial Activities Program," 3–4, and General Accounting Office, *DOD Functions Contracted Out Under OMB Circular A–76: Costs and Status of Certain Displaced Employees* (Washington: 12 July 1985), 2–3.

35. General Accounting Office, *GSA's Cleaning Costs Are Needlessly Higher than in the Private Sector* (Washington: 24 August 1981).

36. Garry L. Briese, "An Overview of the Private Sector Fire Service," *The International Fire Chief* (February 1984).

37. Roger Ahlbrandt, "Efficiency in the Provision of Fire Services," *Public Choice* 16 (Fall 1973): see especially 12, table III.

38. David G. Davies, "The Efficiency of Public versus Private Firms: The Case of Australia's Two Airlines," *Journal of Law and Economics* 14 (April 1971); and "Property Rights and Economic Efficiency—The Australian Airlines Revisited," *Journal of Law and Economics* 20 (April 1977). Davies has also done an equally ambitious but more ideologically strained and hence less convincing comparison of public and private banks in Australia: "Property Rights and Economic Behavior in Private and Government Enterprises: The Case of Australia's Banking System," *Research in Law and Economics* 13 (1981).

39. Cited in Davies, "Efficiency," 155.

40. Ibid., 160, n. 45.

41. Ibid., 163, table 3, and Davies, "Australian Airlines," 226, table 1.

42. See Davies, "Efficiency," 164, table 4. These specific figures cover only the 1959–69 period; the later article included neither a similarly detailed comparison nor data that could be used to calculate it.

43. Davies, "Australian Airlines," 226. It is possibly significant and certainly unfortunate that Davies dealt only with labor productivity and made no mention of capital productivity. If there is

only one right way to turn an airline—one uniquely efficient mix of capital and labor—this is not an issue. But if there is any room for *technical* trade-offs between people and machines, the efficiency question gets more complicated.

44. Douglas W. Caves and Laurits R. Christensen, "The Relative Efficiency of Public and Private Firms in a Competitive Environment: The Case of Canadian Railroads," *Journal of Political Economy* 88 (Dec. 1980); see especially 961, 974. Except for grain and flour transport rates, which continued to be regulated, both railroads were allowed to set rates anywhere between 1 to 2.5 times the total variable costs. Both railroads were also required to maintain certain unprofitable routes through lightly populated areas that they would have preferred to abandon.

45. The precise form of the total factor productivity comparison is significant. See ibid., 970–73, table 3. For productivity comparisons of the Canadian National and the Canadian Pacific, see ibid., 968–69, table 2, 974.

46. James L. Perry and Timlynn T. Babitsky, "Comparative Performance in Urban Bus Transit: Assessing Privatization Strategies," *Public Administration Review* 46 (January–February 1986).

47. See ibid., 62, table 3, for the statistical results.

48. The source for the discussion of Mill's involvement in the London water supply issue is Pedro Schwartz, "John Stuart Mill and Laissez Faire: London Water," *Economica* 33 (February 1966); see especially 80–81.

49. The studies summarized here are Patrick C. Mann and John L. Mikesell, "Ownership and Water System Operation," *Water Works Bulletin* 12 (October 1976); Mark Crain and Asghar Zard-koohi, "A Test of the Property-Rights Theory of the Firm: Water Utilities in the United States," *Journal of Law and Economics* 21 (October 1978); Thomas W. Bruggink, "Public versus Regulated Private Enterprise in the Municipal Water Industry: A Comparison of Operating Costs," *Quarterly Review of Economics and Business* 22 (Spring 1982); Susan Feigenbaum and Ronald Teeples, "Public versus Private Water Delivery: A Hedonic Cost Approach," *Review of Economics and Statistics* (1983); Ronald Teeples, Susan Feigenbaum, and David Glyer, "Public versus Private Water Delivery: Cost Comparisons," *Public Finance Quarterly* 14 (July 1986); Patricia Byrners, Shawn Grosskopf, and Kathy Hayes, "Efficiency and Ownership: Further Evidence," *Review of Economics and Statistics* 68 (May 1986); and Ronald Teeples and David Glyer, "Cost of Water Delivery Systems: Specification and Ownership Effects," *Review of Economics and Statistics* 69 (August 1987).

50. Robert A. McGuire and Robert Ohnsfeldt, "Public versus Private Water Delivery: A Critical Analysis of a Hedonic Cost Approach," *Public Finance Quarterly* 14 (July 1986): 345.

51. It is also worth noting that a study applying modern statistical techniques to historical cost data on British coal-gas utilities of the late 1800s found no significant cost differences between public and private gas suppliers. If anything, the edge was in favor of public gas utilities. Robert Millward and Robert Ward, "The Costs of Public and Private Gas Enterprises in Late 19th Century Britain," *Oxford Economic Papers* 39 (December 1987).

52. The studies comparing electric utility costs are Robert A. Meyer, "Publicly Owned versus Privately Owned Utilities: A Policy Choice," *Review of Economics and Statistics* 57 (November 1975); Leland Neuberg, "Two Issues in the Municipal Ownership of Electric Power Distribution Systems," *The Bell Journal of Economics* 8 (1977); James A. Yonker, "Economic Performance of Public and Private Enterprise: The Case of U.S. Electric Industries," *Journal of Economics and Business* 28 (Fall 1975); Donn R. Pescatrice and John M. Trapani, "The Performance and Objectives of Public and Private Utilities Operating in the United States," *Journal of Public Economics* 13 (1980): R. Fare, S. Grosskopf, and J. Logan, "The Relative Performance in Publicly Owned and Privately Owned Electric Utilities," *Journal of Public Economics* 26 (1985); and Scott E. Atkinson and Robert Halvorsen, "The Relative Efficiency of Public and Private Firms in a Regulated Environment: The Case of U.S. Electric Utilities," *Journal of Public Economics* 29 (April 1986).

53. Richard Wallace and Paul E. Junk, "Economic Inefficiency of Small Municipal Electric Generating Systems," *Land Economics* 66 (February 1970), did find public utilities to be less efficient, but they explicitly defined their "public sector" sample to include only municipal utilities operating at a small scale, and they removed all efficiently large municipal utilities from consideration. Louis De Alessi, "Managerial Tenure under Private and Government Ownership in the Electric Power Industry," *Journal of Political Economy* 82 (May–June 1974), found some evidence that top managers at public utilities enjoy undue job tenure, but he presented no results on overall efficiency.

54. See Yonker, "Economic Performance," 65, table 5, equations 4–7; and Fare, Grosskopf, and Logan, "Relative Performance," 100.

55. Meyer, "Publicly Owned," 398.

56. Neuberg, "Two Issues," 320. De Alessi, "Managerial Tenure," drew exactly the opposite

conclusion from the same set of facts. Neuberg probably did not really believe this was the source of the difference, and I do not.

57. Neuberg, "Two Issues," 321.

58. H. Averch and L. L. Johnson, "Behavior of the Firm under Regulatory Constraint," *American Economic Review* (December 1962).

59. See, for example, Robert M. Spann, "Rate of Return Regulation and Efficiency in Production: An Empirical Test of the Averch-Johnson Thesis," *Bell Journal of Economics* 5 (Spring 1974).

60. Meyer, "Publicly Owned," 399, and Neuberg, "Two Issues," 321. Pescatrice and Trapani, "Performance and Objectives," 273–74, found that investments by public firms tended to lower costs—that their capital decisions looked like sensible responses to technological change and the relative costs of capital, labor, and fuel—but that "the addition of new equipment by private firms does not reduce the cost significantly and may even increase it," just as the Averch-Johnson hypothesis would suggest. For discussions of the Averch-Johnson effect in water utilities, see Crain and Zardkoohi, "Property-Rights Theory," 402–5, and Bruggink, "Public versus Regulated," 121.

61. Glenn Blackmon and Richard Zeckhauser, "Utility Regulation with Fragile Commitments" (discussion paper, Kennedy School of Government, Harvard University, June 1985).

62. Walter Primeaux identified the forty-nine American cities where there was some kind of direct competition between electric utilities, matched this sample with a set of otherwise similar cities, and compared cost levels. He found that competition reduced costs by about 11 percent, on average, regardless of whether utilities are public or private. The results are statistically sound. His conclusions, consistent with those advanced here, are that private monopolies develop the same kind of organizational slack that plagues public agencies, and that regulation cannot really substitute for competition. See Walter Primeaux, "An Assessment of X-Efficiency Gained through Competition," *Review of Economics and Statistics* 59 (1977).

63. This could undercut competition in animal shelter operations, inspection services, and perhaps also in day-care facilities and in programs for the retarded. For example, it took over one year for Massachusetts officials to respond to complaints about the operation of a for-profit methadone maintenance enterprise, which suggests that it would have been fruitless for other potential operators to bid for the contract and, possibly, pointless for the incumbent to offer very high-quality service. See Patricia Wen, "State Stops For-Profit Drug Clinic's Expansion," *Boston Globe*, 9 June 1987.

Chapter 5

1. For one perspective on this tendency, see Charles Wolf, Jr., "A Theory of Nonmarket Failure: Framework for Implementation Analysis," *Journal of Law and Economics* 22 (April 1979): 113.

2. Sometimes, however, government officials may *prefer* to cede discretion over means. When Philadelphia garbage that had been collected under contract ended up floating in the surf at a Haitian beach, Philadelphia officials met Haitian protests with the claim that municipal responsibility ended once the contractor took possession of the trash. "Haiti Says Philadelphia Garbage Was Dumped by Ship on Its Beach," *New York Times*, 8 Feb. 1988.

3. This caveat is likely to matter when it comes to collecting government debt, for example, a point neglected in at least one argument for contracting out federal debt collecting. See James T. Bennett and Manuel H. Johnson, "Tax Reduction without Sacrifice: Private-Sector Production of Public Services," *Public Finance Quarterly* 8 (October 1980): 379.

4. A classic study by James G. March and Herbert A. Simon, *Organizations* (New York: John Wiley & Sons, 1958), 145, includes an analogous set of guidelines for the choice between "product specifications" (corresponding to pure profit-seeking agency) and "activity specifications" (corresponding to pure bureaucratic agency).

5. Niskanen, *Bureaucracy and Representative Government*, 201–9, calls for such a system of competition and of rights to claim cost savings as remedies for the ills of bureaucracy.

6. Such "time and materials" contracts are sometimes used in the private sector but, in the words of an IBM executive, such relationships "require a colossal amount of supervision." E. Raymond Corey, *Procurement Management* (Boston: CBI Publishing Company, 1978), 4.

7. For thoughtful readings on this topic, see Michael Walzer, "Toward a Theory of Social Assignments," in Winthrop Knowlton and Richard Zechhauser, eds., *American Society: Public and Private Responsibilities* (Cambridge, Mass.: Ballinger Publishing, 1986), and Burton A. Weisbrod, *The Nonprofit Economy* (Cambridge, Mass.: Harvard University Press, 1988).

8. See item in "Labor Letter," *Wall Street Journal*, 2 Feb. 1988.

9. Ben A. Franklin, "VA Ends Bonuses to Appeals Board," *New York Times*, 10 June 1988.

10. Deputy director of the Office of Management and Budget, quoted in Robert D. Hershey, Jr., "Bonuses for Bureaucrats? Why Not?" *New York Times*, 29 May 1987.

11. "China Lake," *Wall Street Journal*, 16 May 1986; "Tax Collecting on Commission," *Wall Street Journal*, 1 July 1986.

12. This exchange is recounted in Lawrence Langer, *G.B.S. and the Lunatic* (New York: Atheneum, 1963), 100. I am grateful to Robert Brustein for this reference.

13. According to Mark Menchick, an advisor to the Senate Subcommittee on Intergovernmental Relations, "one of the best results of privatization is that it forces government to reconsider the nature of the service and the rationale for providing it." Menchick is quoted in Thomas B. Darr, "Pondering Privatization May Be Good for Your Government," *Governing* (November 1987): 44.

14. These points apply to private as well as to public bureaucracies. See March and Simon, *Organizations*, 147–48.

15. Jay's role in the negotiations is discussed in Richard B. Morris, *Witnesses at the Creation: Hamilton, Madison, Jay, and the Constitution* (New York: New American Library, 1985), 78–93.

16. Edward Banfield also cites the need for honor—although he is pessimistic as to the likelihood that it will often be forthcoming—in a context where "objectives . . . are numerous, unordered, vague and contradictory." Edward Banfield, "Corruption as a Feature of Governmental Organization," *Journal of Law and Economics* 18 (December 1975): 595.

17. The *Wall Street Journal*'s coverage of the Nobel Prize in economics to public choice scholar James Buchanan shared a page with a feature on Dr. Samuel Broder of the National Cancer Institute, who worked brutal hours and hand-carried samples from lab to lab in his passion to find a cure for HIV infection. On the same day that the *New York Times* reprinted Dr. Buchanan's Nobel acceptance speech warning that bureaucracy "manipulates the agenda for legislative action for the purpose of securing outcomes favorable to its own interests," it ran a profile of Richard Darman, the indefatigable deputy treasury secretary who worked far harder, and for far less money than he could have earned in the private sector, in order to draft, and to push for the passage of, the historic 1986 tax bill. These examples of honorable civil servants simply happened to share newspaper space with the apotheosis of public choice theory, and virtually any other day's news would offer its own examples. See Lindley H. Clark, Jr., "Critic of Politicians Wins Nobel Prize in Economic Science," and Marilyn Chase, "In War Against AIDS, Samuel Broder Serves as General and Private," *Wall Street Journal*, 17 Oct. 1986; James M. Buchanan, "Why Governments Got Out of Hand," and Peter T. Kilborn, "Richard Darman's Invisible Hand," *New York Times*, 26 Oct. 1986. The impressions of C. William Verity, a leading steel-industry executive who served a stint as Reagan's commerce secretary, are also noteworthy: "I had always felt . . . that maybe government people didn't work so hard because they weren't so highly motivated. Well, I was dead wrong. In this department there is a tremendous cadre of professionals highly motivated not by financial incentives but to serve their country. It's as simple as that." Verity is quoted in Clyde H. Farnsworth, "Good Will and Progress Mark a Brief Tenure," *New York Times*, 29 Nov. 1988.

18. Anthony Downs, *Inside Bureaucracy* (Boston: Little, Brown and Company, 1967).

19. Max Weber, "Politics as a Vocation," in Gerth and Mills, eds., *From Max Weber*, 80.

20. As this chapter was being edited, two instances arose where purchasing regulations served to frustrate efforts to base contract awards in part on reputation—in one case, to favor a reliable supplier, in the other, to penalize a troublesome and unresponsive supplier. Calvin Sims, "Navy Broke Bid Rules, Panel Finds," *New York Times*, 9 Dec. 1988; Bob Davis, "U.S. Divides Huge Contract for FTS-2000," *Wall Street Journal*, 8 Dec. 1988. For a related example, see the statement of Milton J. Socolar, *The Postal Service's Sole-Source Contract with Perot Systems Corporation*, prepared for the General Accounting Office (Washington: 10 August 1988).

21. Max Weber noted this difference between European and American culture in 1918: "The social esteem of officials as such is especially low when the demand for expert administration and the dominance of status conventions are weak. This is especially the case in the United States." Max Weber, "Bureaucracy," in Gerth and Mills, eds., *From Max Weber*, 200.

22. Max Weber argued that "a very strong development of the 'right to the office' naturally makes it more difficult to staff bureaucracies with regard to technical efficiency" because incompetent, negligent, or rebellious incumbents cannot easily be removed. Ibid., 203.

23. U.S. Constitution, ARTS. 2 and 3.

24. For examples of studies in the controversial area of public-private pay comparisons, see Sharon P. Smith, "Pay Differentials between Federal Government and Private Sector Workers," *Industrial*

and Labor Relations Review 29 (January 1976); and Joseph F. Quinn, "Wage Differentials among Older Workers in the Public and Private Sectors," *Journal of Human Resources* 14 (Winter 1979).

25. See "Abuses Reported in Assets Agency," *New York Times*, 25 April 1988; "Calls by U.S. Workers Tracked," *New York Times*, 23 June 1986; and Suzanne Daley, "Custodian versus Principal: Stacked Deck," *New York Times*, 25 Feb. 1988. See also pieces by City Council President Andrew Stein in *New York Times*, 6 Nov. 1987 and 6 Feb. 1988, both in Opinions Editorial Section; editorials, *New York Times*, 28 Jan. 1988 and 13 May 1988; and Jane Perlez, "Wagner Says Schools-Custodians Agreement Is Near," *New York Times*, 19 May 1988.

26. William Orzechowski, "Economic Models of Bureaucracy: Survey, Extensions, and Evidence," in Thomas E. Borcherding, ed., *Budgets and Bureaucrats: The Sources of Government Growth* (Durham, N.C.: Duke University Press, 1977), 239.

27. Crystal Nix, "Welfare Hotel Is Said to Show $3 Million Profit," *New York Times*, 23 Nov. 1985, and "City Report Cites a Fifty-Percent Profit at Welfare Hotel," *New York Times*, 11 March 1986. Spurred by such reports, New York City took steps to "deprivatize" the shelter business as it moved to buy one of the biggest welfare hotels and to run it directly. Josh Barbanel, "New York City Seeks to Buy a Welfare Hotel and Renovate It," *New York Times*, 9 March 1988.

28. However, there are limits on the ability of owners to wring rents out of lower levels of profit-seeking organizations. For some interesting discussion and evidence, see Daniel Kahneman, Jack L. Knetsch, and Richard Thaler, "Fairness as a Constraint on Profit Seeking: Entitlements in the Market," *American Economic Review* 76 (September 1986).

29. Keith Schnieder, "Operators Got Millions in Bonuses Despite Hazards at Atom Plants," *New York Times*, 26 Oct. 1988.

30. A pattern of asymmetrical assertion of agent interests—with greater efforts to block cutbacks than to increase spending—may also be explained by the tendency for rents to be *capitalized* into the price of entering rent-rich positions: Individuals might serve in the military in part to gain preference in the civil service system, for example. When, similarly, a Pentagon supplier is acquired by another firm, its most valuable asset is frequently its connections with the government. See the discussion of the sale of the Chrysler Corporation tank division in Robert B. Reich and John D. Donahue, *New Deals* (New York: Times Books, 1985), 241.

31. Bribes from public workers are not unknown. Two judges in Philadelphia were indicted for accepting five hundred dollars from a roofer's union, for example. See Martin Tolchin, "Suddenly, It's Open Season on Public Servants," *New York Times*, 26 Oct. 1986. More commonly, though, civil servants may seek to influence officials through illegitimate favors only somewhat analogous to bribes, including reciprocal back-scratching, special services, flattery, and toadying.

Chapter 6

1. Department of Commerce, *Survey of Current Business* (Washington: July 1988), table 3.9.

2. Office of Management and Budget, *The United States Budget in Brief FY 1989* (Washington, 1988), 104, table 3.

3. See Richard Halloran, *To Arm a Nation* (New York: Macmillan Publishing, 1986), 186–90, 199–203; J. Ronald Fox with James L. Field, *The Defense Management Challenge: Weapons Acquisition* (Boston: Harvard Business School Press, 1988), 327–29; and, for a few specific examples, see Tim Carrington, "Federal Probes of Contractors Rise for Year," *Wall Street Journal*, 23 Feb. 1987; Ellen White Read, "Indictment Seen for Rockwell in Billing Case," *Wall Street Journal*, 22 Jan. 1988; Lindsey Gruson, "Litton Unit to Pay $15 million to U.S.," *New York Times*, 16 July 1986 and "Litton Unit Guilty Plea on Fraud," *New York Times*, 23 July 1986; and Tim Carrington, "Lifting of General Dynamics Suspension Increases Congress-Pentagon Tensions," *Wall Street Journal*, 10 Feb. 1986.

4. See Edward T. Pound, "Pentagon Payoffs: Honored Employee Is a Key in Huge Fraud in Defense Purchasing," *Wall Street Journal*, 2 March 1988; Andy Pasztor, "U.S. Indictment Names Nine People, Five Firms in First Round of Defense-Bribe Charges," *Wall Street Journal*, 4 Feb. 1987 and "Bribery Scandal at Defense Department Center Puts Focus on Problems in Military Procurement," *Wall Street Journal*, 28 May 1986.

5. Cost estimate from Fox and Field, *Defense Management*, 322; comparison figure from Office of Management and Budget, *Budget in Brief FY 1989*, 27, table on "Domestic Discretionary Programs."

6. *The Gallup Report*, no. 260 (May 1987): 3.

7. These historical examples are taken from Halloran, *To Arm a Nation*, 194.

8. This is a quite compressed summary of contracting problems in weapons procurement. Jacques S. Gansler, *The Defense Industry* (Cambridge, Mass.: The MIT Press, 1980), 30–31, enumerates thirty particulars in which military contracting departs from the conditions required for full competitive efficiency; most of these conditions apply also to other types of government contracting. J. Ronald Fox, *Arming America* (Cambridge, Mass.: Harvard University Press, 1974), 4–5, offers a similar diagnosis.

9. For the past several decades, the United States, especially, has adopted a strategy of countering quantitative superiority with technological superiority. See William J. Perry, "Defense Reform and the Quality-Quantity Quandry," in Asa A. Clark IV et al., eds., *The Defense Reform Debate* (London and Baltimore: The Johns Hopkins University Press, 1984).

10. Frederic M. Scherer, *The Weapons Acquisition Process: Economic Incentives* (Boston: Harvard Business School Press, 1964), 143, table 6.2.

11. For examples, see J. Michael Cummins, "Incentive Contracting for National Defense: A Problem of Optimal Risk Sharing," *Bell Journal of Economics* 13 (Spring 1977), especially 169; John R. Hiller and Robert D. Tollison, "Incentive versus Cost-Plus Contracts in Defense Procurement," *Journal of Industrial Economics* 26 (March 1978); and David P. Baron and David Besanko, "Monitoring, Moral Hazard, Asymmetric Information and Risk Sharing in Procurement Contracting," *Rand Journal of Economics* 18, no. 4 (Winter 1978).

12. Figure based on General Accounting Office calculations cited in Bill Thurman, *Reducing the Cost of Weapon Systems Acquisition: Hearing before the Task Force on Selected Defense Procurement Matters of the Senate Committee on Armed Services*, 98th Cong., 1st Sess. (Washington: 18 December, 1984), 25. A Rand Corporation study cited in Fox, *Arming America*, 376–79, found that midcontract changes boosted the final cost of ninety-four Air Force contracts by an average of 40 percent. Gansler, *The Defense Industry*, 94, estimates that the average contract shows cost growth of 45 percent. Fox and Field, *The Defense Management Challenge*, 33–34, cited a Department of Defense Inspector General Office study of fifteen thousand engine parts that found that the cost of the majority of the parts had at least doubled between 1980 and 1982, while the cost of over one-quarter had increased by a factor of five. See also Robert A. Magnan, *In Search of the "End Game": A Comparison of U.S. and Foreign Weapons Acquisition Systems* (Washington: CIA Exceptional Intelligence Analyst Program, 1986), 28–30.

13. For a particularly vigorous statement of this point of view, see Easterbrook, "Sack Weinberger."

14. This occurs, in part, because production must begin before development work is wrapped up. For a discussion of "production concurrency," see Thomas L. McNaughter, "Weapons Procurement: The Futility of Reform," *International Security* 12 (Fall 1987): 75–80. The developer also has an overwhelming edge in production competitions because of the expertise it develops and, perhaps, because of the tooling it acquires, since the urgency that typifies weapons programs makes military officials resist the delay that would be associated with switching to a new firm for production.

15. General Accounting Office, *Analysis of Change Orders on Selected F-16 Airframe Contract*, (Washington: December 1987). See also Fox, *Arming America*, 237–38, as to the ease with which ostensibly fixed-price contracts can be altered.

16. See Richard W. Stevenson, "New Risks in Military Deals," *New York Times*, 24 Feb. 1987. See also The MAC Group, *The Impact on Defense Industrial Capability of Changes in the Procurement and Tax Policy 1984–1987* (Washington: February 1988), especially list of procurement changes 8–12.

17. See Scherer, *Weapons Acquisition*, 32–33.

18. See Magnan, *"End Game,"* 80.

19. See Halloran, *To Arm a Nation*, 191–92.

20. Quoted in Richard Halloran, "Making Arms Makers Do It Right," *New York Times*, 15 June 1986. For related reporting, see John Koten and Tim Carrington, "Beating the Rap: For General Dynamics, Scandal over Billing Hasn't Hurt Business," *Wall Street Journal*, 29 April 1986; and Eileen White, "Pentagon Dodge: Suspended Contractors Often Continue to Get More Defense Business," *Wall Street Journal*, 6 May 1986.

21. See Scherer, *Weapons Acquisition*, and James J. Anton and Dennis A. Yao, "Second Sourcing and the Experience Curve: Price Competition in Defense Procurement," *Rand Journal of Economics* 18 (Spring 1987). When the Air Force brought in Teledyne as a second source to curb the Williams International monopoly on cruise missile engines, it had to pay nearly double the Williams Interna-

tional price. See Tim Carrington, "Defense Contractors Face Less-Receptive Climate as U.S. Budget Tightens and Scrutiny Toughens," *Wall Street Journal*, 15 Sept. 1986.

22. See Fox, *Arming America*, 377, n. 13.

23. See Fox and Field, *The Defense Management Challenge*, 42–43, and Fox, *Arming America*, 4, 471. In the latter, Fox is blunt: "Contracts fail as instruments of control."

24. See Richard W. Stevenson, "The High Cost of an Arms Scandal," *New York Times*, 10 July 1988, and Paula Dwyer, "The Defense Scandal," *Business Week*, 4 July 1988, for discussions of the political sentiment to increase congressional oversight of the Pentagon and its contractors, and to broaden the mandate of the Department of Defense inspector general, in the wake of the 1988 scandals.

25. See "Cookie Mix, Dry," in *Harper's*, Oct. 1985; and Tim Carrington, "In Wake of Foul-Ups, the Pentagon Is Pressured to Shop around for Bargains on Everyday Goods," *Wall Street Journal*, 3 Oct. 1986.

26. Quoted in Halloran, *To Arm a Nation*, 179. For a theoretical discussion of proliferating specifications, see Murray L. Weidenbaum, "Arms and the American Economy: A Domestic Convergence Hypothesis," *American Economic Review* 58 (May 1968): 330–32.

27. Halloran, "Making Arms Makers."

28. Fox and Field, *The Defense Management Challenge*, 302–7.

29. See John E. Steiner and Louise K. Montle, "Changing the Course of U.S. Aviation," *Astronautics and Aeronautics* (May 1983), 10.

30. See Magnan, *"End Game,"* 20–22.

31. See Scherer, *Weapons Acquisition*, 107–8.

32. Ibid., 136–37, 177–84.

33. See Cummins, "Incentive Contracting." Cummins illustrates with an example involving a combat vehicle with two design choices involving a total of four well-defined alternatives, and shows how a schedule of contingent contracts could be negotiated. But real-world applications would involve a more lengthy—and, almost inevitably, still incomplete—set of configurations, thus creating considerable room for dispute in implementation.

34. See Scherer, *Weapons Acquisition*, 252–57, for a discussion of the long history or renegotiation rules. Scherer cites John Perry Miller, *Pricing of Military Procurements* (New Haven: Yale University Press, 1949), 238, who wrote that "it is extremely difficult to negotiate contracts with appropriate incentives to efficient production so long as there is in the background a scheme for recouping excessive profits "

35. See John Strong, "Lockheed and the C-5A" (case study, Harvard University, Kennedy School of Government, 1986); Robert B. Reich and John D. Donahue, *New Deals: The Chrysler Revival and the American System* (New York: Times Books, 1985), 65–69; and Dave Griffiths, "Defense Keeps Tightening the Screws on Contractors," *Business Week*, 2 Feb. 1987.

36. Twelve are listed in General Accounting Office, *DOD Acquisition: Strengthening Capabilities of Key Personnel in Systems Acquisition* (Washington: 1986), 128. The other two are Scherer, *Weapons Acquisition*, and Fox and Field, *The Defense Management Challenge*.

37. See Fox and Field, *The Defense Management Challenge*, 42–44.

38. In Defense Secretary Packard's words, "successful development, production, and deployment of major defense systems are primarily dependent upon competent people, rational priorities, and clearly defined responsibilities." Ibid., 44–45.

39. Packard's 1971 testimony to the House Subcommittee on Defense Appropriations, quoted in Fox, *Arming America*, 385.

40. Ibid., 477–78; see also Fox and Field, *The Defense Management Challenge*, 46, 134.

41. The procurement officer is quoted in Fox and Field, *The Defense Management Challenge*, 132.

42. Ibid., 37.

43. Public Law 97–377, and Public Law 98–212.

44. Public Law 98–369.

45. Public Law 99–145.

46. Public Law 99–591.

47. David Packard, chairman, *An Interim Report to the President by the Blue Ribbon Commission on Defense Management* (Washington: 28 February 1986), 13.

48. Ibid., 19, 21.

49. Ibid., 15. Richard D. DeLauer, former undersecretary of defense, was one of many to share Packard's sentiment. "There's an adversarial environment caused by the present occupants of the

Pentagon. They think everybody's a crook. So everybody's watching everybody else, instead of pushing the product out the door." DeLauer is quoted in Nicholas D. Kristof, "Stern Times for Arms Makers," *New York Times*, 3 July 1986.

50. The *New York Times* noted with some relief that "the various sections of the band do not actually compete musically with one another to achieve the desired effect." John H. Cushman, Jr., "Competition Is Music to Some Ears," *New York Times*, 29 July 1986.

51. Nicholas D. Kristof, "Stern Times for Arms Makers," *New York Times*, 3 July 1986.

52. Tim Carrington, "Defense Contractors Face Less-Receptive Climate as U.S. Budget Tightens and Scrutiny Toughens," *Wall Street Journal*, 15 Sept. 1986; and Richard W. Stevenson, "Competition for Contracts Trims Costs for Pentagon," *New York Times*, 31 March 1988.

53. See John H. Cushman, "Stealth Project Competition Rejected," *New York Times*, 9 Oct. 1987.

54. See John H. Cushman, "Arms-Buying Revisions Imperiled," *New Yorks Times*, 17 Sept. 1987. See also editorial, "Another Failure to Fix the Pentagon," *New York Times*, 21 Sept. 1987, and John H. Cushman, "Pentagon Procurement Has Armor that Repels Reform," *New York Times*, 27 Sept. 1987.

55. The MAC Group, *Impact on Defense*.

56. Arthur D. Little study excerpted in Nicholas D. Kristof, "Stern Times for Arms Makers," *New York Times*, 3 July 1986.

57. Richard W. Stevenson, "Competition for Contracts Trims Costs for Pentagon," *New York Times*, 31 March 1988.

58. President of Martin Marietta is quoted in Thomas Moore, "Why Martin Marietta Loves Mary Cunningham," *Fortune*, 16 March 1987.

59. Donald H. White, president of Hughes, is quoted in Nicholas D. Kristof, "Stern Times for Arms Makers," *New York Times*, 3 July 1986. The three firms leaving the game were Martin Marietta, LTV, and Fairchild Republic; Grumman was rumored to be considering a similar move. William M. Carley, "Grumman's Future in Military Aircraft Is Called into Question by Recent Setback," *Wall Street Journal*, 29 Jan. 1988.

60. Packard, *Interim Report*, 1.

61. Alexander Cockburn, "When National Security Meant Militarizing the Tortugas," *Wall Street Journal*, 29 May 1986.

62. See Merton J. Peck and Frederic M. Scherer, *The Weapons Acquisition Process* (Boston: Harvard Business School Press, 1962), 43–47.

63. Figure from commentary by Murray L. Weidenbaum in Caspar Weinberger, *The Defense Budget* (Washington: American Enterprise Institute, 1972), 24.

64. Office of Management and Budget Circular A–109 requires formal mission analysis before a procurement program can begin, as well as frequent reassessment throughout. But it has proven relatively easy to meet the letter of this circular without asking hard questions about a system's value. See Fox and Field, *The Defense Management Challenge*, 46–47.

65. Alain Enthoven has described "a sort of Parkinson's law of military requirements: they will always expand to use up the supply estimated to be available." Alain C. Enthoven and K. Wayne Smith, *How Much Is Enough?* (New York: Harper and Row, 1971), 201. For thoughtful comments on this general topic, see Enthoven and Smith's chapter 6, "Yardsticks of Sufficiency." Central Intelligence Agency assessments of Soviet aims and capacities frequently differ from those of the Pentagon (see Michael R. Gordon, "C.I.A., Evaluating Soviet Threat, Often Is Not So Grim as Pentagon," *New York Times*, 16 July 1986), and are themselves inconclusive—the "range of uncertainty" about the much-discussed Soviet outspending of the United States in the 1970s varied from an insignificant gap to a hugh disparity. See Gansler, *The Defense Industry*, 24, fig. 1.7.

66. Casper Weinberger, ed., *The Defense Budget* (Washington: American Enterprise Institute, 1972), 4. See also discussion on the conceptual difficulties of measuring the value of armaments, Holland Hunter, *American Economic Review* 58 (May 1968): 442–45.

67. See David Stockman, *The Triumph of Politics* (New York: Harper and Row, 1986), 107–9, 294–95.

68. For examples of weapon-system lead times, see Fox and Field, *The Defense Management Challenge*, 29, table 1.4. For a discussion of problems with both developmental and operational testing in the Army, see General Accounting Office, *The Army Needs More Comprehensive Evaluations to Make Effective Use of Its Weapon System Testing* (Washington: 24 February 1984).

69. Gansler caps a typical—if unusually sophisticated—discussion of the issue with these words of warning: "The preparedness deficiencies of the United States and NATO must be corrected by

appropriate planning, done well in advance, and fully implemented. The response time is too great to do it later, and the potential cost too high to not do it at all." Gansler, *The Defense Industry*, 127. While much of Gansler's discussion is sound, his list of recommended changes, ibid., 274–77, amounts to an expensive and probably unwarranted insurance policy.

70. These figures reported in Fred Kaplan, "Secrecy Is on the Rise in Pentagon's Budget," *Boston Globe*, 12 Jan. 1987. For other discussions of the secrecy issue, see Tim Weiner, "The Dark Secret of the Black Budget," *Washington Monthly*, May 1987; Anthony Ramirez, "The Secret Bomber," *Fortune*, 14 March 1988; and Malcolm W. Browne, "Will the Stealth Bomber Work?" *New York Times Magazine*, 17 July 1988.

71. For example, see "Debating the B-2," *Aviation Week and Space Technology*, 28 Nov. 1988, 11.

72. Contractors often find advantages in this imprecision. See Tim Carrington, "Defense Firms, Facing Budget Squeeze, Mobilize to Fight Plan for an Agency to Measure Profits," *Wall Street Journal*, 21 Jan. 1987.

73. See Douglas R. Bohi, "Profit Performance in the Defense Industry," *Journal of Political Economy* 81 (May–June 1973): 721–23.

74. See Weidenbaum, "Arms and American Economy," 434, table 1.

75. See Bohi, "Profit Performance," 724, table 1, 728.

76. See George J. Stigler and Claire Friedland, "Profits of Defense Contractors," *American Economic Review* 61 (September 1971). The virtue of this study is that it measures return on equity directly at the level of equity securities, thus avoiding ambiguous measures of profitability at the balance sheet level. For a survey of pre-1980 analyses of defense industry profits, see Gansler, *The Defense Industry*, 85–88.

77. See Department of Defense, *Defense Financial and Investment Review* (Washington: June 1985), V30–V33, ex. 12–15.

78. See General Accounting Office, *Government Contracting: Assessment of the Study of Defense Contractor Profitability* (Washington: December 1986); note especially appendix 4 and table 4.8 on p. 91.

79. See RRG Associates, *Financial Analysis of Major Defense Contractors* (May 1987), 18, table 3.

80. For press discussions of defense industry securities, see Charles Stein, "Defense Stocks in Retreat," *Boston Globe*, 23 July 1987; Richard W. Stevenson, "Military Contractors Squeezed," *New York Times*, 16 Nov. 1987; and "The High Cost of an Arms Scandal," *New York Times*, 10 July 1988.

81. These figures from staff working paper by Congressional Budget Office, *Compensation of Aerospace Workers* (Washington: September 1984), 4, table 1.

82. General Accounting Office, *Compensation by Twelve Aerospace Contractors* (Washington: 12 October 1984), 6, chart 2. Lower-level workers earned much smaller premiums, it was found, supporting the chapter 5 arguments on where the rents end up.

83. See Gordon Adams, *The Politics of Defense Contracting* (New Brunswick and London: Transaction Books, 1981), 190–93. Adams also describes a similar corporate campaign mounted by Grumman—involving workers and investors, state officials and representatives, and the vast Grumman network of subcontractors—when the Pentagon sought to delay production of the F-14 Tomcat.

84. See Charles Mohr, "Pentagon Accused by GAO of Illegal Lobbying," *New York Times*, 1 Oct. 1982.

85. Philip M. Stern, *The Best Congress Money Can Buy* (New York: Pantheon Books, 1988), 38.

86. See Nick Kotz, *Wild Blue Yonder: Money, Politics, and the B-1 Bomber* (New York: Pantheon, 1988).

87. John Koten, "McDonnell Douglas Lobbies Congress to Save Apache Helicopter Program," *Wall Street Journal*, 12 March 1987.

88. See Subcommittee on Oversight of Government Management, Senate Committee on Governmental Affairs, *Wedtech: A Review of Federal Procurement Decisions* (Washington: 1988). See also Edward T. Pound, "Weapons Inquiry Soon Will Provide a Look at Consultants' Role," *Wall Street Journal*, 19 July 1988.

89. Fox, *Arming America*, 457.

90. Fox and Field, *The Defense Management Challenge*, 300.

91. Quote in Richard Halloran, "Arms Scandal: More than a Matter of Greed," *New York Times*, 17 July 1988.

92. Richard Halloran, "Arms Industry Urged by Carlucci to Focus on Integrity in Dealings," *New York Times*, 26 July 1988.

93. For a thoughtful statement of this view, see Steven Kelman, "Defense Bureaucracy's Corrupting Influence," *Wall Street Journal*, 7 July 1988. Kelman's proposal to let reputation, as perceived by contracting officials, guide source selection decisions echoes the view of Scherer, *Weapons Acquisition*, chapter 4.

94. This is also the basic recommendation in Fox and Field, *The Defense Management Challenge*, chapters 3, 4, and 8.

95. See Edward A. Kolodzief, *Making and Marketing Arms* (Princeton: Princeton University Press, 1987), 244–54, for an overview of the French procurement service. See also Joginder S. Dhillon and Brent Vardeman Woods, "A Centralized Civilian Acquisition Organization: Analysis of a Proposal for Structural Reform of U.S. Defense Procurement" (third-year paper at Harvard Law School, March 1987).

96. See Peck and Scherer, *The Weapons Acquisition Process*, v, and Fox, *Arming America*, 41. The Watervliet Arsenal still supplies the American armed forces (and those of much of the West) with large-bore cannon. See Harold Faber, "New York Arsenal Celebrates Role as Only Big Gun Producer in U.S.," *New York Times*, 24 July 1988.

97. I have benefited from discussions about the arsenal system with Bruce Gudmundsson and Marc Cancian.

98. See Scherer, *Weapons Acquisition*, 385–98, especially 389. See also *Jane's Weapons Systems 1987–88* (London: Jane's Publishing Co., 1988), 759.

99. Herman Leonard speculated about such a system in a 1987 seminar at Harvard University. Gansler, *The Defense Industry*, 265, urged the separation of development and production, and more recently Thomas McNaughter, "Weapons Procurement: The Futility of Reform," *International Security* (Fall 1987), called for "competition among design alternatives in which production firms would stand more or less neutrally by, waiting to bid on the winning design." Scherer, *Weapons Acquisition*, 189, discussed the weakness of contractual incentives for managing weapons design. The German and, to some extent, the Soviet systems follow this pattern of separating design and production, with a governmental organization mediating the processes. See Magnan, *"End Game,"* 52, 56.

100. See Scherer, *Weapons Acquisition*, 396. Scherer's astute discussion of the arsenal system, ibid., 385–98, merits attention.

101. Eileen White, "Competition Drive: War on Military Waste May Turn on Battles of Small vs. Big Firms," *Wall Street Journal*, 6 March 1986.

102. For a thoughtful theoretical treatment of this issue, see Jean Tirole, "Hierarchies and Bureaucracies: On the Role of Collusion in Organizations" (discussion paper at Massachusetts Institute of Technology, December 1985).

103. See Charles Mohr, "Military Debates Measure of Contractor Efficiency," *New York Times*, 25 March 1986, and the discussion of Tech Mod, IMIP, "Work Measurement," and other attempts to affect contractor operations, rather than results, as described in the statement of Lt. Gen. Bernard P. Randolph, *Reducing the Cost of Weapons Systems Acquisition: Hearing before the Task Force on Selected Defense Procurement Matters of the Senate Committee on Armed Services*, 98th Cong., 2d sess., 18 December 1984, 14–15, 19–20.

Chapter 7

1. Federal employee compensation in 1987 (as a share of total spending): 14 percent; purchases of outside goods and services: 21.6 percent. State and local employee compensation: 53.2 percent; outside purchases: 36.3 percent. From Department of Commerce, *Survey of Current Business* (Washington: June 1988), tables 3.3, 3.7.

2. Number of workers, 1985: 3,021,000 federal, 3,984 state, 9,685,000 local. Department of Commerce, *Statistical Abstract of the United States, 1988* (Washington: 1988), 282, table 462.

3. See Poole, *Cutting Back City Hall*; Bennett and Johnson, *Better Government*; and Savas, *Privatizing the Public Sector*. Each of these early briefs for privatization is largely or entirely concerned with government below the federal level.

4. *Social Responsibilities of Business Corporations* (New York: Committee for Economic Development, 1971), 52.

5. "Dividing the Pie between Public and Private," *American City and County*, Jan. 1984.

6. See Martin Tolchin, "More Cities Paying Industry to Provide Public Services," *New York Times*, 28 May 1985.

7. Figures are from Department of Commerce, *Survey of Current Business* (Washington: Jan. 1980 and June 1988).

8. National Center for Policy Analysis, Dallas, June 1985, i.

9. See *Passing the Bucks: The Contracting Out of Public Services* (Washington: American Federation of State, County, and Municipal Employees, 1983).

10. Sources for this section are Joyce Purnick, "Trump Offers to Rebuild Skating Rink," *New York Times*, 31 May 1986; Martin Gottlieb, "Who Can Fix the Wollman Rink Faster? City and Trump Agree It's Trump," *New York Times*, 6 June 1986; Suzanne Daley, "Trump to Rebuild Wollman Rink at the City's Expense by Dec. 15," *New York Times*, 7 June 1986; Alan Finder, "Ice Rink Project: Mistakes, Delays, and Blame," *New York Times*, 17 June 1986; and Andrew Rosenthal, "Trump Reports Large Profit from Wollman Rink," *New York Times*, 1 April 1987.

11. This section draws on a series of pieces by Andy Logan, "Around City Hall," *New Yorker*, 3 Feb., 3 March, and 31 March 1986; Michael Oreskes, "Suicide by Manes Shifts the Focus of Graft Inquiries," *New York Times*, 15 March 1986; Philip Shenon, "U.S. Officials See Historic Effort to Combat Municipal Corruption," *New York Times*, 30 March 1986; M. A. Farber, "Datacom: A Thriving Collection Agency under Scrutiny for Political Ties," *New York Times*, 7 May 1986; M. A. Farber, "Indictment Names Friedman in Bribe for City Contract," *New York Times*, 28 March 1986; and Richard J. Meislin, "Friedman Is Sentenced to Twelve Years in Corruption Case," *New York Times*, 12 March 1987.

12. This figure is from a study by the Reason Foundation Local Government Center cited in Robert W. Poole, Jr., and Philip E. Fixler, Jr., "Privatization of Public-Sector Services in Practice: Experience and Potential," *Journal of Policy Analysis and Management* 6 (1987): 616. Specific instances cited in these paragraphs are from ibid.; Neil A. Martin, "When Public Services Go Private," *World* (May–June 1986); John Heins, "Government Is on the Defensive," *Forbes*, 15 Dec. 1986; David Seader, "Privatization and America's Cities," *Public Management* (December 1986); Randall Fitzgerald, *When Government Goes Private* (New York: Universe Books, 1988).

13. See John J. Kosowatz and Barbara Lamb, "Questions Shroud Privatization," *ENR*, 9 Jan. 1986.

14. *Passing the Bucks*, 101.

15. See Ronald W. Jensen, "The Phoenix Approach to Privatization" (unpublished paper, November 1987), 5. I should emphasize that there is no evidence this particular case of privatization was motivated by the kind of political sleight of hand described here.

16. See Stuart M. Butler, *Privatizing Federal Spending* (New York: Universe Books, 1985), 13–19.

17. Gerald McEntee, president of the American Federation of State, County, and Municipal Employees, quoted in "More Cities Paying Industry to Provide Public Services," *New York Times*, 28 May 1985.

18. Touche Ross & Co., *Privatization in America* (New York: 1987). The Privatization Council was launched by a coalition of accounting and consulting firms, investment banks, and construction companies. Interestingly, it charges corporate members between five and twelve times as much as it charges public sector members—a suggestive indication of how the benefits of privatization fall.

19. As do many similar efforts, the Touche Ross study attempts to draw a clear distinction between contracting out for municipal services and using privately owned and operated plants, buildings, or other assets. The distinction causes more confusion than it resolves, however, since both forms of privatization raise similar issues of efficiency, competition, and accountability. A third type, asset sales, refers to taking some endeavor entirely out of local government's purview. This *is* clearly different, but it is also beyond the scope of this book. It is also far less significant in U.S. cities than it is at the U.S. federal level, or in many cities overseas.

20. Touche Ross, *Privatization*, 4, fig. 2, 5, fig. 3. The most important impediment to privatization was the loss of control, cited by over one-half of the governments responding. Next came employee resistance.

21. Ibid., 11, fig. 7, 13, fig. 9.

22. Barbara J. Stevens, "Comparing Public- and Private-Sector Productive Efficiency: An Analysis of Eight Activities," *National Productivity Review* (Autumn 1984), hereinafter Stevens, *A*; Barbara J. Stevens, ed., *Delivering Municipal Services Efficiently* (Washington: HUD Office of Policy Development and Research, June 1984), hereafter called Stevens, *B*.

23. John C. Goodman, *Privatization* (Dallas: National Center for Policy Analysis, 1985), 116.

24. Stevens, *B*, section F, 10. These costs range from 5 percent of the total for asphalt laying to 69 percent for payroll preparation. The overall study design is described in Stevens, *A*, 396–97, and Stevens, *B*, 20–23. The quality of these various cost estimates is obviously crucial.

25. Ibid., 399–401; Stevens, *B*, 23–40.

26. Stevens, *B*, 26.

27. Touche Ross, *Privatization*, 13, fig. 9.

28. Roger S. Ahlbrandt, Jr., "Implications of Contracting for a Public Service," *Urban Affairs Quarterly* (March 1974): 348–51.

29. See David Kennedy and Robert Leone, "Cornwall County School Distict" (Kennedy School of Government, case study C16-85-641, used at Harvard University, 1985).

30. Jensen, "Phoenix Approach."

31. Stevens, *A*, 402.

32. Goodman, *Privatization*, 116.

33. Fitzgerald, *When Government Goes Private*, 62. Fitzgerald mentions only asphalt laying, the one service out of seven that departs from the pattern.

34. Payroll preparation is excluded from the next two tables both because there are no cost savings to be explained and because Stevens reported only technical and supervisory salaries for this function.

35. Stevens, *A*, 402.

36. These figures are from Stevens, *B*, 11, ex. 6. Benefit costs are *not* reported directly, but are given as a percentage of labor costs. It is unclear whether this means as a percentage of wages, or as a percentage of wages plus benefits; here I give the calculation that minimizes the difference between municipal and contractor benefits.

37. Ibid., 14, ex. 8.

38. These figures are derived from ibid., 11, ex. 6.

39. This assumes—based on Stevens *B*, 9, ex. 5—that only 75 percent of a contractor's labor costs are payments to his own workers; the other 25 percent represents payments to city workers who monitor the contractor or are otherwise involved in contracting. In fact, this is an overestimate, since Stevens's estimate of noncontractor costs in the total cost of private provision is biased sharply upward by one service, payroll preparation. Again, I interpret ambiguities conservatively here, to minimize the difference between public and private unit labor costs.

40. Fitzgerald, *When Government Goes Private*, 80.

41. Sociologist Paul Starr, quoted in Louis Uchitelle, "Public Services Found Better If Private Agencies Compete," *New York Times*, 26 April 1988.

42. For example, see Grand Jury of Bronx County, "Franchise Emergency Tow and Repair: A Concession to Corruption," (New York: Feb. 1986).

43. See "Labor Letter," *Wall Street Journal*, 1 March 1988.

44. Jeff Myers and Betsy Stephenson, "Service Provision Strategies: Structuring the Privatization Decision-Making Process" (unpublished policy analysis exercise, Harvard University, John F. Kennedy School of Government, April 1988), 38.

45. See Eileen Brettler-Berenyi, "Public and Private Sector Interaction Patterns in the Delivery of Local Public Services," *Governmental Finance* 9 (March 1980): 6.

46. For example, see Richard W. Hurd and Jill K. Kriegle, "You *Can* Fight City Hall," *Labor Studies Journal* (Fall 1985).

Chapter 8

1. See chapter 8, "The Growth of Private Security," in William C. Cunningham and Todd H. Taylor, *Private Security and Police in America* (Portland, Oreg.: Chancellor Press, 1985). See also Peter Kihss, "Protection of Celebrities Remains a Small Part of Security Business," *New York Times*, 21 Dec. 1980; Martin Tolchin, "Private Guards Get New Role in Public Law Enforcement," *New York Times*, 29 Nov. 1985; Marcia Chambers, "California's Swift, Costly Private Judicial System," *New York Times*, 24 Feb. 1986; and Claudia M. Christie, "Private Justice," *New England Business*, 17 Sept. 1984.

2. These figures from Bureau of Justice Statistics *Bulletin* (Washington: July 1986), 2.

3. The figures are for the mid-1980s and come from various tables in Department of Commerce, *Statistical Abstract of the United States* (Washington, D.C.: U.S. Government Printing Office, 1988).

4. The list comes from Equitable Securities research report (June 2, 1988), 2–3. The Texas prisons were scheduled to open in mid-1989.

5. The Corrections Corporation of America bid for the Tennessee prison system is described in Jim Montgomery, "Corrections Corp. Seeks Lease to Run Tennessee's Prisons," *Wall Street Journal*, 13 Sept. 1985; Martin Tolchin, "Private Concern Makes Offer to Run Tennessee's Prisons," *New York Times*, 13 Sept. 1985; and Winthrop Knowlton, "Corrections Corporation of America" (case study C15-85-646, used at Harvard University, Kennedy School of Government, 1985).

6. See Kevin Krajick, "Prisons for Profit: The Private Alternative," *State Legislatures* (April 1984); Martin Tolchin, "As Privately Owned Prisons Increase, So Do Their Critics," *New York Times*, 11 Feb. 1985. Behavioral Systems Southwest also runs local jails.

7. See *Public Works Financing* (January 1988): 6.

8. See Michael Sherman and Gordon Hawkins, *Imprisonment in America* (Chicago: University of Chicago Press, 1981), chapter 1, for an interesting discussion of the "crisis mentality" that, the authors suggest, muddies thinking about corrections reform.

9. Bureau of Justice Statistics *Bulletin* (October 1986); Peter Applebourne, "With Inmates at Record High, Sentence Policy Is Reassessed," *New York Times*, 25 April 1988.

10. See Sherman and Hawkins, *Imprisonment in America*, 46.

11. The source for this and the next several survey citations is the *American Public Opinion* microfiche series, 1985 compilation. The source for this citation is the North Carolina survey, question 64.

12. University of Kentucky October survey, question 64.

13. Florida State University's 1985 Annual Policy Survey, questions 35 and 39.

14. Zia Research Associates, January 1985 survey, question 9.

15. Bureau of Justice Statistics *Bulletin* (Washington: April 1985), table 11. The overcrowding figures are customarily stated as a range, rather than a single estimate, because of ambiguities about the meaning of capacity.

16. See American Correctional Association, *Standards for Adult Local Detention Facilities*, 2d ed. (April 1981). Private prisons, it is worth noting, more often meet the standards than public facilities.

17. Massachusetts Legislative Research Council, *Report Relative to Prisons for Profit* (Boston: 31 July 1986), 40, hereinafter LRC, *Report*. This is one of the best and most comprehensive compilations of information on the private prison issue.

18. Bella English, "Prisons: System in Crisis—Toll Tells on Everyone," *Boston Globe*, 1 June 1987.

19. A number of studies are cited in Stephen D. Gottfredson and Ralph B. Taylor, *The Correctional Crisis: Prison Populations and Public Policy* (Washington: U.S. Department of Justice, National Institute of Justice, June 1983), 1.

20. LRC, *Report*, 86.

21. State Senator Stuart Greenleaf, quoted in Martin Tolchin, "Prospect of Privately Run Prisons Divides Pennsylvania Legislators," *New York Times*, 15 Dec. 1985.

22. Editorial, "Prisons for Profit," *Wall Street Journal*, 5 Feb. 1987.

23. Chairman Thomas W. Beasley, quoted in Erik Larson, "Captive Company," *Inc.* (June 1988): 88.

24. Memo by cofounder Lucius Burch excerpted in Knowlton, "Corrections Corporation of America," 9–11.

25. Corporate head Ted Nissen, quoted in Martin Tolchin, "As Privately Owned Prisons Increase, So Do Their Critics," *New York Times*, 11 Feb. 1985. If private prisons draw from the same population of criminals as public prisons; if recidivism is accurately measured and contracts fully enforced; and if forfeiture would impose real losses on prison entrepreneurs large enough to ensure realistic bids and best efforts to deliver, this kind of results-based contract would be highly desirable. There are reasons to doubt that these conditions would hold, however, as later sections relate.

26. From a 1985 American Correctional Association position statement cited in LRC, *Report*, 85.

27. President's Commission on Privatization, David F. Linowes, chairman, *Privatization: Toward More Efficient Government* (Washington: March 1988).

28. Cited in LRC, *Report*, 48–49.

29. J. Michael Keating, Jr., *Seeking Profit in Punishment* (Washington: AFSCME, 1985), quoted in LRC, *Report*, 51.

30. American Bar Association, Section of Criminal Justice, *Report to the House of Delegates* (February 1986), 1. The reservations were reaffirmed in 1988; see Amy Dockser, "Prison Managers Remain Unproven, Law Group Finds," *Wall Street Journal*, 1 Dec. 1988.

31. Quoted in LRC, *Report*, 82.

32. Michael Walzer, "Hold the Justice," *The New Republic*, 8 April 1985.

33. Robert Lekachman, *Visions and Nightmares* (New York: Macmillan Publishing Company, 1987), 106.

34. American Bar Association, *Report*, 12–13.

35. Charles R. Ring, "Private Prisons Need a Fair Trial," *Wall Street Journal*, 8 May 1987.

36. See Joan Mullen et al., *The Privatization of Corrections* (U.S. Department of Justice, National Institute of Justice, February 1985), 56–58; LRC, *Report*, 48–49.

37. Cost data are for 1984, calculated from Department of Commerce, *Statistical Abstract 1987*, 172.

38. Administrative director quoted in Hirsch, "What's New in Private Prisons."

39. See Mullen, *The Privatization of Corrections*, 68.

40. For example, see Regina E. Herzlinger and William S. Karasker, "Who profits from Non-profits," *Harvard Business Review* (January–February 1987), and the responsive letters on that article in *Harvard Business Review* (March 1987), especially the letter by Arnold Relman, editor of *New England Journal of Medicine*. See also Tamar Lewin, "A Sharp Debate on Hospitals," *New York Times*, 2 March 1987.

41. See Dudley Clendinen, "Officials of Counties Debate Private Jail Operation," *New York Times*, 14 Nov. 1985.

42. See Judith Hackett et al., *Issues in Contracting for the Private Operation of Prisons and Jails* (Washington: National Institute of Justice Research Report, October 1987), chapter 2, for a summary of experience to date.

43. See LRC, *Report*, 80, table 1.

44. See the statement of Richard Crane in Congress, House Committee on the Judiciary, *Hearings on the Privatization of Corrections*, 99th Cong., 1st sess., 13 November 1985 and 18 March 1986, 42.

45. Bureau of Justice Statistics, *Bulletin* (Washington: July 1986).

46. English, "Prisons: System in Crisis."

47. Department of Commerce, Bureau of the Census, *1980 Census of Population: Earnings by Occupations and Education*, vol. 2 (Washington: May 1984), table 1. Interestingly, female guards earned 8 percent *more* than the nationwide average.

48. One possible labor cost *disadvantage* for private prisons is that private sector employees, unlike civil servants, generally cannot be denied the right to strike. A prison cannot easily be shut down, and temporarily replacing strikers—even if possible—is likely to be expensive and disruptive. Private prison guards, then, could command considerable bargaining leverage, and may eventually negotiate better wage and benefit deals than those achieved by public guards.

49. See Hackett et al., *Issues in Contracting*, 31–33, for observations on competition in prison contracting.

50. See Williamson, *Markets and Hierarchies* (New York: The Free Press, 1975), 68.

51. Prudential-Bache Securities, *Company Report on CCA* (New York: 3 April 1987): 9.

52. The official is quoted in Mullen, *The Privatization of Corrections*, 69.

53. Commonwealth of Kentucky, *Finance and Administration Cabinet Document SR–903–85 CON* (Frankfort, Ky.: April 1985).

54. A report by the American Correctional Association cites the contracting issue without really recognizing the difficulty of writing and enforcing comprehensive contracts. A private corrections center, it explains, "is only as good as the staff, management, program, facilities, resources and support that it receives; the formula for success is no different than for publicly operated institutions. What does differ, though, is the need to have a tightly structured contract in order that the private sector . . . be held accountable," American Correctional Association, *Private Sector Operation of a Correctional Institution* (Washington: Department of Justice, April 1985), 60.

55. See Martin Tolchin, "Privately Operated Prison in Tennessee Reports $200,000 in Cost Overruns," *New York Times*, 21 May 1985.

56. See Larson, "Captive Company," 90.

57. See Krajick, "Prisons for Profit," 10, and LRC, *Report*, 64, 75.

58. Title 42 United States Code, section 1983.

59. *Medina v. O'Neill*, 589 F. Supp. 1028 (1984).

60. Mary R. Woolley, "Prisons for Profit: Policy Considerations for Government Officials," *Dickinson Law Review* (Winter 1985): 330. LRC, *Report*, lists a number of other precedents supporting the same expectation. See also American Bar Association, Section of Criminal Justice, *Report to the House* of Delegates (Washington: February 1986), 3.

61. See the statement by Richard Crane of the Corrections Corporation of America in *Hearings*

on Privatization, 102, in which he explicitly concedes that governments remain fully liable for a prison contractor's actions.

62. The Corrections Corporation of America (CCA) made a minuscule quarterly profit for the first time in the fall of 1988. For more detailed information, see the company's Form 10–K submission to the Securities and Exchange Commission for 1987, dated 29 Feb. 1988, especially the consolidated financial statements beginning on page 20. Individual CCA facilities do cover their direct costs, but by a margin of less than 8 percent—far too little to cover corporate overhead and debt.

63. Statistics here are from Department of Commerce, *Statistical Abstract 1987* (Washington: 1988), 262, table 446; 172, table 305; and 463, table 774.

64. John J. DiIulio, Jr., "Private Prisons" (unpublished discussion paper, Princeton University, May 1987), 8.

65. A detainee suffered an untreated mental breakdown while in the custody of the Corrections Corporation of America (CCA), as described in Martin Tolchin, "Jails Run by Private Company Force It to Face Question of Accountability," *New York Times*, 19 Feb. 1985. Another CCA inmate died of an undiagnosed ectopic pregnancy.

66. The Reverend Thomas Sheehy, who serves as chaplain at the Corrections Corporation of America Houston detention center, endorses private management: "If I had my choice of this private organization, or it being run by the Immigration and Naturalization Service, I would take this private organization. They're much more humane. The guards haven't been in the business that long, so they're not calloused." Quoted in Tolchin, "As Privately Owned Prisons Increase."

67. See prepared statement of Richard Crane in *Hearings on Privatization*, 37.

68. Executive Vice-President T. Don Hutto, quoted in Tolchin, "As Privately Owned Prisons Increase."

69. Unnamed Corrections Corporation of America official, quoted in Hirsch, "What's New in Private Prisons."

70. LRC, *Report*, 61.

71. See Mullen, *The Privatization of Corrections*.

72. Jeremy Bentham, *Panopticon, Or, the Inspection-House, Containing the Idea of a New Principle of Construction applicable to any sort of Establishment, in which persons are to be kept under Inspection, and in particular to Penitentiary-Houses* (London: Thomas Payne, 1791). I am grateful to Dennis Thompson for calling *Panopticon* to my attention.

73. Ibid., 42–43, 48. Note that, as the Inspector could put prisoners to work, running the panopticon would be a money-making proposition, and the "best terms" might be the highest payment *to* the public, not the lowest price.

74. Ibid., 67–71. Bentham's proposal on this point is intriguing in its treatment of the allocation of risk, the costs of monitoring behavior, and the merits of contingent contracts based on deviations from actuarially determined expectations. In all these areas he anticipates recent developments in agency theory by nearly two centuries.

75. Ibid., 45–46.

76. Ibid., 29, 33.

77. Ibid., 45–46, 49.

78. Oral presentation by Thomas Beasley at a San Francisco conference, September 1985, quoted in LRC, *Report*, 60.

79. The National Institute of Justice study notes this potential. "On balance, it is entirely likely that private institutions will receive fairly intense scrutiny, in the short term. . . . Whether this interest will be sustained in the long term remains unclear." Mullen, *The Privatization of Corrections*, 74.

80. Hackett et al., *Issues in Contracting*, 61; see also 42–44.

81. Gordon Chase, "Implementing a Human Services Program: How Hard Will It Be?" *Public Policy* 27 (Fall 1979): 399.

82. See Martin Tolchin, "Companies Easing Crowded Prisons," *New York Times*, 17 Feb. 1985, and Krajick, "Prisons for Profits," 9.

83. While the overall male population ages twenty to twenty-nine peaked in 1984 and is expected to decline, the number of *black* males in that age group is expected to keep rising, according to two scholars. "If black incarceration rates continue at their current level . . . the expected decrease in prison populations may not happen." James Austin and Barry Krisberg, "Incarceration in the United States," *Annals of the American Academy of Political and Social Science* (March 1985): 24.

84. See Mullen, *The Privatization of Corrections*, 73–74; and LRC, *Report*, 62.

85. See statement by Edward Koren of the American Civil Liberties Union in *Hearings on Privatization*, 6–7, and the accompanying notes citing legal opinions.

86. Detention center chief quoted in Tolchin, "Jails Run by Private Company."

87. Martin Tolchin, "Experts Foresee Adverse Effects from Private Control of Prisons," *New York Times*, 17 Sept. 1985.

88. Kenneth F. Schoen, "Private Prison Operators," *New York Times*, 28 March 1985.

89. LRC, *Report*, 57.

Chapter 9

1. *Public Papers of Ronald Reagan*, vol. 2 (Washington: 1982); Seth Kind, "President Signs Job Training Bill, Calling It an End to Boondoggle," *New York Times*, 14 Oct. 1982.

2. The shifting manpower programs of the 1960s and 1970s are discussed in Dave M. O'Neill, *The Federal Government and Manpower* (Washington American Enterprise Institute, 1973); Ewan Clague and Leo Kramer, *Manpower Politics and Programs: A Review 1935–75* (Kalamazoo: Upjohn Institute for Employment Research, 1976); Sar Lavitan, Garth L. Mangum, and Ray Marshall, *Human Resources and Labor Markets: Employment and Training in the American Economy* (New York: Harper & Row, 1972); Jeffrey Pressman and Aaron Wildavsky, *Implementation* (Berkeley: California University Press, 1979); and Peter Kobrak, *Private Assumptions of Public Responsibilities: The Role of American Business in Urban Manpower* (New York: Praeger, 1975).

3. Robert F. Cook et al., *Public Service Employment: The Experience of a Decade* (Kalamazoo: W. E. Upjohn Institute, 1985), 12.

4. Gary Orfield et al., *Job Training under the New Federalism* (Chicago: Illinois Unemployment and Job Training Research Project, University of Chicago, 1986), 66–69, charts 4.1 and 4.2. In real terms, the growth was much more modest—measured in 1972 dollars, the total budget went from around $4 billion in 1975 to around $6 billion in 1980.

5. See Robert Taggart, *A Fisherman's Guide: An Assessment of Training and Remediation Strategies* (Kalamazoo: W. E. Upjohn Institute, 1981), 42, table 2.3.

6. For evidence on this point, see Alan Fechter, *Public Employment Programs* (Washington: American Enterprise Institute, 1975). It is worth stressing that contracting between governments invites agency problems similar (if not identical) to those later diagnosed in the JTPA. For a related discussion see William Mirengoff et al., *CETA: Assessment of Public Service Employment Programs* (Washington: National Academy of Sciences, 1980), 10.

7. James Cameron, "How CETA Came to Be a Four-Letter Word," *Fortune*, 9 April 1979.

8. R. K. Bennett, "CETA: $11 Billion Boondoggle," *Reader's Digest*, Aug. 1978. Critics found sinister, as well as silly, aspects of CETA: In several cities, political connections determined access to the better public jobs, and many ward-heelers and their associates showed up on CETA payrolls. See James Bovard, "The Failure of Federal Job Training," (Washington: Cato Institute Policy Analysis Paper, August 1986), 5.

9. For a review of JTPA's legislative history, see William J. Lanouette, "Life after Death—CETA's Demise Won't Mean the End of Manpower Training," *National Journal*, 6 Feb. 1982.

10. Another major change is an enlarged role for the states. In the JTPA, unlike CETA, the link between local programs and the Labor Department is mediated by state governments. For a discussion of the shift from a federal to a state-based program, see General Accounting Office, *Concerns within the Job Training Community over Labor's Ability to Implement the Job Training Partnership Act* (Washington, D.C.: April 1985).

11. Governors keep 22 percent of the state allocations for administration, demonstration projects, statewide programs, and discretionary grants. (JTPA, Public Law 97–300, sec. 201–202, 13 Oct. 1982. All further JTPA section and title references are to Public Law 97–300.) For further details on state administration, see General Accounting Office, *Job Training Partnership Act: Initial Implementation of Program for Disadvantaged Youth and Adults* (Washington: March 1985).

12. The standard terminology is "service delivery area" (SDA) which may refer to a single city, a county, a consortium of local and/or county governments, or a large, thinly populated area. To spare readers unfamiliar with manpower policy jargon the need to learn a whole vocabulary of acronyms I use the (not entirely accurate) term "local programs" to refer to SDAs.

13. Sec. 102–103.

14. Sec. 204

15. Sec. 203(b)(1). This is in addition to the summer jobs program and the Job Corps, youth programs funded under separate titles that are not discussed here.

16. Sec. 108. For a discussion of support-cost spending, see Gary Walker et al., *JTPA: Implementation and Performance* (New York: Grinker-Walker and Associates, 1986), 41. This study is hereinafter called Walker, *I.*

17. Sec. 141(a).

18. Sec. 203(b)(3).

19. Sec. 141(b).

20. Gary Walker et al., *An Independent Sector Assessment of the Job Training Partnership Act (Phase II)* (unpublished study, 1985), 23–28. This report is hereinafter called Walker, *II.*

21. Senator Hatch is quoted in Orfield et al., *Job Training,* 51. For a further discussion of the JTPA "performance driven" system of accountability "based on prescribed outcomes rather than on [the CETA] prescribed service descriptions," see Stanley S. Litow and Susan Amlung, "Reducing Youth Unemployment: The Case for a Fresh Approach," in *Jobs for the Future: Strategies in a New Framework* (Washington, D.C.: Center for National Policy, 1984), esp. 55.

22. Sec. 106.

23. Sec. 106(b)(3).

24. Sec. 106(h)(1).

25. To be precise, performance indicators were introduced in CETA, primarily in its later years, but the General Accounting Office found that they were never "fully implemented or required," unlike those under the JTPA. See General Accounting Office, *The Job Training Partnership Act: An Analysis of Support Cost Limits and Participant Characteristics* (Washington: November 1985), 2.

26. Taggart, *A Fisherman's Guide,* 250–51.

27. Walker, *I,* 23; table 2-C.

28. *Is the Job Training Partnership Working?* (Washington: National Alliance of Business, 1986).

29. Sec. 106(b)(2). "Competency certification" programs for youths include everything from instruction in labor market trends and technical training to a variety of socialization, nonverbal communication, and attitude-improving exercises. It is somewhat unfair to characterize "positive termination" as so hopelessly broad a category that it validates as a success, in James Bovard's words, "anything short of suicide," James Bovard, "Son of CETA," *New Republic,* 14 April 1986. At the same time, it is impossible to assess how much value these certifications actually do represent, or to estimate what fraction of "positive terminations" represent such certification. A Department of Labor initiative to define and measure competency certification was quashed by the Office of Management and Budget as unduly intrusive. See General Accounting Office, *Youth Job Training: Problems Measuring Attainment of Employment Competencies* (Washington: February 1987) 18, 57–60.

30. Walker, *I,* 27, table 2-E. While nearly as many officials cited improved management practices, a better public image for subsidized training, and expanded private sector participation, only 8 percent of officials reported major impacts on local social problems.

31. The official is quoted in Orfield et al., *Job Training,* 138. For more data on this point see Walker, *I,* 5.

32. General Accounting Office, *Initial Implementation of Program,* 43–44.

33. Department of Labor, Bureau of Labor Statistics, *How Workers Get Their Training,* bulletin 2226 (Washington: February 1985), tables 2, 10, and 24.

34. Taggart, *A Fisherman's Guide,* 6–7. The federal government spent $36 billion on human capital development in 1984, but only around $2 billion on the types of efforts discussed here. Department of Commerce, Bureau of the Census, *Statistical Abstract of the United States 1986* (Washington: 1986), 129.

35. See Taggart, *A Fisherman's Guide,* and Richard Anderson and Elizabeth Kasl, *The Costs and Financing of Adult Education and Training* (Lexington, Mass.: Lexington Books, 1982), the latter cited in William Spring, "Training and Industrial Policy" (unpublished discussion draft, Harvard Faculty Seminar on Industrial Policy, November 1982), 7.

36. The IBM figure is from Partricia Seller, "How IBM Teaches Techies to Sell," *Fortune,* 6 June 1988, 142.

37. Department of Labor, *How Workers Get Their Training,* table 33.

38. Lee A. Lillard and Hong W. Tan, *Private Sector Training* (Santa Monica: Rand Corporation, 1986), 11–17.

39. Becker introduced the notion in "Investment in Human Capital: A Theoretical Analysis, " *Journal of Political Economy* (October 1962) and elaborated it further in *Human Capital,* 2d ed. (Chicago: University of Chicago Press, 1975).

40. The appropriability problem and the threat of "hold-up in the post-investment period" are

discussed in Masanori Hashimoto and Ben T. Yu, "Specific Capital, Employment Contracts, and Wage Rigidity," *Bell Journal of Economics* 11 (Autumn 1980).

41. For a discussion of such devices, see Jeremy Bulow and Lawrence Summers, "A Theory of Dual Labor Markets," working paper no. 1666 (National Bureau for Economic Research, October 1985).

42. People can also pay for on-the-job training in general skills through apprenticeships and similar low-paying positions, which amounts to financing investments through lower consumption. If a worker could commit to stay with the firm, he could effectively "borrow" to finance general skill development by collecting wages in excess of productivity during training and wages lower than productivity for a time thereafter. For an economist's perspective on this and some related issues, see Jacob Mincer, "On-the-job Training: Costs, Returns, and Some Implications," *Journal of Political Economy* (October 1962), especially 52.

43. See David Levhari and Yoram Weiss, "The Effect of Risk on Investment in Human Capital," *American Economic Review* (December 1974), especially 950. On a related point, see Theodore Schultz, "Reflections on Investment in Man," *Journal of Political Economy* (October 1962): 8.

44. Pat Choate, *Retooling the American Work Force* (Washington: Northeast-Midwest Institute, 1982), 35.

45. Sec. 141(b).

46. Lillard and Tan, *Private Sector Training*, 14, table 2.6. Some of the workers probably got their training through CETA or other government programs, but most did not—CETA never covered so large a fraction of the disadvantaged, and most of the reported training was on the job or at business and technical schools.

47. Sec. 141(2).

48. See Mary Jo Bane and David T. Ellwood, "Slipping into and out of Poverty: The Dynamics of Spells" (unpublished discussion draft, August 1985). The precise pattern is significant: While about half of the people counted below the poverty line *at any one time* are long-term poor, most of the people who experience poverty *at some point in their lives* will escape within a few years, and a substantial fraction of the poverty population consists of the transitory poor.

49. See General Accounting Office, *Job Training Partnership Act: Data Collection Efforts and Needs,* (Washington: March 1986), 5, 7.

50. Department of Labor, *Division of Performance Management and Evaluations, Summary of JTLS Data for JTPA Title IIA and III Enrollments and Terminations during Program Year 1985* (Washington: 1986), appendix B.

51. See General Accounting Office, *Data Collection Efforts,* 13–21. The contrast between the dearth of data about the JTPA and the glut of data about the CETA is striking. In 1979, the Department of Labor published a bibliography of research on subsidized training—a six-hundred-page volume of closely printed, single-paragraph abstracts. Department of Labor, Employment and Training Administration, *Research and Development: A Sixteen-Year Compendium* (Washington: 1979). While some of these studies were of dubious validity, the sheer number of them attests to the scale of research under the CETA. A relatively small three-year pilot program, the Youth Employment and Demonstration Projects Act initiative, generated more than four hundred reports. National Research Council, *Youth Employment and Training Programs* (Washington National Academy Press, 1985).

52. General Accounting Office, *Federal Evaluation: Fewer Units, Reduced Resources, Different Studies from 1980* (Washington: January 1987), 77.

53. The main data source is the summary of the Job Training Longitudinal Survey published each fall by the Department of Labor.

54. Department of Labor, "JTPA Economically Disadvantaged Population, Used for Allocation Purposes (unpublished data sheet provided by department to author).

55. Sec. 203(a)(2).

56. General Accounting Office, *Analysis of Support Cost Limits,* 10–13.

57. Agency head quoted in Walker, *I,* 27.

58. Jay Ostrower, director of ABCD's Center for Jobs, Education, and Training, quoted in Sarah Snyder, "Antipoverty Agency Adapts to New Limits," *Boston Globe,* 21 April 1987.

59. Walker, *I,* 38.

60. Ibid., 24.

61. Walker, *II,* 27.

62. These figures are from National Alliance of Business, *Is the Job Training Partnership Working?* 54–55. The Alliance draws somewhat different conclusions from the data.

63. Michael E. Borus, *Measuring the Impact of Employment-Related Social Programs* (Kalamazoo: W. E. Upjohn Institute, 1979).

64. The four types of programs covered in the table account for about 63 percent of CETA's 1980 enrollment, and about 89 percent of JTPA's 1985 enrollment. The remainder for CETA is mostly public service employment and youth transition services; the remainder for JTPA is "other."

65. General Accounting Office, *Job Training Partnership Act: Participants, Services, and Outcomes*, (Washington: 29 September 1988).

66. Orfield et al., *Job Training*, 190.

67. Michael E. Borus, "Indicators of CETA Performance," *Industrial and Labor Relations Review* 32 (October 1978).

68. Ibid., 8, table 2. The mean estimated difference for 1974 earnings was $662, mean weeks employed was 8.25, and mean welfare received a negative $650, all significant at the .001 level.

69. Ibid., 11, table 3. Program completion explained 8 percent of the earnings differences four years after training. Both proxies were significant at .001. Program completion, of course, is more likely a proxy for participant characteristics than for program characteristics.

70. From Continuous Longitudinal Manpower Survey and Current Population Survey data compiled in Taggart, *A Fisherman's Guide*, 57.

71. Walker, *I*, 24.

72. Taggart, *A Fisherman's Guide*, 221. For an extensive analysis of the long-run effects of different forms of training—and some evidence hinting at the long-run superiority of classroom training—see David Card and Daniel Sullivan, "Measuring the Effect of Subsidized Training Programs on Movements in and out of Employment," *Econometrica* 56 (May 1988), especially 503, table 2.

73. Westat, Inc., *Impact on 1978 Earnings of New FY 1976 CETA Enrollees in Selected Program Activities* (Washington: Employment and Training Administration, Feb. 1981).

74. Sec. 108(k), 205(d)(3)(B).

75. Sec. 108(g).

76. General Accounting Office, *Participants, Services, and Outcomes*, 12.

77. Walker, *I*, 54. Other examples in this section are drawn from Karen Blumenthal, "Job Training Effort, Critics Say, Fails Many Who Need Help Most," *Wall Street Journal*, 9 Feb. 1987; James Bovard, writing in the *New Republic*, April 1986, and "The Failure of Federal Job Training"; Orfield et al., *Job Training*, 12. See also Labor Market Analysis Policy Research Project, *Local Employment Policy in a High-Growth Economy: Matching Training and Jobs in Austin, Texas* (Austin: Lyndon B. Johnson School of Public Affairs, 1982).

78. Quoted in Bovard, "The Failure of Federal Job Training," 13.

79. The annual report is quoted in Blumenthal, "Job Training Effort."

80. National Alliance of Business, *Is the Job Training Partnership Working?* 67.

81. Walker, *I*, 19.

82. Bane and Ellwood, "Slipping Into," 32, table 2.

83. Sources on the Job Corps include Taggart, *A Fisherman's Guide*, and National Research Council, *Youth Employment and Training Programs*. See also Dave M. O'Neill, *The Federal Government and Manpower* (Washington: American Enterprise Institute, 1973); Charles Mallar et al., *The Lasting Impacts of Job Corps Participation* (Washington: Department of Labor, Employment and Training Administration, May 1980); and General Accounting Office, *Job Corps: Its Costs, Employment Outcomes, and Service to the Public* (Washington: July 1986).

84. General Accounting Office, *Job Corps*, 6; Taggart, *A Fisherman's Guide*, 264.

85. Taggart, *A Fisherman's Guide*, 265.

86. See ibid., 263, and Mallar et al., *Lasting Impacts*, 8–9.

87. See National Research Council, *Youth Employment and Training Programs*, 113, table 5.3; O'Neill, *The Federal Government and Manpower*, 42–43; Mallar et al., *Lasting Impacts*; and General Accounting Office, *Job Corps*. Taggart, *A Fisherman's Guide*, 266, concludes that although "there is no magic in private sector management per se, competitive contracting assures options in the case of poor performance and some incentives to maintain the performance of staff."

88. See the later Mallar/Mathematica study cited in National Research Council, *Youth Employment and Training Programs*, 112–16.

Chapter 10

1. See William K. Stevens, "Developers Expanding Role in Social Services," *New York Times*, 28 Nov. 1987.

2. See William K. Stevens, "Confusion for Philadelphia Homeless," *The New York Times*, 8 Oct. 1988. The mayor of Philadelphia and the brother of President Bush are cochairmen of the Privatization Council.

3. See Laurie McGinley, "Airline Industry Makes Controversial Bid to Take Air-Traffic Control System Away from the FAA," *Wall Street Journal*, 26 Nov. 1986; and the President's Commission on Privatization, David F. Linowes, chairman, *Privatization: Toward More Efficient Government* (Washington: March 1988), chapter 5.

4. Elizabeth M. Fowler, "Temporary Job Needs of Government," *New York Times*, 8 Nov. 1988, and Michael J. McCarthy, "Temp-Services Industry Stands to Gain under New Federal Hiring Proposal," *Wall Street Journal*, 21 Oct. 1988.

5. Philip Shabecoff, "Interior Department Again Weighs Plan to Shift Jobs to Industry," *New York Times*, 29 Oct. 1988.

6. See Edward M. Gramlich and Patricia P. Koshel, "Is Real-World Experimentation Possible? The Case of Educational Performance Contracting," in Robert H. Haveman and Julius Margolis, eds., *Public Expenditure and Policy Analysis*, 2d ed. (Chicago: Rand McNally, 1977); and Gramlich and Koshel, *Education Performance Contracting* (Washington: Brookings Institution, 1975). See also Polly Carpenter and George R. Hall, *Case Studies in Educational Performance Contracting: Conclusions and Implications* (Santa Monica, Calif.: Rand Corporation, 1971).

7. See Alex Kotlowitz and Dale D. Buss, "Localities' Giveaways to Lure Corporations Cause Growing Outcry," *Wall Street Journal*, 19 Feb. 1987; Michael Kranish, "A New Twist in New Bedford," *Boston Globe*, 19 May 1987; and Patrick Houston, "When a City's Deal to Save Jobs Sours," *New York Times*, 24 June 1988.

8. There is an enormous literature on this topic. See, for example, Jerry Green, "Physician-Induced Demand for Medical Care," *Journal of Human Resources* 13 (Dec. 1978); Robert G. Evans, "Supplier-Induced Demand: Some Empirical Evidence and Implications," in Mark Perlman, ed., *The Economics of Health and Medical Care* (New York: Stockton Press, 1974); Donald W. Simborg, "DRG Creep: A New Hospital-Acquired Disease," *New England Journal of Medicine* 304 (June 1981); Randall R. Bovbjerg, Philip J. Held, and Mark V. Pauly, "Privatization and Bidding in the Health-Care Sector," *Journal of Policy Analysis and Management* 6 (Dec. 1987); and Richard P. Jusserow, *Preliminary Analysis of Hospital Profit Margins in the Third Year of the Prospective Payment System*, memorandum from Department of Health and Human Services Inspector General (Washington: 25 Jan. 1988).

INDEX

A2F attack plane, 110
Accountability, 10–11, 23–24, 223; civil
  servants and profit seekers' rents and,
  93; fidelity to public's values and, 12;
  layered structure of, 43; military procurement systems' lack of, 103; organizational form and problems of, 85;
  private contractors' allocation of, 141;
  in private prisons, Bentham's proposed
  mechanisms for, 172; problems in public realm, special, 49–54; in profit-seeking agency relationship, 40; special
  burden accompanying grants of public
  authority, 11
Adams, Gordon, 239n83
Advancement, opportunity for, 143
Aerospace stocks, Standard & Poor index
  of, 120
AFL-CIO, 29
Agency relationship, 38–39; overcoming
  problems of, 43–45; risk in, 41, 42,
  56, 228n7
Agents: citizen as both principal and, 54,
  94–97; civil servants, 39, 46–48; excess payments for, 51–52; honor of,
  87; profit-seekers, 39, 40–45; public
  interest vs. interests of, 93, 94–97, 98,
  235n30
Ahlbrandt, Roger, 70–71
Airlines in Australia, 71–72, 231n43
Allegiance vs. results, contracting for, 79–
  85

Ambiguity about value of defense goods,
  115–17
American Bar Association, 155, 156
American City and County (magazine), 131
American Civil Liberties Union (ACLU),
  155, 176
American Correctional Association, 153,
  154–55, 244n54
American Federation of State, County, and
  Municipal Employees, 136, 147, 155
American Legion, 120–21
Americans for Democratic Action, 29
American Water Works Association, 74
Ansett Australian National Airways, 71
Antipoverty policy, manpower policy as,
  191–92, 194–95
Apache helicopters, 121
Appalachian Mountain Club, 28
Apprenticeship programs, 206, 248n42
Area Redevelopment Act (1961), 180
Argentina, privatization in, 6
Armed forces: contractor links with, 122;
  mercenary armies, 34; priorities of,
  127–28. *See also* Pentagon, military
  procurement of
Army Signal Corps, 124
Arsenal network, federal, 124–25
Atkinson, Scott E., 76
Australia: airlines in, 71–72, 231n43; pub-
  lic and private banks in, 231n38
Averch, H., 77
Averch-Johnson effect, 233n60

251